971
.4
Gra

10313

GRAHAM, R.
THE FRENCH QUARTER.

$27.95

DEC 2 9 199

33969

10313

971
.4
Gra

GRAHAM, R.
THE FRENCH QUARTER.

M W
& R

The French Quarter

The epic struggle of a family –

and a nation – divided

The
FRENCH
QUARTER

Ron Graham

Macfarlane Walter & Ross

Toronto

Macfarlane Walter & Ross
37A Hazelton Avenue
Toronto, Canada   M5R 2E3

Canadian Cataloguing in Publication Data
Graham, Ron, 1948–
     The French quarter : the epic struggle of a family and a nation divided
Includes bibliographical references and index.
ISBN 0-921912-37-4

1. Canada – English-French relations. 2. Graham family.
I. Title

FC144.G73 1992   971.4   C92-095107-4
FI027.G73 1992

The publisher gratefully acknowledges the assistance
of the Ontario Arts Council

Printed and bound in Canada

To James and Mimi –
the fourteenth generation –
and to the memory of
René Edouard Moncel
(1880–1958)

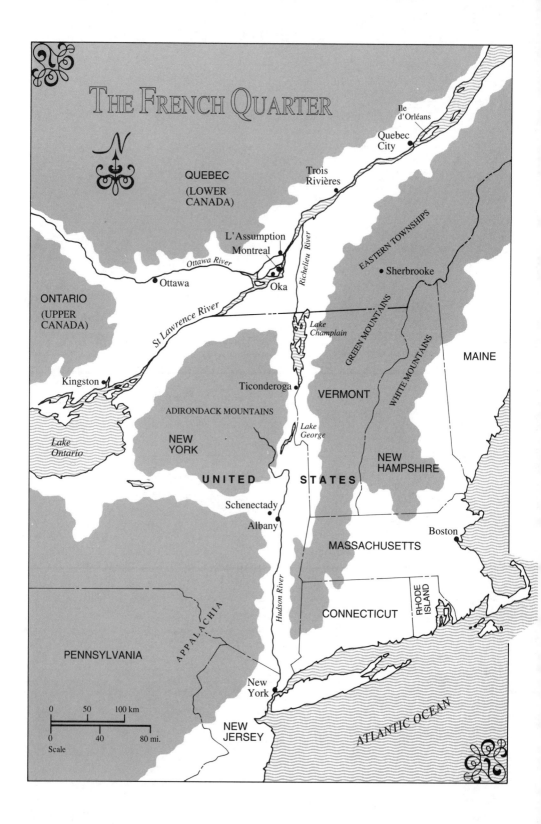

THE FRENCH QUARTER

N

QUEBEC
(LOWER
CANADA)

Ile
d'Orléans

Quebec
City

Trois
Rivières

L'Assumption
Montreal

Richelieu River

Ottawa River

EASTERN TOWNSHIPS

• Sherbrooke

• Ottawa

Oka

St Lawrence River

ONTARIO
(UPPER
CANADA)

Lake
Champlain

GREEN MOUNTAINS

WHITE MOUNTAINS

MAINE

Kingston

Lake
Ontario

Ticonderoga

VERMONT

ADIRONDACK MOUNTAINS

Lake
George

NEW
YORK

NEW
HAMPSHIRE

UNITED   STATES

Schenectady

Albany

MASSACHUSETTS

Boston

Hudson River

APPALACHIA

CONNECTICUT

RHODE
ISLAND

PENNSYLVANIA

0   50   100 km

0   40   80 mi.
Scale

New
York

NEW
JERSEY

ATLANTIC OCEAN

CONTENTS

FAMILY CIRCLE

"In all his life, he had never seen an English Canadian and a French Canadian hostile to each other face to face. When they disliked, they disliked entirely in the group."

— Hugh MacLennan
Two Solitudes
(1945)

The Walled Garden, 1955

I GREW UP in a large Tudor graystone near the top of Westmount, one of the three volcanic hills that dominate the island of Montreal. The house was perched like a stronghold above a steep and wooded cliff; its undulating gardens were enclosed behind a long stone wall. Beyond it, a small cul-de-sac ringed a park of birch trees, gabbro outcrops, and a huge oak. To my family, the house and road were simply the Circle.

The Circle was my childhood. Day or night, in January or July, the city seemed far away, little more than a hum or glow, and there were many times when we had difficulty getting up from it in a blizzard and no desire to go down into it in a heat wave. From spring to autumn the children of its half-dozen homes had the street almost exclusively for our bicycle races and ball games – the only danger was Mr Thomson speeding around the corner in his Sunbeam convertible – and in winter we had the high banks of snow that the Westmount roads department had piled around the edge of the park into an invincible fortress. We had the run of the lawns and groves of the immense estate next door, the conkers from Mrs Molson's chestnut tree, the toboggan track beside the Dawes', and our own swings and slide.

As much as an earthly paradise, the Circle was an imaginary realm: the house soared like King Arthur's castle, Robin Hood hunted for pheasants and rabbits, the twisted hawthorn became Captain Hook's brig, the cliff was the hill up which the Grand Old Duke of York marched his ten thousand men. The Circle itself was the circumference of the globe around which Sir Francis Drake sailed the *Golden Hind.*

By the 1950s the British Raj had long since passed, but its memory lingered in this Canadian hill station. Scottish nannies in uniform pushed black perambulators through King George Park. The Avenue Theatre showed the latest British comedy. The telephone exchange was Fitzroy (and then Wellington 5). The town council sent a gift of maple syrup to the queen each year. Indeed, my earliest memories are associated with the United Kingdom: the Playbox biscuits with silhouettes of trains and teddy bears on their colored glaze, the wooden puzzle blocks that formed a Devonshire farm scene, a pair of blue shoes with straps, lead soldiers, a cable-stitch sweater, and Mr Toad of Toad Hall. Most vivid of all was the coronation of Queen Elizabeth II in 1953, when I was five. Almost forty years later I can picture the room in which I watched the ceremony, not just because of the glittering crown, the golden carriage, the queen of Tonga, or the plumed Guards on horseback, but also because it was the first time I saw television.

The royal family set the standard for the dress and behavior of Westmount, and Westmount was proud to uphold the Empire's archaic codes. In 1955, for example, a prominent businessman spent a quarter of a million dollars to establish a foundation to combat modern art, which threatened in his judgment "to uproot and demolish the tradition that has been built up through the centuries." Westmounters golfed at the Royal Montreal Golf Club, curled at the Royal Montreal Curling Club, and yachted at the Royal St Lawrence

Yacht Club. They banked at the Royal Bank of Canada and went to Her Majesty's for theater. Each day they followed the comings and goings at Buckingham Palace published in the court circular, and each year they lured some idle duke with the promise of a free meal to lend distinction to the St Andrew's Ball. Families dined out for generations on the smallest connection to royalty. "Lord Atholstan turned his first home into a residence *par excellence* for old ladies," an old lady once told me with pride, "and my grandmother was one of the eight or nine lucky ones who got in. Her bedroom had been used by the Prince of Wales. His feathers were carved on the walnut headboard of her bed, and her toilet was covered by a huge wicker armchair padded with velvet. She had to go up three steps to get to the throne."

Atholstan had been one of the lords and knights who had built Montreal into the capital of the British Empire in Canada, the equivalent of Bombay, and made themselves the local maharajahs. Almost all of them had begun without title or coin, as crofters' sons or Yankee engineers, and risen by toil and luck and cunning to control most of the wealth in the huge Dominion that reached from the Atlantic to the Pacific to the Arctic Sea. Nothing escaped their grasp – furs, grain, ships, banks, beer, sugar, tobacco, textiles, steel, railways, newsprint, electricity, insurance, and all the accompanying profits in law, real estate, accounting, and the stock market. They established family alliances and dynasties; they set the conditions for taste and entrée; they supported obedient politicians and imperial tariffs; and they pandered to all things royal and British in exchange for capital, culture, and self-esteem.

They named their streets after British governors such as Lord Dorchester and Sir John Coape Sherbrooke, after London notables such as Robert Peel and Lord Stanley, or – in the case of McTavish, Simpson, Drummond, and Redpath – after themselves. They put up a monument to Admiral Nelson and a statue of Robbie Burns. They set Queen Victoria in bronze upon her throne in Victoria Square and in front of Royal Victoria College and also honored her name with a bridge, a hospital, and a rink. Her son, Edward VII, gazed down upon the fashionable shoppers crossing from Morgan's emporium to Birks the jeweler.

At the foot of Mount Royal's southern slope, in what became known as the Square Mile, they constructed their Victorian fantasies amid orchards and gardens: Florentine palazzos and Tuscan villas with observation towers and two-storey ballrooms, Second Empire mansions and Beaux-Arts palaces with Louis XV drawing rooms and Louis XVI boudoirs, Scottish Baronial castles and American Romanesque fancies with round turrets and oriental smoking rooms, English Classical revivals and English Renaissance variants with paneled libraries and billiard dens, and weird or wonderful combinations of several different styles compressed into extravagant and intimidating declarations of money and power. Nearby, and with the same sense of grandeur, they erected their Anglican and Presbyterian churches, their gentlemen's clubs, McGill University, the Montreal Museum of Fine Arts, and, in 1912, their favorite home away from home, the Ritz-Carlton Hotel.

"You may hear the older men explaining that the country is going to absolute ruin, and the younger ones explaining that the country is forging ahead as it never did before," Stephen Leacock observed of them, "but chiefly they love to talk of great national questions, such as the protective tariff and the need of raising it, the sad decline of the morality of the working man, the spread of syndicalism and the lack of Christianity in the labour class, and the awful growth of selfishness among the mass of people."

In time, just as the nineteenth-century nobs had fled the dust and congestion of Old Montreal for the green fields of Sherbrooke Street, so their twentieth-century offspring fled Sherbrooke Street for the green trees of Westmount. Once a forest marked by Indian trails, then land granted to French settlers, then the country estates of English merchants, Westmount emerged after 1874 as a separate town for the well-to-do. "To think that a daughter of mine would live in Westmount!" a Square Mile matron lamented in the 1920s, but the new cantonment offered fresh air, fine views, open spaces, and an efficient police force, all within minutes of downtown. The sidewalks were shaded with elms, maples, and chestnuts. There were no hotels, no bars, no industries, and only a couple of high streets with small shops and village services. Such were its splendors that, in 1933, a certain Charles Benedict felt moved to compose an entire volume of verse to Westmount's parks and traffic lights, its fire brigade and general manager, even to its mosquitoes.

> If I should ever hang my harp
> By Babylonia's waters,
> I'll ne'er forget thee, Westmount, or
> Thy short-skirt, bob-hair'd daughters.

One by one the great houses of the Square Mile were buried under office towers and apartment buildings, donated to McGill University, or purchased by clubs and governments. The American consul worked where once the Aulds of Canadian Cork Cutting had held sway; the Society of African Missions plotted to save Congolese souls in Senator Wilson's old home. One by one, smaller versions of the old mansions appeared in Westmount, more appropriate to divided inheritances and fewer servants, all the way to the summit, in a rich and eclectic mix of architecture that got grander as the elevation got higher. And there the descendants of the Square Mile carried on as a colonial aristocracy, long after industry and investment had ebbed away to Toronto or New York or the west.

Westmount became such a backwater that it did not even realize it was a backwater. Its old families continued to behave as if they were the true rulers of Canada and, through loyalty to London, of the world. They bashed on as expected, from their private schools to their conservative firms to their elaborate mausoleums, from champagne

7

at the debutante parties to cocktails on the summer veranda to gin on the deathbed. If they were no longer allowed titles, they still had totemic names, known across Canada as a brand of beer or a gold mine up north; and if they no longer had power, they could still intimidate outsiders with their voices and their sang-froid. "He talked about business," the *Gazette* reported upon the death of a local financier in 1990. "He never talked about personal feelings, *if there were such things*."

Their money was presumed rather than flaunted. They preferred station wagons to Rolls-Royces and looked more comfortable in Harris tweeds than in black tie. Though they liked to think of themselves as cosmopolitans, at ease with the world and its ways, they relaxed only among themselves. Often they were each other's cousins, after all, sharing a pleasant and isolated community built upon similar pretensions, inherited prejudices, and memories of grander days. They knew who had slept with whom that summer in Métis; they knew what a nerd the Cabinet minister had been at school; and they knew who had paraded naked and drunk down Aberdeen Avenue one Saturday afternoon. That sense of family let them be loud and even madcap with one another at weddings or the Ritz Café.

One Friday in June 1955, when I was seven, I was taken to the Ritz for lunch with my grandparents, who lived in a suite on the eighth floor, with the rogues' gallery of family photographs on the walls and bowls of chocolate ladyfingers beside each chair. I loved visiting them, not least because I associated their humor and kindness with the *luxe, calme et volupté* of the hotel itself, where painted fishes swam on the aquamarine ceiling of the Maritime Bar above the smoke and din of the double-martini regulars, where a quartet of sombre men in black tie played chamber music and Cole Porter tunes during high tea in the Palm Court, and where ducklings quacked for pieces of bread on summer nights in the Garden. I always experienced a slight lift in my spirits when I passed under its wrought-iron marquee on Sherbrooke Street and entered its black and gold lobby.

Down we drove from the Circle, down Belvedere Road past Sam Bronfman's lawyer and the steel family and the *Gazette* family and the terraced garden of the man who wore black tie every night at dinner, down past the ornate gates of Sam Bronfman's own palace and the house in which my mother's aunt and uncle had lived before they went bust, down by Daulac Road, where my father's parents had built their home during the Depression, and down by the massive Gleneagles, where my mother's parents had had an apartment before they moved to the Ritz, down past the gray and formidable Convent of the Sacred Heart, where my sister went to school, and down past the elm-lined street where Selwyn House School sat empty until I returned to it in September, all the way down to Sherbrooke Street – where I met a surprise.

Crowds were lining the sidewalks for as far as I could see. There was going to be a parade, apparently, and these people had come from all over Quebec to see it. It was some sort of holiday for the French Canadians, I was told, some sort of religious celebration. It was bound to be fun.

Growing up in a mock British enclave, I had only a vague awareness of being surrounded by people who spoke French. They were out there somewhere, in the countryside or at the bottom of the hill, as abstract as the Hindoos I read about in Kipling or the Mau Maus terrorizing the British settlers of Kenya according to that morning's *Gazette* (which led, however, with the reassuring headline, "Norwegians Salute Queen, Duke").

To most of Westmount, French Canada was a landscape to be traversed en route to Knowlton in the summer or Sainte-Agathe in the winter. It was a servant, a factory hand, a bribeable politician. It was an old romance about skating parties, toboggan races, and sleigh rides, canoe trips, fishing camps, and hunting lodges. While there had been several wealthy French Canadians within the Square Mile, they were accepted into the clubs and boardrooms only if they conformed to British standards; and while all the children of the Square Mile had been expected to learn French as the language of diplomacy, no one was expected to speak it in the offices and shops of Montreal – not even the French and Swiss hoteliers imported to manage the Ritz.

There were no French Canadians on the Circle, not even as servants, and I did not know any at school. I was familiar with streets called Décarie and Côte-Saint-Antoine, districts called Notre-Dame-de-Grâce and Outremont, bridges called Jacques Cartier and Mercier, but they were no more connected to a people and a history than the names of Massachusetts and Louisiana.

If I thought of French Canadians at all when I was a child, it was in a make-believe way gathered from French textbooks, hearsay, holidays in the countryside, and the fantasies of their own traditionalists: as rural folk who went to church a lot, picked raspberries in summer and chopped wood in winter, loved beer and pea soup, danced to the fiddle, made maple syrup, had dozens of kids and an enviable *joie de vivre*, and spoke a peasant tongue that had little to do with "good" French. If I ever observed a discrepancy between the rustic domain I imagined and the rough-and-tumble quarters through which we drove whenever we left the city, it never puzzled me. I saw another make-believe life in the boys playing hockey among the cars, the girls marking the pavement with chalk, the mothers in curlers and aprons on the balconies at the top of spiraling iron stairways, and the fathers smoking in groups outside the corner stores. However foreign to me, they were not threatening – except perhaps for the French Canadian policemen, who had a reputation in those days for corruption and brutality.

For a brief while in the early 1950s I caught a slightly closer, though no less romantic glimpse into French Canada. When television started up in Montreal, there was only one channel, and the few hours of daily programming were divided between French and English. Eager to watch anything on the new wonder, I became as familiar with Capucine and Pépinot as with Howdy Doody and Maggie Muggins. But if that was the small start to some sort of shared experience, it was discontinued in 1954 when the Canadian Broadcasting Corporation set up a separate English-language station. After that, my only French connection was through the English version of "La Famille Plouffe," an extremely popular sitcom about an elderly plumber, an adorable matriarch, and their four adult children in Quebec City. Each week the actors more or less repeated the French episode live in English, and their heavy accents and unfamiliar names (Théophile! Onésime! Père Gédéon!) made the show particularly amusing and endearing to English Canadians. It was a rare window, as true and as false as Amos and Andy were to black America, and it lulled me into the illusion that, whatever their financial worries and emotional crises, the families I passed on the streets and the farms were as happy as my own.

When the Plouffes left the air after a few years, French Canadians again became anonymous masses shopping on St Catherine Street or cheering the Montreal Canadiens at the Forum. Nicknamed the "Habs" after the *habitants* who had farmed along the banks of the St Lawrence for three hundred years, but in fact owned by several grand families of Westmount, the hockey team was a unique rallying point for both French and English Montrealers. Both considered it their own; both basked in its Stanley Cup victories. To have seen the Canadiens play in the 1950s was like having seen Olivier on the stage as Hamlet – an experience never matched and never forgotten – and my most valuable treasure as a boy was a stick signed by "Rocket" Richard, "Boom Boom" Geoffrion, Jacques Plante, and all the other stars of the day.

In hindsight, my ignorance of French Canadians seems especially odd, given that my mother's father, who greeted me in the lobby of the Ritz with a big hug and escorted us into the Oval Room for lunch, was himself a French Canadian.

———————————

I knew Granddaddy as well as a child can know an old man. Less well, perhaps, because I adored him, a liability when it comes to judging character. There seemed nothing self-righteous about his gentleness, nothing proud about his courtliness, nothing mean about his laughter. His was a style warm yet patrician, familiar to Canadians in the 1950s as that of "Uncle Louis" St Laurent, the prime minister, or Georges Vanier, the governor general. It was based on old-fashioned manners and elegance. I never saw him dressed in other than a gray or navy blue suit, a starched white shirt, and gleaming black shoes. Nor did I ever hear him speak anything but English – not to a waiter at the Ritz, not to his closest relations.

As a result, despite his French name – René Edouard Moncel – and his French accent, I never connected him with the hinterland of peasants, Plouffes, and hockey players. He seemed apart, just himself; as indeed he was. Nevertheless, when my friends referred to French Canadians as "Frogs" or "Pepsis," I always felt perplexed. Subconsciously my love for my grandfather had enveloped his people. Indeed, my most insidious prejudice was to assume that French Canadians were not so different from me, except that they thought the same things in another language.

Most people assumed that René Moncel had gone over to the "English side" because of Edith Brady, my plump and petite grandmother with the vivid blue eyes and Irish wit, who had married him and become a Roman Catholic over the objections of her widowed mother and seven sisters, stalwart Presbyterians. (It was not a rare story: I know a man in Westmount who had never allowed himself to admire the French Canadian girls of his youth lest he scandalize his family by falling for a Catholic.) But even before his marriage my grandfather had been drawn to the commercial world of English Montreal. He was a modern man who had studied electrical engineering at McGill, trained in the profession in New York City, and had as his first partner a chap named Bennett. When he built Devoe Electric Switch into a major manufacturer of switches and switchboards, his clients were mostly English-speaking, whether the Sun Life Assurance Company or Sir William Van Horne. When he moved to Westmount, he sent his three children to English-speaking schools and hoped they would not have his accent.

Two languages had created two worlds in Montreal, and the two worlds tended to break families into two branches that seldom met except for weddings, funerals, and New Year's Day levees. My grandfather rarely talked about his own parents or childhood, and I knew his brothers and sisters only as quaint names such as Ninette and Guillaume or as faces in a few family photographs. Once, and only once, they all showed up in our house for Sunday lunch. Born in the previous century, sharing my grandfather's dignified bearing and his fine white hair, they seemed to have come from another time as well as another place. Years later, reading *A la recherche du temps perdu*, I remembered them on that afternoon as if they had been the frail and elegant guests Proust saw for the last time in the drawing room of the Prince de Guermantes; but they went as mysteriously as they had come, leaving behind a haze of cigarette smoke, a scent of Shalimar, an impression of sweetness, and – deep within me – a sense of loss.

My grandfather never appeared to feel that anything had been lost, however; nor did his children. My Aunt Marguerite married Leslie Wichbold Wade, the grandson of a British knight, before illness carried her away at the age of thirty-seven. My Uncle Robert, christened Robert Guillaume Napoléon Moncel, changed Guillaume to William, converted to the Church of England, became the youngest brigadier in the Canadian Army during the Second World

War, and remained a professional soldier before retiring as vice-chief of defence staff to sail and garden with his wife Nancy in Nova Scotia. As for my mother, named Renée but nicknamed Mimi, she went to schools called Trafalgar and King's Hall, married an Irish-Catholic Westmount boy just before he went overseas with the Calgary Regiment tanks, and settled down to raise six children on the Circle. But, deeply attached to her father, she imbued us with a zest and sensitivity she attributed to the Moncels, and she linked us by anecdotes and pride to a vast – though somewhat arcane – kinship of French Canadian "cousins" we never met.

———————

When the first French settlers came to North America in the seventeenth century, they brought with them the custom of lighting bonfires for the saint whose feast day had long been associated with the summer solstice. Their gratitude for the light and warmth was all the greater after Canada's savage winter and dismal spring, and it was not long before St John the Baptist became their guardian angel. He even became a personification of them, like John Bull for the English and Uncle Sam for Americans. The Saint-Jean-Baptiste Society, founded in 1834, became the main patriotic organization of French Canada, and Saint-Jean-Baptiste Day became the annual celebration of the French Canadian heritage.

For decades it had been highlighted by a big parade in Montreal, always marked by a theme such as "Homage to the Patriots" or "Homage to the Peasant Family" or "Homage to Marital Fidelity." In 1955, when I watched from the Ritz as though from a private loge, the theme was "L'Acadie rayonnante," Radiant Acadia, a tribute to the French-speaking community in Canada's Atlantic provinces. Three hundred and fifty years earlier the French had established their first important foothold in North America at Port-Royal in present-day Nova Scotia. One hundred and fifty years after that, in 1755, the

English had enforced their cruel solution to a century and a half of fighting over the territory by deporting most of the thirteen thousand French settlers to England or its American colonies. The rest escaped to Quebec or hid in the woods. In time some of them returned, and by swearing allegiance to the king of England they earned the right to stay. The vast majority, however, never again saw the paradise whose name had been inspired by Arcadia and whose moment they never forgot. They remembered by their songs in Louisiana, where they are still called Cajuns. They remembered by the legends of Evangeline, who wandered all her life throughout America in search of her beloved Gabriel. They remembered by their religion and their language. "Only suffering produces great individuals and peoples," Archbishop Léger said on the eve of the parade when he blessed the four hundred evergreens to be ignited in honor of Saint-Jean-Baptiste.

On the street below me there were four floats devoted to Evangeline. (I had not yet heard the famous poem about her by Longfellow, though I already knew of Hiawatha, the village smithy, and the midnight ride of Paul Revere.) Then Samuel de Champlain, the great explorer and one of the founders of Port-Royal, danced by on a float sponsored by the Slater Shoe Company, followed by twenty-eight marching bands and nineteen tributes to Acadian tenacity, from the Happy Times to the Great Dispersal to the Resurrection. At last, as the grandest and final highlight of the two-hour, five-mile extravaganza, there came St John the Baptist himself. As depicted by tradition, the saint was a boy in shepherd's garb, with blond curls, a cherubic countenance, and a lamb by his side: Purity leading the Agnus Dei, prophet of Christ in the wilderness of Canada.

Two storeys above, from the window of the Vice-Regal Suite, I watched him roll by amid a fanfare of trumpets and flurry of flags as though I had come from the garrison to see the devotees of Krishna pull the Juggernaut through Calcutta. Though I did not know it, I too, of course, was a representative of my people, the heirs of the British soldiers who had conquered French Canada in 1763, the Protestant families of the Square Mile and Westmount, the bosses of the pulp mills and textile factories, "the damn English."

There were at that time more than a half-million English-speaking Quebeckers. They were middle-class managers in the suburbs of Montreal West and Pointe-Claire. They were working-class laborers in the slums of Verdun and Saint-Henri. They were fishermen in the Gaspé, loggers in the Ottawa Valley, farmers in the Eastern Townships, and miners on the North Shore. They were Jews on Saint-Urbain Street, blacks below the railway tracks, Chinese in Chinatown, Italians on Saint-Laurent, Greeks on Park Avenue, and Mohawks at Caughnawaga. Fewer than twenty thousand of us lived in Westmount. But when French Canadians spoke of *les maudits Anglais*, they usually associated everyone with the privileged few on the top of the hill who, after several generations in Quebec, did not understand a word of French. "It's simple," said old Théophile Plouffe in the novel on which the television series was based. "We have been, we are, and we shall always be against the English."

If any of the hundreds of thousands of people on Sherbrooke Street had looked up from the parade and seen the child standing high above them in his white shirt, white shorts, and black and gold blazer on the breast pocket of which a lion roared "Veritas," they would have seen the perfect incarnation of the Raj in Quebec. At age seven, standing at the window of the Ritz, I stood in the dock of history, condemned for having perpetrated crimes I could not yet imagine.

Someone did look up. It was the other blue-eyed boy, advancing out of the east on a golden throne. He was my own age, from my own city, of my own religion and color, yet we saw each other as abstractions. I was the symbol of a battle won, the fruit of triumph of the past. He was the memory of a paradise lost, the herald of the kingdom to come. From the center of the horde who marched with him, he smiled up at me and gave a victorious wave.

An Old Romance, 1964

A COUPLE OF DAYS before Christmas 1958, René Moncel died in hospital at the age of seventy-eight. Granddaddy's death was a shock, for his stroke had been minor and he would have returned to his room at the Ritz within a week if he had not developed an infection. My gift for him – a bottle of Yardley's cologne from Kane's drugstore – sat under the tree, like a concrete manifestation of love unexpressed, until the tree itself was removed. At first, unaccustomed to tragedy, I did not know what to do with death. It seemed a temporary absence. In the basement I found an album of French love songs, which seemed appropriate, and I played Josephine Baker's version of "J'ai deux amours" as if to induce bereavement. But it was not until I followed the casket down the aisle of St Patrick's, the grandest "Irish" church in Montreal, that I discovered my own grief. When the funeral music began and I walked in the procession between my stoic grandmother and my dry-eyed uncle, tears flooded down my cheeks.

Outside, it was too cold and wet for consolations. I have only the dimmest recollection of my great-aunts and great-uncles getting into the black Cadillacs for the drive to the Moncel plot in Notre-Dame-des-Neiges. It was only the second time I had seen the Moncel family together. It was the last time I would see any of them again. Several died soon afterward, and with Granddaddy gone, the others drifted back to the unknown land from which they had come.

If my grandfather had lived another ten years, I would have asked him questions I had never thought to ask and learned things that took me thirty years to discover. Perhaps I would have come to know the French Canadian part of me that was borne away when the heavy rear door of the hearse slammed shut.

By the time of Granddaddy's death I had been sent from the Circle to follow my distinguished uncle's footsteps to Bishop's College School, a boarding school founded in 1836 by the Reverend Lucius Doolittle for the enlightenment of "right English-looking youths of a gentlemanly stamp." Set in the Eastern Townships, one hundred miles from Montreal, Bishop's was like a garrison within a cantonment within an enclave. The Townships had been carved out of the Quebec countryside for the English-speaking immigrants of the early nineteenth century. The nearest town had been named for Lord Sherbrooke, who is also remembered by Montreal's most fashionable street; the nearest village had been named for the Duke of Richmond and Lennox; the school itself had been named for the Anglican bishop.

"The boys are more like English boys than any I have seen out here, and pride themselves on their English cheer," a British visitor observed in 1864. "They seem to have the same love and respect for their college as the Eton boys have for Eton."

Things were not so different a hundred years later. The younger boys suffered a fagging discipline. The prefects were allowed to cane for sins such as unpolished shoes. There were hymns every morning and prayers every night; there were cricket matches and tea dances; and there was a cadet corps affiliated with the Royal Highland Regiment of Canada. "Always stand up to sing 'God Save the King,'" my Uncle Robert had been instructed as a cadet, "but you needn't stand up for 'O Canada.' It's just a French Canadian folk song."

There were very few French Canadians in this corner of a foreign field that was forever England, of course, and even fewer opportunities to meet French Canadian girls. Except for the school stud, who climbed out the dormitory window to rendezvous with the prettier maids who served us meals, we were restricted to the female versions of ourselves who were bused over from King's Hall for heavily chaperoned dances. The gods intervened, however, in the spring of 1964, when the Sherbrooke Rotary Club sent four local students to a model assembly of the United Nations in Plymouth, New Hampshire. I was the very unlikely ambassador from Castro's Cuba. Jocelyne was the more plausible delegate from Italy. Dark, poised, slender, and intelligent, she reminded me of Leslie Caron, a Gigi more interested in discussing nuclear disarmament than learning to drink champagne.

It was normal when I was entering puberty to consider French Canada feminine. French Canada was the benign and long-suffering Maman Plouffe or Madeleine de Verchères, the fourteen-year-old heroine who had withstood an Iroquois seige near Montreal for a week in 1692. French Canada was the sway of the maids in the school dining room, the ecstasies of the repressed nuns in our histories of New France, the rumors of the brothels on Rue de Bullion, the electric signs for "danseuses nues" outside the hotel bars in the Laurentians. If Canada was a marriage between the English and the French – usually on the edge of a divorce – everyone understood who was the husband, who the wife. The federal Parliament buildings in Ottawa, Ontario, were distinguished by an enormous and erect tower; but when the business of the day was done, the statesmen hurried across the river to the dark and dirty alleys of Hull, Quebec, for the pleasures of the night. And even French Canada's own writers, politicians, and priests often encouraged their people to remain submissive to "our master the past."

But that began to change after 1960. "Masters in our own house!" was the new slogan of French Canadians, and in the Saint-Jean-Baptiste parade of 1964 the boy-saint with the golden curls was replaced by a brawny man with a black beard.

That June I invited Jocelyne to my graduation dance in Montreal.

If tongues wagged, I did not hear them. If some girls thought her dress pinker than appropriate in Westmount and some boys wondered why she wore her corsage on her wrist, I did not care: she looked lovely, she danced well, she laughed gaily, and she was not stuck up. Like the best of my mother, in fact. But had anyone, including myself, been sensitive to what she felt about the young lions and long-nailed cats among whom she had been thrown? What had she made of the houses we visited from the cocktail hour to the dinner party to the midnight swim to the breakfast feast? Had she been cut by the looks of intimate friends, repelled by the crudeness of drunken snots, entranced by the insouciance with which we treated these expensive rooms? If so, she was courageous, for she displayed nothing but the confidence that she deserved to be there as much as anybody else.

In September 1964 I entered McGill University, which sits in the very center of Montreal. All around the gates of the campus the political and economic transformation of French Quebec known as the Quiet Revolution was expressing itself in song and prose, on the stage and at the galleries, at the same time that Montreal was experiencing a French-language version of the hippie culture that flowed from London and San Francisco. Among the young, and especially among young French Canadians, there was a spirit of freedom and creativity that would charm visitors to the world's fair in 1967 and shatter my attachment to the Circle.

It was first shattered when three armed men with stockings over their faces broke into the house one night. I was away with my father at the time, but the rest of the family were held in terror for several hours while the thieves ransacked the cupboards for jewels and silver. Not long afterward we moved to a more secure apartment downtown. Just as well, I thought, for at seventeen I had outgrown the quiet and secluded life of the Circle and become embarrassed to say I was from Westmount. If I thought of England, I thought of the Beatles and the Rolling Stones. Dylan no longer meant the Welsh poet. Martin Luther King was more important than Queen Elizabeth. My long hair was not the look of an English schoolboy any more. After my Grandmother Moncel's death I marched in front of the Ritz in demonstrations against the war in Vietnam more often than I entered it for lunch. As much as I had loved the Circle, it was time to break from it. Instead of loss, I felt liberty.

It was only a couple of miles from Westmount to the small apartment I took in the so-called student ghetto in 1967, but I felt I had changed cities. I imagined I was an expatriate in Paris. I began to pass my waking hours from Friday night to Sunday evening in the Bistro on Rue de la Montagne or in one of the cafés on Saint-Denis, reading the cultural pages of *Le Devoir* and arguing about the student uprisings in Europe. I smoked Gitanes, lived on French bread and pâté, and rushed to any film by Truffaut or Godard. Once I drove all the way to the Gaspé to study habitant houses and old church carvings along the St Lawrence River. I read Réjean Ducharme and Emile Nelligan as well as Dostoevsky and Yeats. I went to the first plays of Michel Tremblay and the small *boîtes de chanson* where Gilles Vigneault sang. I narrowed my interests to Quebec history and politics and got a part-time job as a researcher at McGill's French Canada Studies center.

Inspired by a sense of justice and a sense of guilt, pushed by a rebellious instinct in myself and the times, perhaps even envious of an exuberant people with a just cause, I sympathized with Quebec nationalism. But unlike some of my friends I never bought the radical line that French Canadians were the "white niggers" of America (they had never known anything like slavery or segregation) or the separatist line that Quebec's liberation was comparable to the post-colonial struggles in Asia and Africa (Quebeckers had ruled their own state for a hundred years). Nor did I try to recover my own French Canadian roots. Without once thinking about it, I understood that my grandfather would have felt disgraced if the Moncel name had been linked to a movement of poorly dressed leftists who glorified French slang and pilloried English businessmen.

In truth, I looked upon French Canada as I had once looked upon the Christmas window at Ogilvy's: speechless at the wonders and delights, my nose pressed against the glass, my heart desperate to play among the remote figures moving in a magical winterland. It was a soft-hearted, even erotic feeling that had almost as little basis in reality as the Plouffes or the advertisements by which the Quebec Department of Tourism tried to lure Americans to the ski hills and the Winter Carnival. One snowy midnight, walking along Sherbrooke Street, I found a piece of paper on the ground. It was a page from a journal or perhaps a novel, handwritten in French, full of abstract meditations about loneliness and life. I never forgot it, because it represented what I so wanted in those days – an intimate connection with a French Canadian friend.

There were remarkably few meeting places. French and English still tended to keep to their own. Cultural institutions and student associations were usually divided according to language or religion. Even chance encounters in bars and at parties were constrained by the natural tendency to huddle within the "two solitudes" and the growing tensions that affected personal relationships. In my case things were worse because my French, like that of Henry v, hung upon my tongue "like a new-married wife about her husband's neck, hardly to be shook off." My comprehension and reading were fluent enough, but my speaking remained a game leg: awkward at best and liable to give way completely. Nor did I ever master the French Canadian accent known as *joual* (after the way *cheval*, horse, is pronounced), which can be so strong in parts of Quebec that a film about farmers on the Gaspé peninsula had to be shown in Montreal with French subtitles.

Language itself had become an act of politics. French Canadians were less and less tolerant of having to speak English at work or in stores, less easily appeased by a token "Bonjour" at parties or in taverns. Despite the arrogant assumption among English Canadians that other peoples have a natural gift for bilingualism, most French Canadians had felt the fatigue and handicap of speaking a second language. It bred a condition of inadequacy or uncertainty, made worse by the fact that English had been forced upon them.

This would seem neurotic in most parts of the world, where various languages live side by side and English serves without remorse as the lingua franca; but even the reasons the anglos gave for not speaking French sounded arrogant. "I have a tin ear" meant "You do my work for me." "It's hard to practise" meant "It's easy to live in Montreal without knowing the language of the majority." "It's not what I learned at high school" meant "French Canadians speak a rotten French with a thick accent that no Parisian could understand." Indeed, to nationalistic French Canadians, Parisian French was only a marginal improvement over atrocious French: both betrayed the speaker as a stranger.

"The most effective way to learn French is in bed," went a popular adage. "It's also the most pleasant." When Jocelyne came to Montreal for the Saint-Jean-Baptiste holiday in June 1966, I had not seen much of her in two years – she was at university in Sherbrooke – but I harbored the fantasy that one thing would lead to another. When she called to invite me to watch the parade from an apartment near Rue Saint-Urbain with some of her friends, it seemed the opportunity I had been wishing for.

I soon realized, however, that my university French could not keep pace with a dozen drunken students who shared jokes, slang, songs, and references I did not follow. As I grew quieter and more intimidated, I saw myself acting out the part French Canadians often assigned to the anglo "squareheads" – the stiff, silent, humorless outsider – but I seemed powerless to break from the role. I was paralyzed in this world, which contrasted so dramatically with the one to which I had escorted Jocelyne on graduation night. A group laughed wildly at someone's comical imitation of an Englishman trying to speak French. It was funny and accurate, but I sensed the same contempt I was used to hearing when my friends mocked the broken accents of French Canadians.

There was a young man, however, who seemed anxious to practise his English and connect with *les autres*. He was amiable to the point of deference. "I have lived all my life in Montreal," he said, "and I have never been to Westmount."

"You haven't missed much," I answered.

"But I am curious. What kind of people live in those big houses?"

"I'll take you there someday," I promised, but I never did.

Why not? Because of a remark by Jocelyne, perhaps. In appearance she had not changed much, she was pert and intelligent, but now there was an angry edge to her voice when she spoke of politics. University had done to her what it had done to me – joined a set of leftist dogmas to a spirit of intolerant conviction – except that she held the moral ground as an "oppressed" French Canadian.

"Come," I said to her after the parade, eager to get away from the others. "We'll take a ride on my motorcycle. It's my new toy."

"It must be nice to have a rich father to buy you toys."

I never saw her again.

We Want a Country! 1990

TWENTY-FOUR YEARS later I was back again at the Saint-Jean-Baptiste parade. The 1990 parade was only the second held in Montreal since 1969, when a mob of French Canadian nationalists had attacked a giant statue of the saint and – shades of Salome! – cut off his head.

"When I heard that they had decapitated Saint-Jean-Baptiste," said Lise Payette, a popular talk-show host who later became a Cabinet minister in René Lévesque's separatist government, "I thought that it was very important to kill a symbol in order to move forward. They were breaking with the idea of a nation of followers, a sweet and submissive people who never reacted. I think that people sometimes used to identify more with the sheep than with the little Saint-Jean-Baptiste!" When she herself organized the festivities in 1975, not as a parade but as music and fireworks in the park on top of Mount Royal, the theme song went, "Adieu le mouton, salut les Québécois," Goodbye sheep, hello Quebeckers!

The theme of the 1990 parade was "Thirty Years of Quiet Revolution." Here came a float dedicated to Quebec women to commemorate the fiftieth anniversary of their right to vote in Quebec. Here came tractors pulling cages of cows and pigs, in tribute to Quebec agriculture. Here on roller skates came teenagers with three-piece suits and briefcases, to personify the vitality of Quebec business. Here came a monument to Hydro-Québec, in the form of a plaster dam being painted in rainbow colors by several men. Between the floats came clowns on stilts, unicyclists, gymnasts, dancers, sports and television celebrities waving little flags or gesturing V for victory in the back of white Ford Fairlane convertibles, and school bands in elaborate uniforms (sponsored by gas companies and credit unions) marching to the tune of "Auprès de ma blonde" or "Alouette." One of the loudest cheers went to the couples sitting in opera boxes up in the air on forklifts: million-dollar winners in the Quebec lottery.

Whenever the parade slowed down, the crowds around me picked up the rhythmic chants that ebbed and flowed up and down the three-mile route. "Qué-bec fran-çais!" shouted a spry old man, a handsome middle-aged couple in natty summer clothes, two graceful girls, and a tattooed biker whose hairy paunch was exposed beneath an abbreviated black T-shirt that proclaimed "Eat the Rich." Others had literally wrapped themselves in the Quebec flag; its fleurs-de-lis were painted on Sherbrooke Street and many faces. "On veut un pays!" read a placard hanging from countless apartment balconies and ice-cream wagons – We want a country! – and from tens of thousands of mouths came the chant "Le Québec aux Québécois!"

By an extraordinary coincidence, the holiday came immediately after the failure of the latest attempt to keep the French-speaking majority of Quebec happy and secure within the English-speaking majority of Canada. As much a psychological symbol as a constitutional reform, the deal – known as the Meech Lake Accord – had been the center of three years of political and emotional debate about the place of Quebec within the Canadian federation and the pride of the six and one-half million French Canadians who make up a quarter of Canada's population. Its dramatic, last-minute failure was widely interpreted as a rejection of Quebec by English Canada, an utter humiliation, and the polls were reporting that 60 per cent of Quebeckers would vote for independence if a referendum were held.

"Forgetting the past quarrels we may have had, forgetting the accusations we may have said to each other that may have hurt, I say to my premier, let us try to get together," Jacques Parizeau, the leader of the pro-independence Parti Québécois, said in the legislature to Robert Bourassa, the head of the ruling Quebec Liberal Party. "Since we find ourselves all together among ourselves, *entre nous*, let us accept simply to get together and discuss among ourselves – not with all sorts of other people, among ourselves – our future and what must happen to us."

"Entre nous" – more than anger or tension, the predominant emotion in Quebec was a palpable desire to come together. Few people in the world are quicker to rally for collective joy or comfort than French Canadians. "It's a family thing," a priest once told me, trying to explain why huge numbers had turned out to welcome Pope John Paul II to Montreal, even though hardly anyone goes to church anymore. "We all used to come from big families, and we remain a gregarious and tightly knit people as a result. In the face of modern, urban alienation, it doesn't take much to pull us back into the bosom of the family."

At first the mood of the quarter-million people lining the parade route was remarkably tranquil – as if the world had been expected to end at midnight and everyone was too drained to celebrate, or rue, that it had not – but the sun, the floats, the marching bands, and the political chants generated a spirit of euphoria. A long siege seemed to be over; these people seemed to have emerged triumphant.

And then, as if to confirm that feeling, the final float approached. The saint had been replaced by a colossal sheep called (strangely enough) "le mouton de Troie," the Trojan Sheep. Huge and highly abstract, pulled through the city by youths dressed in black, it was little more than a black mask attached to a metallic skeleton filled with overexcited children who looked like a school group that had been allowed to play inside a museum dinosaur. Its intent had been ironic, according to its designer: a symbol of docility had been magnified into a statement of liberation; the hidden soldiers had been revealed as the hope of future generations. It was as much a god as any golden calf or Hindu bull – a sign of summer, a portent of power – and there was pride in the grins around me, joy in the hurrahs, as the shadow of the swaying idol blessed the crowds.

The sheep was back, bigger and bolder than ever.

All around me the crowd fell in behind it and a line of political dignitaries. "Québécois, dans la rue!" became the chant, and take to the street they did, a mighty procession of citizens for as far as I could see in both directions, a turbulent St Lawrence of blue and white flags flowing eastward under the dazzling sun, a spectacular manifestation of solidarity and purpose not unlike those I had seen on television from Tiananmen Square, Wenceslas Square, and the Brandenburg

Gate. These aren't people who would leave Canada, I thought. These are people who have already left.

———————

Unlike the reporters from Germany and Finland, from CBS and the BBC, I had not been drawn to the parade by rumors that Canada was about to end with a bang. I had come from Toronto, from a kind of exile, to the province I love more than any other, the place of my childhood, the place of my maternal ancestors, in search of what I jocularly called my French quarter.

I had become intrigued by a paradox about myself and my country. I had always known of my French Canadian side. I had adored my Grandfather Moncel; I had become infatuated with Quebec history and politics at university; I had covered French Canadian politicians and businessmen as a journalist for more than ten years. I had visited every corner of Quebec, from James Bay to the Beauce. I had built a log cabin beside a quick stream in the woods of the Eastern Townships, which bound my heart to Quebec whenever my life took me elsewhere. I had become proficient enough in French to lose most of my inhibition and shame; I had found the intimate friendships with French Canadians I had craved. Yet I had not been moved to ask about my French Canadian relatives or probe into the lives of my French Canadian ancestors until I was over forty and the father of a child who might someday ask me about my grandfather.

In the same way, it seems, English Canada has been obsessed, irritated, or charmed by French Canada. Countless commissions, conferences, studies, speeches, and news reports have been dedicated to the "problem" of Quebec since Canada was created in 1867. Yet throughout English Canada I still heard the refrain, "I don't understand those French Canadians. What do they want, anyway?" Like me, three-quarters of Canada had accepted its French quarter as a given, just there, never looking at it closely or loving it intensely. It was both mundane and foreign. It was intimidating as well as intriguing. It was family, but it was other.

Indeed, my own French Canadian family was so other that I hardly knew where to look for it. I began with a long-distance operator and, through her, found André Moncel, the son of one of my grandfather's brothers and the last of my relatives to bear the family name in Quebec. He invited me for coffee at his home in the Town of Mount Royal, an English-speaking suburb of crescents and boulevards to the north of downtown Montreal. As I set off to meet him, I felt an irrational anticipation that I was going to recover some profound knowledge that had been lost. I was unaccountably nervous.

When André Moncel greeted me at the door, we noticed in one another a family resemblance. He was on the eve of his seventieth birthday. My grandfather must have been about the same age when I knew him at the Ritz, but his nephew seemed younger and less august. My grandfather would have worn a dark blue suit; André wore beige slacks and a yellow sportshirt. My grandfather would have been quiet and ceremonious; André was energetic and affable. He introduced me to Françoise, his wife, as we passed through the kitchen on our way to the patio overlooking a long, narrow garden. On the kitchen counter Saturday's *Gazette* and a portable radio, tuned to an English-language station, carried the news of the constitutional crisis.

"What do you think of this business?" I asked André.

"I'm sick of hearing about it," he said. "The Moncels were never great nationalists. You know, I've never even been to a Saint-Jean-Baptiste parade."

Like my mother, André had grown up in lower Westmount. Unlike her, he had grown up in French. But he had learned English as a child playing in the neighborhood, studied engineering in English at McGill, and dealt mostly in English with the senior management of a heavy-equipment manufacturer before retiring to run his own card and gift shop in Verdun. Still, he made a clear distinction between himself and me. "Growing up, I had the impression that your grandfather and his children were the English side of the family," he said, "because of Auntie Edith. I only saw them once or twice a year, usually at New Year's, when we would go around and shake hands with all the family. In my mind the Moncels weren't close. They tended to get lost in the lives of their wives or husbands."

Even when my forebears were alive, according to André, they had been as silent as the grave. Dead, they were doubly entombed by silence. They seemed further away from me, not nearer, and I felt cut off from them forever. It was not just that André knew so little – his grandfather's occupation, for example, or his own father's childhood memories – and it was not even that he was less curious about the Moncels than I. It was that he himself had not fit what I was expecting or hoping for. His life seemed so *familiar*: the Westmount childhood, the McGill fraternity, the Town of Mount Royal bungalow, the *Gazette* in the kitchen, the disdain for Quebec nationalism. I had wanted to connect with something different, make a link with the people who had paraded on Sherbrooke Street before they marched out of view altogether. I had wanted to understand why they were determined to leave Canada when they were more prosperous and powerful than ever before. I had wanted to know them better than I had known my grandfather, so that I would not feel the loss of them as deeply as I had felt his loss.

"Just a minute," André said as I was about to go. "I have something, I don't know, it might be a help." He went into the house, leaving Françoise and me to talk about the time the nuns at the Sacred Heart had dressed the girls in peasant costumes, "as though we were habitantes," she laughed, for she had been the daughter of a sophisticated insurance broker. The small living room was filled with French antiques and French books that had belonged to him.

André returned with a thick, leather-bound book. "It's the Moncel family tree," he said, passing it to me. "It was done in the forties by a genealogist called Drouin. He gave it to Dad as a Christmas present or in return for some favor. Borrow it, if you want. I have no need for it."

I was surprised by my own emotion when I opened the book and saw, elegantly presented on a couple of hundred ornate pages, my own blood. Here were the names of my French Canadian ancestors. Here were the dates and places of their marriages. In many cases Drouin had listed their occupations and their villages of origin in France. In some cases he had added a note or two about them – "Came at the time of Champlain" or "Killed by the Iroquois." It was as if I had been handed a long-buried treasure box, something I had heard of as a child but never expected to find. Thumbing through the book, I felt the dizziness I get when I look into the night sky and glimpse my connection to infinity.

On October 22, 1653, I saw, Marie-Madeleine Sevestre was married at Quebec to Jacques Loyer, a sergeant in the fort. The precision of the date startled me. I could not remember who was the governor of New France in that year or what military campaigns were being waged, but neither fact would have mattered to these two young people on that day. More memorable, no doubt, was the taste of their kiss at the altar and what her father, a businessman and judge, had thought of this young sergeant.

From that kiss, almost three hundred years later, I had emerged. So had this man sitting beside me in a garden on a sunny morning in June 1990. We were not strangers, after all, and suddenly his life was not so ordinary. It was as extraordinary as the lives of Marie-Madeleine Sevestre and Jacques Loyer now seemed, as mysterious as history, as marvelous as existence.

Why had I presumed that André would fit a stereotype? He and Françoise were French Canadians, certainly, in the language and style of their home, but that did not necessarily define them. They were also North Americans at the end of the twentieth century, for instance, who traveled broadly and subscribed to the *Gazette*. To deny that reality was to place them in the anonymous masses following the Sheep or to dress them in the folkloric get-up at the Sacred

Heart. The book in my hand had the authority of a birth certificate, affirming André Moncel's rightful place in the French Canadian family, but the French Canadian family was more complex than I had supposed.

If I hoped to know the family, I had to put aside my presumptions and go back to the beginning. If I hoped to fill the empty space of my not belonging, I had to explore its uncharted territory. With the genealogy as my only luggage, I kissed my cousins goodbye and departed for a wilderness called Canada. The word is derived, apparently, from the Huron-Iroquois word *kanata*, meaning "home."

FAMILY LEGENDS

"The walls of all the formal salons in the homes are hung with pictures of various ancestors. From frequent discussions of these relatives and their personal characteristics the smallest child comes to know them very well, not as mere names but as individuals in the family."

— Horace Miner
St. Denis: A French-Canadian Parish
(1939)

The Patriarch, 1634

Z ACHERIE CLOUTIER lived in a time and place – seventeenth-century France – when God spoke to people more often, or at least more directly, than He does today. He told some of them about Canada. One night in 1632 He showed a young nun in Tours "a large and spacious place that had no roof but the sky," with a "pavement as white as alabaster" and "a wonderful silence." A couple of years later He restored the health of a noble lady after she promised to dedicate her life and her fortune to the conversion of heathen girls.

Now the Lord said to Zacherie Cloutier, "Get thee out of thy country, and from thy kindred, and from thy father's house, unto a land that I will show thee; and I will make of thee a great nation." But Zacherie was no mystic. He was a carpenter in the province of Perche, and he needed a sign as down-to-earth as the notarized contract and guarantee of two thousand acres of land on the banks of the St Lawrence River offered to him by a local doctor named Robert Giffard.

"This place is no delusion. I've been there," Giffard told Zacherie in early 1634, with all the authority of a man of science. "Seven years ago. I used to go often to Dieppe and Rouen. I'd see the ships heading off to New France and coming back heavy with fish and furs, and I'd say to myself, 'Giffard, someday you'll go with them.' You know how much I love to fish and hunt in our hills! Well, as it happened, I met some traders who needed a doctor on board, so off I went. It was heaven. The beauty, the solitude, the fishing. I had a little cabin on the Beauport, and I fished every day until the ship sailed home. If I caught anything smaller than *this*, I'd throw it back!"

While in New France, Giffard had met the family of his fellow apothecary Louis Hébert, who had died recently after slipping on some ice. Giffard was impressed by what the Hébert family had accomplished. Despite the opposition of the fur traders, agents of the French merchants who looked on settlers as an expense and a nuisance, the Héberts had cleared away ten acres of trees near the *habitation* at Quebec that Samuel de Champlain had founded in 1608 (a year after the English founded Jamestown in Virginia), raised vegetables and grain, imported cattle and apple trees, and created a little bit of France in the wilderness. Robert Giffard hoped to do the same, if and when God willed it.

God seemed ready to help almost at once through Cardinal Richelieu, who was chief minister to the king of France as well as a servant of the Lord. In 1627, while the good doctor had been off fishing, Richelieu had labored to bring financial and administrative stability to the affairs of Canada after more than thirty years of fits and starts by a series of private companies. He had created a new monopoly, known as the Company of One Hundred Associates, which basically received control over all the land and trade of French North America, except the fish business, in exchange for developing the place as the English and Dutch were beginning to do to the south. Richelieu hoped to lure at least four thousand French settlers within fifteen years and to send a squad of missionaries to capture the souls of the natives. Driven by the imperial and spiritual ambitions of the court, flush with the money squeezed out of the one hundred investors, the company had managed to pack four hundred people into four boats and wave them off from Dieppe in 1628. Among their number, with enough belongings to suggest he might have been going ahead to prepare a hearth for his bride of two months, was Dr Giffard.

"No words can describe the suffering that we endure in this miserable vessel," one transatlantic passenger to New France wrote on behalf of all who did the trip. "The lurching is horrible and continuous. We don't know where to place ourselves or how to hold on. We could break our necks at any moment. The almost continuous beating of the waves inundates us with vile salt water. It is not a mere matter of buckets of water; our animals and fowl are dying by the numbers. I won't even speak of the damp and cold that must be endured without a fire and out in the open every day. The despotic lurching rules more than our lives, our movements, our attitudes, our rest; we must fight it every morsel we bring to our lips and every time we must satisfy a need."

As the French fleet finally sailed into the St Lawrence River after three wretched months at sea, there came out of the mist between Gaspé and Tadoussac three English ships commanded by the privateer David Kirke. War had broken out between England and France after Richelieu laid siege to the Protestant stronghold of La Rochelle, and Charles I and some London investors had sent Kirke with his brothers to take Canada. For fifteen hours the two flags fired at each other with little apparent effect. The French admiral – prompted perhaps by the wound to his leg – surrendered just before his ammunition gave out. His ships, his crews, his supplies, and his passengers were seized. Dr Giffard soon found himself back in France.

That had been a minor setback compared to the news that reached him a year later in Mortagne, a small town about halfway between Paris and the western coast. Taking advantage of the weakness of the tiny colony at Quebec, Kirke had forced its surrender in July 1629. In the courts of England and France, Champlain agitated for the colony's return to French possession, on the solid ground that the capitulation had come two months after the two kings had made peace. But the issue was mixed up with other disputes, and Giffard realized he might never again see his cabin in Canada.

Almost three years later, however, Louis XIII had regained his North American lands in exchange for paying some money he owed to the king of England. The Company of One Hundred Associates wobbled back into business, and Robert Giffard was able to negotiate a contract with it. He received the feudal title of seigneur, or lord of the manor, and several square miles of land where his beloved Beauport met the St Lawrence, on condition that he help to fulfill the company's obligation to deliver settlers. His first need, he knew, would be a house in a clearing. He immediately recruited two local tradesmen, a master mason named Jean Guyon and his pal, the master carpenter Zacherie Cloutier.

The great-great-great-great-great-grandfather of my great-great-great-great-great-grandmother, twelve generations back, Zacherie Cloutier was in his mid-forties in 1634. He and Xainte Dupont had been married almost eighteen years; they had five children (a sixth had died at the age of nine). Given his trade and the rootedness of most Percherons, he was an unlikely candidate for emigration. But France was in bad shape in the early part of the seventeenth century. The king faced foreign armies and civil insurrection. The Church was trying to beat back the Protestant heretics and the devils who had possessed the Ursuline nuns at Loudun. The nobles were losing power and money. The merchants were tottering on the edge of ruin. The peasants suffered from disease, hunger, and taxes, while aristocrats and soldiers and priests and traders used their backs to step above the mud. Most people resigned themselves to death and the promise of the happier kingdom to come; some took up arms or tramped off to another corner of France. A few, a very few, were gripped by the idea of Canada.

"What about the savages?" my ancestor asked Dr Giffard.

"Bah, they are no worse than the mosquitoes compared to the armies that have smashed through our streets and laid waste our fields – and will do again, mark my words! What are some naked heathens to us, the Christian sons of Mortagne, where in our own childhood twenty-eight brave citizens held Notre-Dame against the onslaught of sixteen hundred well-armed partisans of Charles de Lorraine? Away with doubt, *mon ami*. Let us put our troubles behind us. A new life awaits you, if you'll just sign here."

Zacherie wanted the contract read to him once more. It seemed sweeter each time. He had only to build Giffard a house and help clear the land. His family's needs would be Giffard's responsibility. After three years Giffard would be obliged to give him "deux mille arpents de terre" for nominal seigneurial dues, with hunting and fishing rights included. There were nobles with less land than that! Not knowing how to write, Zacherie Cloutier made his mark: a drawing of a small axe.

According to the contract, only the master carpenter and his sixteen-year-old son were to go at first. Xainte and their other children were to follow in a couple of years when there was a house and garden to receive them. At the beginning of April, however, with their iron pots and copper kettles, their pewter dishes and spinning wheels, their woolen clothes and construction tools, their wooden furniture and vegetable seeds, the whole family left together for Dieppe. After praying at Notre-Dame for a safe journey, the Cloutiers, the Giffards, the Guyons, and two other families set off in horse-drawn carts, the men intent upon the labors ahead, the children excited by the adventure, the women gazing back until the spire of the church disappeared from sight. On the wharf in Dieppe they met the rest of Giffard's party. More afraid than excited, everyone boarded Captain de Nesle's small ship, less than ninety feet in length and two hundred tons in weight, one of four the company was loading with supplies (and priests) for Canada.

The passage was not particularly rough – on bad days Zacherie merely stayed on his bunk in the "wooden prison" with one of his tools suspended above his head, exclaiming "Oh, that was a good one!" whenever a big swell caused it to swing – and he passed the eight weeks of the voyage climbing down into the hold to satisfy his professional curiosity about how the vessel was made. Still, two months of stench and sickness, of salt pork and hardtack, of thin mattresses and crying children in the crowded steerage became reason enough never to return to France.

At last, beyond the dangers of the fog and the chill of the icebergs on the Grand Banks, land appeared, as welcome and as uninviting as it had seemed to the explorer Jacques Cartier in his search for a passage to China exactly one hundred years earlier – land "composed of stones and horrible rugged rocks," nurturing "nothing but moss and short, stunted shrub," no better than "the land God gave to Cain." But as they sailed into the gulf and up the mighty St Lawrence, Zacherie's heart lifted. The sky became huge and blue, the cliffs leveled into forests of oaks and elms and cedars, and the desolate shores gave way to fertile meadows. At Tadoussac, Zacherie saw his first Indians, who looked wild enough with their painted faces and tattooed bodies but seemed no more threatening than the Huguenot merchants back home. On June 4 he got his first glimpse of Quebec, with its great promontory and cultivated fields.

Quebec – named after the Algonquin word for "where the river narrows" – proved no more civilized than a rat's hole. It was less a town than a building, a two-storey compound of lodgings and storage built in birch and stone, topped by gables and chimneys, and surrounded by a high wall and a six-foot-deep moat. It was not even much of a building. Three years of English occupation had left little intact except for stone walls and a few dilapidated sheds that left the couple of dozen surviving settlers and the forty-three new arrivals vulnerable to rain, wind, mud, and the stink of animal shit, rotten hay, and mildew. It was a pathetic monument to more than a century of French presence on the continent and twenty-five years of effort to domesticate the site. European wars, religious conflict, Indian attacks, political intrigues, financial corruption, and the rivalry of the ambitious English and Dutch colonies to the south had conspired to produce little more than a ruin. (There were scarcely a hundred French at Quebec in 1627; New Netherlands had twice as many Dutch, and there were more than two thousand English in Virginia alone.) France's traders had preferred to dash over, grab as much fish and fur as they could, and hustle home before winter; its kings had neither the interest nor the strength to make the place more than what one missionary called "a store for the pelts of dead beasts."

"We have more curiosity than capacity," the essayist Montaigne observed of France's overseas adventures, "for we grasp at everything and catch nothing but air."

By the time Zacherie arrived at Quebec, Samuel de Champlain himself had been back a year to govern the colony for the company and the king. Although he was almost sixty-five years old, Champlain had begun to repair the *habitation* by the river, rebuild the fort (which had been knocked down by lightning) up on the cliff, and erect a new chapel in gratitude to the Virgin Mary for restoring Quebec to France. He was the very spirit of optimism and adventure. As a young man he had fought under Henri IV and sailed with a Spanish fleet to the West Indies. In 1603, on his first voyage to Canada, he had traveled as far as the island Cartier had named Montreal; a year later he had helped to build the first French settlement in Acadia and passed three winters there, raising the spirits of his companions by establishing the Order of Good Cheer. He had hopped back and forth across the Atlantic as if it were a ditch, roved from Lake Huron to Cape Cod as if on a stroll, laughed off scurvy and arrow wounds, shot dangerous rapids and more dangerous Iroquois, won over feathered chiefs and the king of France to his economic schemes and imperial visions, and settled Quebec. As skilled with paddle and arquebus as with quill and astrolabe, devout and funny, far-sighted and practical, Champlain seemed indestructible.

"Eager to see everything, to know everything, he was always out to make discoveries, whether it was a matter of examining a harbour, studying a type of soil or a tribe, looking for a mine," wrote one of his biographers. "He was observant; it was while stalking a strange bird that he lost his way in the forests of the Huron country."

That had been twenty years earlier, while on a deer hunt with his Huron allies. For three days, limping from wounds he had received while leading the assault on an Iroquois fort near Lake Ontario, Champlain wandered lost and alone, with no provisions but his wits, till God led him back to his friends. The elusive bird, the three days, the miraculous reappearance – they were spiritual symbols, of course, and their symbolism would not be lost on Zacherie Cloutier and the others in the *habitation* at Quebec when Champlain regaled them with his mishaps by the fire during the long nights of winter. He was their leader, their *chef*. When he was with them, they worked harder and bore their crosses more lightly; when he was away, they fell into sloth and despair. Now he drew, in his own words, "new courage" from the sight of Giffard's settlers. Champlain led them across the filthy courtyard to the wooden chapel to hear the Jesuits give thanks for their arrival. Then he set them to work, work, work, for the glory of their God and their king.

Zacherie Cloutier did not have much time for fishing that summer of 1634. The season was short, and he and Jean Guyon had to put up Giffard's "manor house" as well as a house for their own families. After erecting a cross on the highest point of the property, they cut down the hardwood forest, burned the brush, and moved the rocks. "They work like horses or oxen," observed Father Paul Le Jeune, the Jesuit superior, but they could clear no more than a couple of acres a summer. While they waited for the stumps to rot, their help was required by the governors and the company, the priests and the nuns, the officials and traders who arrived by the boatload each year. Zacherie was hired to put a roof on the convent, and he built a half-timbered house with rubblework for the gunsmith. It was almost three years, therefore, before he could turn the earth and sow the seeds of wheat and oats.

On February 3, 1637, Robert Giffard tramped through the snow to the home that Jean Guyon and Zacherie Cloutier shared near Rivière du Buisson. There, with an engineer, a surgeon, and the old pioneer Abraham Martin as witnesses, he completed his part of the contract by handing over to his two habitants two thousand acres of land, to be divided into equal fiefs known as du Buisson and La Clouterie.

"No, no," they protested. "You owe us four thousand acres – two thousand acres each! That's what our contract said, 'à chacun deux mille arpents.'"

"You heard it wrong," Giffard replied. "It said, 'à chacun d'eux mille arpents,' to each of them a thousand acres. There's an apostrophe in there."

"We didn't hear any damn apostrophe!" they shouted.

Their deal with Giffard had stipulated that, once they took possession of their land, they owed their seigneur respect and some small dues. These were far less burdensome obligations than the military commitments and taxes in France, intended in Canada only as formalities to preserve a sense of social order. Now, however, Zacherie Cloutier and Jean Guyon refused to get down on their knees and swear *foi et hommage* to Robert Giffard.

Whether they had harbored rebellion in their hearts back in Mortagne or simply assumed new dignity with the thought of so much land, my ancestor and his friend found in New France the conditions that encouraged defiance. One hundred and fifty years before the French Revolution there was liberty in this remote and unmapped landscape. Despite the risks and isolation, farmers preferred to live apart, not in villages. Besides, it was obvious that Giffard now needed Cloutier and Guyon more than they needed him – and if he no longer needed them, plenty of others did. Father Le Jeune noted, as a general effect of Canada, that men who had been working "in the shadows" in France underwent a physical and psychological change in the colony: they became prouder and more confident.

"A contract is a contract," Giffard insisted. He did not much care about the land or the trappings of his position – a grand name, a sword, and the duty to erect a maypole – but he had a French passion for the letter of the law. Almost every transaction was a good excuse for another elaborate contract, and the recalcitrance of Jean Guyon and Zacherie Cloutier justified his opinion that you could not trust the word of a Percheron or a Norman. To be suspicious was merely to be prudent, he liked to think. Had he not bent the knee before the acting governor in the fort on Christmas Day 1635, the day of Champlain's death, in compliance with his own legal duty to render fealty and homage to the company for the granting of the Beauport lands? If he could do it, so should these two scoundrels. He pursued the matter by petitions to the new governor for the next decade.

On July 19, 1646, Jean Guyon and Zacherie Cloutier finally lost their argument and were ordered to fulfill their obligations within two weeks. They waited until July 30, when Giffard was away from home. Then, with bared heads and bended knees, they swore their allegiance before one of his servants!

It was not a deep rift – Giffard served as a witness when one of Zacherie's sons was married a couple of years later – but the incident revealed much about the mind of my ancestor. He was ready to yield to the king's representative and honored to walk at the head of a religious procession; he simply did not wish to bow to a swindler. That simple wish was perhaps the revelation that had taken him from his country and kindred to this fierce wilderness. Unlike Robert Giffard or even Jean Guyon, he never assumed noble pretensions for himself or his family. Though he lived to be almost ninety, he never stopped quarreling with his oldest friends and closest neighbors. He had come to the banks of the St Lawrence, it seemed, in order to cultivate his garden with some sense of pride.

There are more famous contenders for the title of patriarch of the

French Canadian nation – Jacques Cartier, the first explorer; Samuel de Champlain, the first leader; Louis Hébert, the first farmer – but according to an astonishing, if not exaggerated little note beside his name in the Moncel family record, Zacherie Cloutier alone is the ancestor of every French Quebecker. "There is not a genealogy," it says, "that does not mention him once or more." The others may have left as their legacy the foundations of a vast empire, but – like Abraham, the father of Isaac, or Zacharias, the father of Jean-Baptiste – the master carpenter from Mortagne bequeathed to his fifty grand-children and all his descendants his sturdy physique, his swarthy complexion, and the spirit in his blood.

Mother Courage, 1635

H ELENE DESPORTES was related to Zacherie Cloutier by mar-
riage – one of her daughters married one of his sons – but the Moncels, according to the genealogy given me by my cousin, are related to Hélène directly through her son Alphonse Morin. She binds Granddaddy's family, therefore, to the handful of colonists who had come with Champlain before 1620 and hung on as remnants of the French empire in America during the English occupation ten years later. And so she binds me.

Little is known of Hélène's father, Pierre Desportes, except that he could write his name. Her mother, Françoise, had been a Langlois and a sister to the wife of Abraham Martin. Françoise Desportes and Marguerite Martin are rivals in history – as they may have been in life – for the honor of being the mother of the first European child born in Canada. Some give the glory to Eustache Martin, born in the fall of 1621, but others insist that Hélène Desportes beat him by a year – the same year the *Mayflower* landed at Plymouth Rock in Massachusetts with its cargo of Puritan dissenters from England. Either way, Hélène was the first Frenchwoman never to have seen the land of her ancestors.

She knew nothing other than the cold of January and the black flies of July, the squalid conditions of the outpost and the Algonquins coming in canoes to trade. Her childhood inured her to hunger and illness. She grew up in a masculine world of filthy traders and dissolute sailors who drank, gambled, and harassed the few women with rude songs. By the time she was seven she had seen the ice kill Louis Hébert and the natives murder his servant. If that made her half-savage, an orphan of Europe, it was also her strength. As Champlain had said about the Indians, "Their lives are wretched by comparison with ours, but happy for them since they have not tasted a better and believe that none more excellent can be found."

During the 1620s Hélène and her cousins had ranged over Abraham Martin's acres (the Plains of Abraham, they were called) like a native tribe all their own, feasting on wild berries, chasing rabbits, and dancing around the bonfire on the eve of Saint-Jean-Baptiste's holy day. When the ships arrived in spring, they rushed to the dock – not, like the adults, desperate for news from home, but rather, like the Indians, astonished by the arrival of letters, linen, plumed hats, velvet cloaks, and exotic foods from a mythical domain.

Then, in 1628, no ships came. Instead there came reports that the English had seized control of the gulf and were demanding the surrender of Quebec. Everyone's daily ration of seven ounces of peas was reduced immediately, and reduced again when the Héberts' crop did not last the winter. By spring Hélène was foraging in the woods for edible roots with every other person still able to crawl.

"Patience! Patience!" Champlain had shouted. "Relief is coming soon! The worst is over, my dear people!" But when the Kirkes arrived before help from France, there was no more bluff left in him. On July 22 he gave up Quebec to the English. Two days later, he was taken away as their captive, leaving behind the Héberts, the Martins, the Desportes, and a few others who preferred to take their chances under the temporary rule of the English tongue and Protestant faith rather than to be tossed back on to the dunghill of their old world.

The colonists were accustomed to going down to the quay each autumn to wave away the ships returning to France. After the frenzy of last-minute preparations, after the rush of memories and of homesickness, they always felt let down and left behind. They were returned to themselves, *entre eux*. The *habitation* was eerily silent; the distances seemed strangely greater. Soon the frigid darkness of winter would be upon them, disturbed only by the howling of wolves and the cracking of branches from the weight of ice. Words themselves were frozen by the air, people believed, like invisible icicles. But isolation brought a kind of freedom, and there was security in knowing that the ships would be back with the spring. In 1629, however, as they gathered to say goodbye to Champlain, there was no such comfort. A war in Europe had abandoned them to fate and to *les Anglais*.

The French settlers and their religion were treated with courtesy – the Kirke brothers had been born and raised in Dieppe, after all, where their father had worked as an English importer, and there was no advantage to razing the settlement – but the English occupation took its toll. Buildings crumbled, spirits fell with each passing season, and life became steadily more grueling as the trade patterns were broken and the support system collapsed. In one winter, Champlain heard, "fourteen died of want and misery," and the very lack of evidence about the deaths of Hélène Desportes's parents is strong indication that they were victims of the English interregnum.

Hélène still had her aunt and uncle, but there was something discomfiting about the way Uncle Abraham looked at her while she darned by the fire or the way he stroked her hair as she wept herself to

47

sleep. (Years later, his lust for young girls landed him in jail.) Mostly Hélène turned to her spiritual family, Father God, Mother Mary, and Baby Jesus.

In July 1632 they answered her prayers. The English privateers were commanded by treaty to hand back Quebec. The following May, to shouts of hosanna, Samuel de Champlain kept his promise and returned to take charge of a bigger and better colony. Dr Giffard arrived the next summer with his settlers, including Zacherie Cloutier, and suddenly the *habitation* again hummed with the din of construction and voices. Hélène moved from the putrid shed into the Martins' new and private quarters, and for a short while happiness shines through the old documents. In October 1634 she married Guillaume Hébert, the only son of Louis and Marie. She was no more than fourteen years old. Though he was ten years older, she had known him in close proximity all her life, through sorrow and joy. There had been few men to choose from, of course, but I like to imagine that my ancestress had nursed a childhood infatuation for him while he, in turn, had not been able to hide his impatience for her to grow up. They had three children in almost as many years, of whom a boy and a girl survived infancy.

And then the sadness began to close in again. Champlain fell ill, became paralyzed, and bequeathed his estate to the Virgin Mary in a fit of madness. He had been striding through Hélène's life for as long as she could remember, leaving but always returning, vivacious and inspiring, and though he was not yet seen as the Father of New France, he was a fatherly figure none the less. Champlain's wife, who had had an unhappy stay in Quebec from 1620 to 1624, was Hélène's godmother – best remembered for the small mirror in which she promised to keep the image of her goddaughter beside her heart forever – and his reappearance in 1633 had helped to heal the loss Hélène had felt since her own father's death. Champlain was old enough to be her grandfather, however, and sixty-five years of adventure had worn him out. His death on Christmas Day 1635 was a terrible shock. "Monsieur de Champlain has been reborn in heaven," Father Le Jeune informed the crowd, and the superstitious understood the connection between the savior of mankind and the savior of Canada. Seated in the pew reserved for the Hébert family in Notre-Dame-de-la-Recouvrance, huddled in grief, Hélène sobbed as I had sobbed at my grandfather's funeral, while Father Le Jeune spoke of the great explorer's service to God, who was now guiding him to a kingdom more glorious than China.

Worse was to come for Hélène. She was back in the same church less than four years later to mourn the death of her husband, who had perished from an illness before he was thirty.

Hélène was comforted by a sweet and stately nun recently arrived from Tours, the nun who had dreamed of Canada as a spacious place paved with alabaster and full of wonderful silence. Born Marie Guyart, married early, widowed young with an infant son whom she deserted to marry Christ, Marie de l'Incarnation had come to Canada to found a school for French and Indian girls. She soon became the spiritual mentor to the whole colony, who flocked to her cold, cramped room in the small house by the wharf for advice. "Yes, there are ice floes, brambles, and thorns here, but the Holy Spirit has a sovereign power to consume all these – and even to split rocks," she told Hélène, as she told others, drawing on her mystical experiences with whips of nettles, the burning of her flesh, and other self-mortifications. "There are no objects here to charm the senses, but there are divine feelings, for here God wishes the heart to be stripped of all material things. Oh my God, how rich the soul would be in a little time if it desired to be and were faithful! We see here a sort of necessity to become holy, Hélène. One must either give one's assent to this or die!"

Hélène Desportes built no buildings and left no famous organizations. She was not a protégée of Parisian princesses or a confidante of great men. But she was the first to draw her first breath in Canada. She survived the deaths of her parents under the English. She buried a husband before she was twenty. She married another, Noël Morin, within a year, and helped him to climb from being a maker of wheels to seigneur of Saint-Luc. She raised more than a dozen children by him to serve God and the king of France. She bore the loss of Joseph Hébert, her only son by Guillaume, who was wounded during an Iroquois ambush, traded to an Oneida tribe, tortured, and knifed to death during an alcoholic debauchery. She attended the birth of Joseph's son, who was born after his father's capture, and she prepared her grandson's funeral when he died soon afterward. She gave her eldest surviving son, Germain Morin, into the hands of the Jesuits and saw him ordained as the first priest born in Canada. She gave her daughter, Marie Morin, to the Religious Hospitalers and saw her become the first cloistered nun born in Canada.

Unlike the many heroines of French Canada's history and literature, my ancestress is not generally remembered. That may be appropriate, however, for Hélène Desportes epitomizes the unsung matriarchs of the French Canadian family who, generation after generation, toiled on the mother earth, passed on the mother tongue, prayed in the mother church, and suffered a mother's heart in strength and silence.

Dynasty, 1636

IN JUNE 1636, six months after Champlain's death, Hélène had strolled down to the shore at Quebec to watch the arrival of the new governor general, Charles Huault de Montmagny, though her mother-in-law had warned her that a hot and excited crowd was no place for a pregnant woman. Hélène was curious, however, and would have been sorry to miss the spectacle. Montmagny disembarked like a god from a cloud, trailing an impressive lineage that went back to Henri II and a glorious career that included combat against pirates and Turks. He cut an imposing figure – the Indians translated his name into "Onontio," Great Mountain – as he proceeded with his entourage to the church to offer thanks to God and receive an official welcome at the fort.

In his wake had come the oddest and most aristocratic group of settlers yet: an extended family of Norman nobs and their servants, eighteen in all, headed by two widows, Catherine de Cordé Legardeur de Tilly and Jeanne La Marchant Leneuf du Hérisson. Each came with two sons and a daughter, and they were all linked by the marriage of the Legardeur girl to the younger Leneuf boy. The elder Leneuf, Michel, then in his mid-thirties, brought no wife, but he did bring a four-year-old girl named Anne, either his adopted daughter or "the fruit of a misalliance," as one historian put it. (And so the Moncels' slender link to the French aristocracy is made even more slender.) He led her with one hand and, overcome by the stink of compost and manure that greeted him, used the other to apply a silk kerchief to the very long nose down which he had been looking. "The most reputable people have now struck root in our forests," Father Le Jeune gushed, "in order that they may live in freedom."

Clearly Michel Leneuf du Hérisson was no apothecary putting on airs as a lord of snow and bush. But equally clearly, he and his family would not have graced this fly-ridden sty if they had not been strapped for cash. Though they shared a noble aloofness with few beyond the highest-ranking officials in New France, they were not shy about trading status for financial advantage.

The new governor general set up the two families almost immediately with a small kingdom of their own, at Trois-Rivières, established in 1634 under a local governor on the north shore of the St Lawrence about eighty miles upstream from Quebec. (Even today the oldest families of Trois-Rivières are notoriously snobbish.) There the brothers Legardeur and the brothers Leneuf, heaped with land and offices, manipulated their power to fill their coffers. It did not take my ancestors long to begin dabbling in the most important business of New France, the beaver trade. On paper, and sometimes in practice, it was a perfect opportunity to buy low and sell high. The Indians brought in the thick furs; the traders swapped them for cheap goods and baubles; the ships carried them off; and the merchants sold them at a huge profit in Paris to satisfy the craze for beaver hats. But there were risks, expenses, and plenty of competitors, too.

After fifteen years in business the Company of One Hundred Associates, which never really recovered from the enormous start-up costs of ships and settlers, was almost broke. Pierre Legardeur, who became Governor General Montmagny's lieutenant, used his position to help convince most of the leading figures in the colony that they themselves should take over the fur monopoly from the One Hundred Associates – and effective control of the entire economy of New France – in exchange for giving the company an annual fee of pelts and assuming its obligations. He helped to sell the deal in Paris, and by March 1645 the new enterprise – the Community of Habitants – was in business. It was mostly the seigneurs who were in business, of course, and it was the Legardeurs, the Leneufs, and their relations who were in charge.

Following the custom of European aristocrats, the family maintained and expanded its power by love as well as war. Many of its marriages were really corporate and political alliances. One daughter of Pierre Legardeur married the nephew of Louis d'Ailleboust, Montmagny's successor as governor general. Pierre Legardeur's brother, who by 1648 was governor of Trois-Rivières, married into the Juchereaus, a prosperous and influential clan of seigneurs, officials, and merchants who had come to Canada with Dr Giffard. Not to be outdone, the Leneuf brothers quickly hitched their sister to Jean Godefroy, a former Indian interpreter turned seigneur and fur trader in Trois-Rivières with good connections in Paris. (Jean himself was made a noble by the king and founded a well-known dynasty from which sprang public servants, business leaders, and my own great-aunt Albertine de Tonnancour, renowned in family lore for the fiery way she flung her cards across the room when dealt a bad hand at bridge.)

This family network was not very subtle about manipulating the regulations, taxes, and profits of the fur trade for its own gain. Within a year of the founding of the Community of Habitants there was a popular revolt, backed by some disgruntled leaders such as Robert Giffard and the Jesuits. The revolt caught the ear of the French court, which set up a small managing council that included several elected representatives of the people to help the governors manage the trade and defense of New France. That democratic concession proved little hindrance to the ambitions of my kin. In 1648 and 1649 Michel Leneuf du Hérisson was able to get himself elected to the council by the habitants of Trois-Rivières, not least because he and his relatives were their seigneurs. And though the new council soon discovered that Pierre Legardeur's "methods of bookkeeping were inadequate and that he was not niggardly about expenses," as one historian wrote, his connections kept him director of transport until his premature death in 1648.

Pierre's sister Marguerite demonstrates that even the womenfolk shared the spirit of family enterprise. While her husband Jacques Leneuf was governor of Trois-Rivières and her brother-in-law Michel was a local judge, she ran a lucrative – and illegal – trade in alcohol to the Indians until "they swarmed round her house in droves," according to an official investigator, "drinking, fighting, urinating, and spitting" in the frenzy to swap their moose hides and beaver pelts for her liquor. Indeed, Michel Leneuf's family established the pattern of political corruption and economic nepotism that would reach its apogee three hundred years later in another son of Trois-Rivières, the premier of Quebec when I was a boy, Maurice Duplessis.

If the intention of the Leneufs and Legardeurs had been to make a financial killing in Canada and return to France, they failed. They stayed on, often in a state of penury. Though Michel Leneuf did well enough, acquiring several properties and a mill, his seigneuries brought more responsibilities than income, and his forays into the fur business remained vulnerable to every whim of politics, corruption, taste, and the Indians. The two families did much better with public service – and its perks and pensions. They produced governors, councilors, military officers, naval captains, and diplomats who defended New France against the English and the Iroquois for the next hundred years. Michel Leneuf himself was made a royal judge, and he discovered that he had as much enthusiasm for the law as for making money.

"He was a typical Norman country squire," his biographer wrote, "intelligent and wily, but fond of legal quibbles." This was a particularly Norman trait, evident through the centuries, from Dr Giffard's contracts to Quebec's constitutional demands, and Michel Leneuf brought to it his own bad temper. Like Monsieur Chicaneau in Racine's play *Les Plaideurs*, who spent twenty years suing a farmer whose donkey had eaten some hay, Leneuf delighted in suing his habitants, taking on his neighbors, and fighting off investigations about his brother and himself "by pleas, declarations, arguments and warrants, experts' reports, injunctions, writs of error, statements of grievance, and fresh evidence, with affidavits, royal letters patent, and confutations." He once locked his housekeeper's clothes in a cupboard to prevent her from leaving his service to marry. In 1650 his tantrums drove away four servants, who fled at night by canoe to Quebec and were not seen again.

———————

Everyone in the colony was under great stress in those days, full of penance and prayers, because of the latest Iroquois attacks. Despite

Jacques Cartier, who had kidnaped Indians as prizes for the king of France, and despite the devastating effect of French diseases and the arrogant behavior of French traders, Champlain had managed to secure a friendship with the nomadic Algonquins around the St Lawrence and the agricultural Hurons to the northwest. But the price of peace – and of a stable supply of furs – was no peace at all. The French had to join the Algonquins and the Hurons in their ongoing wars against the Five Nations of the Iroquois – Seneca, Onondaga, Cayuga, Oneida, Mohawk – a prosperous, powerful, and politically sophisticated people who lived south of the St Lawrence and the Great Lakes along the border that now separates Canada from New York State. "It was very necessary to assist them," Champlain later wrote of his alliance with the Algonquins and Hurons, "both to put them the more under obigation to love us and to facilitate my undertakings and discoveries, which, as it seemed, could only be accomplished with their help, and also as this would lead to and prepare their conversion to Christianity."

From the first blast of Champlain's matchlock against an Iroquois army near present-day Ticonderoga in New York State, the French colonists and traders had become part of an intertribal conflict for economic supremacy and territorial domination. That blast sent the Iroquois to seek firearms and help from the Dutch traders who had moved into the Hudson River valley, and it signaled the start of a military and economic drama that took a century and a half to play itself out. In 1652 more than a hundred warriors raided Trois-Rivières and carried off seven men, one of whom was Thomas Godefroy, the brother of Michel Leneuf's brother-in-law Jean.

"I pity the poor Indians to have to put up with him for more than a day," Michel said as a way of consoling his sister. "They'll send him back once they see how mad he is, just like they've done before."

Thomas and Jean Godefroy had come to Canada in 1626 and worked for Champlain as intermediaries with the Indians. It was a crucial job, for the French were dependent upon the good will of the

Algonquins and Hurons for furs and for life itself, and it attracted single young men who yearned for more freedom and adventure than settlers such as Zacherie Cloutier or Michel Leneuf would have. The Godefroys had wandered like the tribes, living off the land and sleeping beneath the stars. They picked up the various languages and indigenous customs; they got used to the boiled corn mush known as sagamite and the overcrowded long houses whose smoke damaged the lungs and the eyes; they learned about the reality of dreams and the meaning of bravery; and they became so removed from the political and social authority of the colony that they hardly noticed when the English held Quebec for three years. The Godefroy brothers simply remained in the wilderness until Champlain returned in 1633.

Shortly afterward they had been lured to Trois-Rivières by grants of land and promises of profit. Jean adapted well enough as a seigneur, a trader, the husband of Marie Leneuf, and the father of eleven children. Thomas, however, longed to escape. Though he was given an elegant new name – Godefroy de Normanville – he found the parochial pretensions intolerable; and though he was a devout man who wanted to bring the word of God to the heathens, he considered the company of the natives more civilized than the Community of Habitants. "Gone Indian," people said, and he continued going out in his deerskin gaiters and beaded moccasins, patching together deals with France's aboriginal allies, guiding the missionaries into remote villages, or hunting for moose by himself in the woods. He was famous for having outraced an Indian chief on foot and on snowshoes.

"In order to practice patience in good earnest and to endure hardships beyond the limit of human strength," wrote one of Thomas's less enchanted contemporaries, "it is only necessary to make journeys with the savages, and long ones especially, such as we did; because besides the danger of death on the way, one must make up one's mind to endure and suffer more than could be imagined, from hunger, from sleeping always on the bare ground in the open country, from walking with great labor in water and logs, and in some places over rocks, and through dark thick woods, from rain on one's back and all the evils that the season and weather can inflict, and from being bitten by a countless swarm of mosquitoes and midges, together with difficulties of language in explaining clearly and showing them one's needs, and having no Christian beside one for communication and consolation in the midst of one's toil." But, as compensation, there were magnificent vistas and profound wisdoms; there was silence, solitude, and liberty.

While on a hunt in 1641 Thomas Godefroy and a fellow interpreter had been captured by some Iroquois and held long enough to learn their language. They would have been killed, except that they were to be bait for an ambush near Trois-Rivières. They managed to arrange a last-minute truce that spared both the town and themselves. In early 1648 Thomas was again captured by Iroquois; again he was able to sweet-talk his way out of death by his knowledge of their language and their ways. When he was taken the third time, in 1652, along with six others, he had the presence of mind to scribble a note on an Indian shield with a piece of charred wood – and the wit to add a macabre joke.

"Normanville, Francheville, Poisson, LaPalme, Turcot, Chaillou, Saint-Germain," he wrote, naming the captives and reporting that they had been taken by Onondagas and Mohawks. "So far," he scrawled, "I've only lost a fingernail."

He was soon to lose more than that. His charm and patter now failed him. Like the Jesuit missionaries murdered three years earlier when twelve hundred Iroquois raided Huron territory, Thomas and the others did not die quickly. Stripped naked, beaten with sticks, they were tied to posts by willow thongs and methodically tortured. Their hands and feet were cut off. They were forced to drink their own blood. The flesh from their arms and legs was sliced into pieces, roasted in the fire, and devoured before their eyes. They were made to eat morsels of themselves. Their wounds, their penises, and their armpits were branded with burning birchbark, and red-hot hatchets were strung around their necks and bellies. Boiling water was poured over their heads in a mock baptism; their tongues were pulled from their mouths, to let them speak no more lies or call no more to the Father who had forsaken them. Finally, as the flames rose beneath them, they were scalped.

Michel Leneuf had never much cared for Thomas's sort. He thought such adventurers vulgar, greedy, untrustworthy, immoral, and beyond the control of the family. In his eyes they betrayed the great civilization of France and jeopardized the company's monopoly of the fur trade. Leneuf grieved more for poor Jean Turcot, a local farmer whose name had been recorded by Godefroy on the Indian shield. Indeed, Michel Leneuf helped to raise Turcot's son Jacques, born a month after his father's death, into a prosperous farmer and respected judge who eventually owned four farms and one of the finest libraries in New France. If such generosity seemed out of character for Michel Leneuf du Hérisson, it was not completely selfless: one of the last acts of his life was to arrange a final marriage of convenience between Jacques Turcot and his own granddaughter Anne Desrosiers, the daughter of the mysterious girl Michel had brought to Canada and hitched to another bright farmer-turned-judge. If he could not find men worthy of his class in New France, it seemed, he created them: they became class by becoming family.

In this way these ancestors of mine, the Leneufs and the Legardeurs, helped to create an ethos as well as a dynasty in Canada. That ethos exalted land, title, and public service above mere profit; it made seigneurs, judges, and soldiers more esteemed than traders in spite of the whole colony's dependence on trade; it glorified the pride of Michel Leneuf instead of the courage of Thomas Godefroy. "There is a great fondness for keeping up one's position, and nearly no one amuses himself by thrift," a Jesuit observed a hundred years later. "The English colonist amasses means and makes no superfluous expense; the French enjoys what he has and often parades what he has not. The former works for his heirs; the latter leaves his in the need in which he is himself to get along as best he can."

The Foolish Enterprise, 1653

THE RAID on Trois-Rivières in 1652 that had cost Thomas Gode-froy and Jean Turcot their lives was a boost to the confidence of the Iroquois nations, and six hundred warriors returned the next year to blockade the settlement and control the trade on the St Lawrence River. Panic spread among the settlers and reached its pitch on the western front line at Montreal, then known as Ville-Marie, the City of Mary. "No one dared open his door at night," wrote Dollier de Casson, a Sulpician missionary, describing the anxiety of the outpost's one hundred and fifty inhabitants, "and in the daytime no one dared to go more than four steps from the house without being armed with musket, sword, and pistol."

Small and isolated, on the edge of Iroquois territory where the St Lawrence meets the Ottawa, Montreal had been subject to guerrilla attack ever since its founding as the third settlement in New France, but it seemed especially vulnerable now. A short peace with the Mohawks had just collapsed; the villages of the ten thousand Huron allies to the west had been destroyed by the Iroquois advances; the English and Dutch to the south had been fortifying the Five Nations, which may have numbered as many as seventy-five thousand people, with weapons and booze; and the blockade downstream had reduced the chances of help from Quebec.

Anne Archambault had come from France as a child with her

parents, and in 1647 married Michel Chauvin at Quebec. Then they had moved with her family to the little bastion at Ville-Marie, had one child, and were expecting a second. In time Anne got used to the idea that an Iroquois might leap from behind a bush at any moment – one of her brothers had been killed in an attack – and she practiced the dash from the house to the stone fort whenever the cannon sounded a warning. How, though, could she have known that the Devil was under her own roof and in her own bed?

One day, while her husband was in the field and the colony on alert, she received a visit from a neighbor, Louis Prud'homme. An ancestor of my great-uncle Hector Prud'homme, Louis, a brewer, had been among the first settlers in Montreal and still carried a certain authority as a close friend of its founder and governor, Paul de Chomedey de Maisonneuve. Prud'homme was pious and civic-minded, but Anne thought him a self-righteous busybody – *prud-hommesque*, in fact, which the dictionary translates as sententious or pompous. When he entered with a long face and began, "I come with bad news, I'm afraid," she braced herself.

"I don't know how to put this, Madame, it is so distressing," said Prud'homme. "As you know, I have been to France recently – I was asked by Monsieur de Maisonneuve to attend to some important affairs pertaining to the financial future of Ville-Marie, and, God be blessed, I had the honor to be presented to our beloved benefactress, whose name I cannot mention but who is, you have my word, a lady of the greatest virtue – but I digress. While there, I learned – I cannot say from whom, for I was sworn to secrecy, as indeed I was with that very noble and very generous woman whom I had the privilege of meeting – but please, Madame, please sit down, you look rather pale."

Prud'homme's concern did not conceal the pleasure he derived from prolonging her agony. "Oh, poor dear, to think the shameless scoundrel has made you heavy with child yet again while all the time he – but I am getting ahead of myself." He paused to collect his wits, sucked in too much air, and had a coughing fit, which sent him to the keg of water for a drink. He wiped his lips with his fingers and then used them to dampen the twisted ends of his upturned mustache. "While in France, as I said, I learned to my shock that your husband – may God have mercy on his wretched soul! – is not your husband. I mean to say, he cannot be your husband, for he has another wife. In France. From an earlier marriage."

This would have been a rude shock anywhere; it was particularly so in Ville-Marie. The town was really a religious commune, full of mystics and devotees; it had been willed into existence not by royal strategists or fur traders but by direct edicts from God. It was a child of the Catholic Counter Reformation, then in full swing in France, which promoted piety, self-flagellation, spiritual visions, and evangelical missions as responses to the Protestant movement that had changed the face of Europe in the sixteenth century.

The exploration of Canada was undertaken at a time when religion was considered to be worth fighting and dying for. Indeed, religion was the direct or indirect cause of most of France's wars and civil unrest. Jacques Cartier's first voyages in the 1530s, for example, had coincided with Henry VIII of England's break with Rome over the issue of divorce and the founding of the Jesuit and Ursuline orders to combat the Protestant heresies. Cartier had returned home to discover French Catholics setting fire to French Protestants with all the enthusiasm of Iroquois warriors. New France became an idealized battleground to conquer Satan. In salons and convents across France, faithful men and women were inspired to join that crusade, either in person or with gold. One result was the founding in 1640 of the Société de Notre Dame de Montréal to establish a community in the hinterland of Canada dedicated to winning heathen souls for Christ and the Roman Catholic Church.

"The hand of the Almighty, shown each day in its workings, willed in the fortieth year of this century to manifest itself in a special manner by the foundation of Montreal," Dollier de Casson wrote in his history, "planning the enterprise in the minds of a number of people in a way which showed the great good will of God to this country, in desiring to give this post to it as the buckler and wall of its defense."

Even though the Society of Montreal was not empowered to trade in furs and the proposed setting was an easy target for the infidels who would rather not hear about their eternal damnation, the money and the organization soon fell into place. More practical heads, looking strictly at cost benefits and military advantages, dubbed it the Foolish Enterprise, but Maisonneuve and his dreamy followers were not dissuaded. "Breathing an atmosphere of miracle," as the historian Francis Parkman put it, "compassed about with angels and devils, urged with stimulants most powerful though unreal, their minds drugged as it were to preternatural excitement," five dozen people landed at Montreal on May 17, 1642, and passed from sunny morning to starry night in prayer, with a meadow as their cathedral, wildflowers as their offering, and fireflies as their altar lamps.

God ruled here through his humble servants. The proof was that the settlement survived flood, famine, frostbite, and the Iroquois furies. Montreal had begun as a sacred center, dedicated to the Virgin Mary; to this day it commemorates its origins by an electric cross atop Mount Royal and a cruciform skyscraper called Place Ville-Marie.

That was why poor Anne Archambault felt less sinned against than sinning when she found she had been fornicating out of wedlock. The rogue Chauvin was immediately banished by Maisonneuve, who had threatened an "immoral" soldier with execution only a few years earlier. The governor general of New France and a nurse named Jeanne Mance, one of New France's most saintly pioneers, volunteered at once to be the godparents of Anne's second baby. There remained, however, the awkward problem of what to do with Anne herself. No one thought she should be punished as an adultress, of course, but she was an uncomfortable reminder of evil and misfortune amid so much sanctity and benediction.

There came another answer to another prayer, in the person of Jean Gervaise. He was one of a hundred new settlers, soldiers, laborers, and religious who had been fetched by Maisonneuve to reinforce the colony – without them, the leader had confessed to his people before he left, "everything will have to be abandoned, for indeed the place would be untenable." This group arrived at Quebec in September 1653, rather the worse for wear after three months of contagious disease and vicious gales aboard the *Saint-Nicolas*, and they were greeted as a miracle. By God's grace, too, the Iroquois had decided to lift their siege of Trois-Rivières in exchange for prisoners, so Maisonneuve and his contingent were able to reach Montreal without a fight.

Jean Gervaise, trained in the law in Anjou, had been caught up in the religious fervor of the period, and it had led him to Canada. By all accounts he was a solid and respected citizen; one historian characterized him as "solemn and sensible." In 1657 he became one of the three "most honorable" settlers elected as wardens of Notre-Dame Church, "esteemed because of their virtues, their piety, and the zeal with which they worked for the good of the colony." (Louis Prud'homme was another of the wardens, and almost two hundred and fifty years later my great-grandfather Moncel joined them on the list of *les marguilliers*.) In 1673 Gervaise was appointed the public prosecutor and quickly rose to become a judge.

So I have almost no justification for the aversion I have developed toward my grandparent of ten generations ago except for the speed with which he offered to solve Maisonneuve's knotty conundrum about Anne Archambault and her kids. "I shall marry the pathetic creature myself," I hear him saying, "and raise her bastards to fear God and love the king!" Perhaps I do him a great injustice – perhaps he took one look at her and threw over all his solemnity and sensibleness – but I cannot help thinking he was an ambitious newcomer eager to score a few holier-than-thou points with the pious governor, who indeed rewarded him with thirty acres where Rue Saint-Sulpice now runs through Old Montreal.

Anne was in no position to be ungrateful. She married Jean Gervaise on February 4, 1654, less than five months after his arrival. They had, according to Dollier de Casson, "a very numerous family whose members combine with their tender years the good manners of maturity. They make a blessed family, in good repute throughout the country, with an endowment of virtue exceeding that of this world's goods."

Behind all the manners and virtue of their nine children, though, I see a rod in the hand of Jean Gervaise and the severity of God on his face. New France was never the puritanical theocracy that some historians later conceived it to be – despite the fervent attempts of its bishops, its missionaries, and its pious ones to create a kingdom of God on earth – but reactionary Catholicism did indeed have a hold on the governors, the traders, the settlers, and even the Indians. No Protestants were allowed to live in the colony, for example, and the clergy had power in the parish and the court. The Church waged war against liberty and libertinism. It preached obedience to fathers such as Jean Gervaise, to mothers such as Hélène Desportes, and to God, who – according to a seventeenth-century catechism – "also orders us to be submissive toward and have respect for those who represent Him and who are clothed with His authority; for those who resist the order He established in the world become worthy of eternal damnation."

Family Business, 1663

CHARLES SEVESTRE had much in common with Michel Leneuf du Hérisson, the aristocratic hustler of Trois-Rivières, besides the fact that both were ancestors of mine. Both had come to New

France in 1636; both had brought a widowed mother and the rest of the family (a wife, some children, and in Sevestre's case three of his four brothers); both had held important positions in the Community of Habitants; and both had risen to judgeships. But if the one accumulated land and influence through his prestige and connections as a Leneuf, the other belonged to Jean Gervaise's school of strategic self-abnegation. Charles Sevestre advanced primarily by kowtowing to the rich and powerful, turning a blind eye to their larcenous foibles, and riding his patrons' coattails to high office.

By the time the Community of Habitants was formed in New France in 1645, its sly directors had already recognized Sevestre's qualities. They had placed him in a sensitive post, in charge of the fur warehouse. But his golden opportunity had come in 1651 with the arrival of Jean de Lauson as governor general of New France. Lauson, a French lawyer and public figure, had been the first managing director of the Company of One Hundred Associates. He had plunged into the mercantile world by appropriating huge tracts of land for himself and his family, including the island of Montreal, which he later tried to sell to the mystics behind the Ville-Marie mission for a sum that was truly out of this world. It was not long before Lauson owned or controlled more of New France than anyone else. To protect this investment against financial ruin and the Iroquois, and to augment it by hands-on manipulation, he had got himself appointed governor general when he was past sixty-five years old.

What was good for the Lausons was good for Canada, or so he claimed. He gave his three sons yet more land, advantageous marriages, and important positions. He made his son Charles the acting governor general after his own return to France. He negotiated a peace with the Mohawks, the quick collapse of which hastened his departure and led to the slaying of his brave and much-loved son Jean. Most boldly of all, he tried to seize the monopoly over the fur trade for himself and his friends, one of whom was Charles Sevestre.

This ancestor had probably performed small kindnesses for the Lausons from afar. Why else would the new governor general, barely off the boat, have made a mere warehouse clerk the first judge of the Lauson seigneury and the first deputy judge of the seigneurial court of Quebec? The wealth Sevestre accrued even allowed him to buy the warehouse he had managed. When Lauson's stupid and avaricious attempt to grab the fur profits eventually brought the wrath of the traders, the One Hundred Associates, and the king himself down upon his head, Sevestre helped him to flee to France in 1656 with a stolen fortune in pelts and an illicit three thousand livres in cash.

This was precisely the sort of creative accounting for which Charles Sevestre would be remembered long after his death in 1657. Perhaps he understood that he could climb no higher; maybe he sensed that he would fall much lower. In any case, he left his soul to the Lord and his reputation to his son-in-law.

Though Sevestre had seven children, none was capable of picking up the responsibilities he passed posthumously to his daughter Catherine's husband. Louis Rouer de Villeray was another impover-ished young nobleman who had come to New France to seek his fortune, first as a soldier, then as a business agent in Trois-Rivières, then as secretary to Jean de Lauson. He prospered as a notary because of Lauson, and he met Charles Sevestre through Lauson. By the time he marched down the aisle with Catherine Sevestre, her father had been buried two months. That did not prevent the ambitious groom from inheriting choice land, most of his father-in-law's occupations, and all the headaches caused by what one historian described as Sevestre's "somewhat muddled financial records."

Villeray spent years trying to clean up the mess. In 1659 he was forbidden to take Sevestre's titles until he went to France and proved to the managers of the Company of One Hundred Associates that he had cleared Sevestre's debts. In 1660 and again in 1662 he was forced to return to France to show them why he should not be held accountable for the money Sevestre had squandered. In 1663 he faced a full investigation of Sevestre's affairs by a lawyer who had been sent to Canada to snoop for the company.

Fifteen years earlier the One Hundred Associates had sublet its control of New France to the Community of Habitants for an annual fee. For at least ten years its directors had been bothered by reports of mismanagement, corruption, and nepotism in the colony. Worse, they had not received an ounce of the ten thousand pounds of beaver skins due since 1650. There had been excuses, of course, with Indians at the top of the list, but there was reason to suspect that something was rotten. In 1660 the company hired Jean Peronne Dumesnil to go and check the books; he soon became the most despised man in New France.

If my relatives are any indication, almost everyone in the Community of Habitants had an interest in hiding incompetence or dishonesty. Even the innocent were offended to see this weasel going through their old records. For one thing, his authority as a "sovereign judge" was in question, since he had been appointed by the company and not by the king. For another, he was a stubborn and obnoxious little nosy parker. Such was the public loathing for him that when a distant kin of mine was accused of kicking Dumesnil's son to death in a brawl, the settlers responded by electing the alleged killer the first mayor of Quebec.

Encountering a solid wall of obstruction, Dumesnil resorted to burglary: he crept into a notary's home and stole the Community of Habitant's documents. The powers-that-be were incensed, naturally, and they dispatched Villeray, an associate, and ten soldiers to retrieve the files and summon the thief. Dumesnil avoided prison only by being expelled at gunpoint from New France.

Needless to say, Dumesnil's report did not sing the praises of the colony's officials and traders. He heaped abuse on the governors and councilors; he hurled charges at the Jesuit missionaries and the bishop himself; he accused the directors of the Community of Habitants of pilfering "three million livres or thereabouts"; and he singled out for special condemnation Louis Rouer de Villeray and the late Charles Sevestre.

Dumesnil was an unstable man of limited credibility, driven to exaggeration and derangement by his experiences in Canada. But where there was smoke, there was fire, and whenever Louis XIV glanced toward New France, he saw nothing but thick, black smoke. The Company of One Hundred Associates was now an empty shell. The Community of Habitants had become a financial fiasco. The Jesuits of Quebec were feuding with the Sulpicians of Montreal for the attention of the bishop who had arrived in 1659. Bishop Laval was fighting with the governor general for control of the merchants. The merchants were battling the bishop and the governor over the right to trade liquor to the Indians. The Iroquois were rampaging through the settlements at will. The population still numbered fewer than three thousand people, and in February 1663 a mighty earthquake devastated the St Lawrence Valley as if, according to one nun's prophetic vision, "four furious and enraged demons at the four corners of Quebec" were tossing the land because "God was ready to punish the country for the sins committed here."

"Even while God shook the mountains and marble rocks of these regions, He took pleasure in shaking consciences," Marie de l'Incarnation remarked. "The days of carnival were changed into days of penitence and sadness." The message reached as far as France, apparently, for Louis XIV also decided it was time to turn over a new leaf. To hell with the One Hundred Associates and the Habitants. If private enterprise could not do the job, he and his brilliant minister of marine, Jean-Baptiste Colbert, would take personal responsibility for the development and defense of New France. There would be a governor general for military matters, local governors for local matters, an intendant for administrative matters, a bishop for religious matters, and an appointed council for judicial and legislative matters (on which the governor general, the intendant, and the bishop sat too).

It looked neat on paper, but when the king's commissioner arrived in New France, he discovered many of the old scoundrels back in power with new titles – including Michel Leneuf du Hérisson and Louis Rouer de Villeray. "There were none more capable to be found," he concluded, provoking Dumesnil to shout in the streets of Paris that the commissioner was in the pay of Canada's "family compact." As it turned out, my ancestors and their colleagues had entrenched more than themselves: they had entrenched the legitimacy of a paternalistic local elite presiding in its own interests over the destiny of the French Canadian people.

Runner of the Woods, 1666

AT FIRST BLUSH the king's reorganization of the administration of New France in 1663 was seen by the good people of Montreal as a divine intercession. Their financial supporters had run out of money or turned their zeal toward the Levant, but the Sulpician priests themselves became their new seigneurs and Maisonneuve remained the governor of their town. In 1665, when royal word arrived that more than twelve hundred musketeers and pikemen were on their way to save Canada, Dollier de Casson reported "very great rejoicing at the king's goodness in making his victorious arms to shine" among the five hundred people of Ville-Marie de Montréal.

The rejoicing soon turned to dismay. Within months the Marquis de Tracy, commander-in-chief of the king's troops in the Americas, consolidated Quebec's hold on Montreal by sending Maisonneuve home to early retirement. Then Montreal was overrun by three companies of pissed-off, pissed-up fighters led by the cantankerous Marquis de Salières. No saint to start with, Salières showed up in particularly foul humor after nine days of hail, white water, and terror in a shallop one hundred and fifty miles from Quebec. His mood was shared by his men, who were chilled, exhausted, sick, and – in Dollier de Casson's words – without "the same regard for the exclusion of vices" as the righteous folk now looking aghast upon their saviors.

Salières was colonel of the Carignan-Salières Regiment, a thousand men – twenty companies of fifty men each – chosen along with Tracy's four companies "to destroy utterly these barbarians," the Iroquois, who had been butchering the settlers and traders in Canada. Scattering most of his infantry to defend the established towns or build new forts from which to launch attacks, Salières kept three units with him: his own company, the Contrecoeur Company (whose wine-loving captain was to demonstrate valor beyond the call of duty by marrying, at the age of seventy-one, a fifteen-year-old girl), and the La Fredière Company under Balthazard de La Flotte de La Fredière, whom history honors as a "repulsive, avaricious, and debauched man, disliked by all except his uncle, the Marquis de Salières."

Among their ranks was my ancestor Mathurin Bernier. He was from Saint-Jean-de-Bessay, a farming village not far from the Atlantic port of La Rochelle, to which he had come in search of work. There had not been any work, but a drummer on the quayside had been calling attention to another opportunity: military service against les sauvages. A regiment had been assembled from the far corners of France, a sergeant explained, but there were still a few places open. Hurry, hurry, step right up, the boats will be sailing shortly. "Why not?" Mathurin thought. "It's food, it's adventure, it's only three years. It can't be harder than haying, and it might be as much fun as a hunt." He did not pause to wonder why veteran officers were deserting like rats or why the sergeant smirked when he ordered the new recruit to report to Major de La Fredière.

That had been in early April 1665. By November his mood had changed entirely. "Two hundred and three days down, eight hundred and ninety-two days to go," he mumbled to the beat of the march into Ville-Marie, "if I get out of this goddamn place alive." He had kept the tally in his head: thirty-eight days in a tent on the Ile de Ré off the coast from La Rochelle, waiting for the worm-infested *Aigle d'Or* to be made seaworthy. Ninety-eight days of terror and nausea on the Atlantic (including the time spent plugging leaks so that the ship would not sink within sight of the cheering crowds at Quebec). Barely ten days to recover his sanity and strength. Then he had tramped for twenty-six days to reach the fort that Captain Jacques de Chambly was building on the Richelieu River, where he was given but one day's rest. He had hardly sat down before he was ordered out again for a twelve-mile hike in the shivering downpour to where Salières wanted his own fort built. Twenty-five days later, without adequate tools or dry clothing or hot meals, the regiment had cleared the cedar forest, dug a trench for the palisade mostly with their bare hands, erected the twenty-foot logs into an outer wall approximately one hundred and fifty feet long and one hundred feet wide, cut other logs into boards, and constructed several barracks and storehouses. Fort Sainte-Thérèse was ready for war; Mathurin Bernier and most of his friends were sick, hungry, and ready for bed. They raised an enervated hurrah when told they would be wintering in Montreal with Salières.

Chicken soup! Fur blankets! White women! Their joy was even greater when, soon after their arrival in Ville-Marie, they watched dozens of Indian leaders come paddling downriver to talk peace. Four of the five Iroquois nations had heard about the French army, seen the new forts, and got the message; and what with smallpox and measles and the flu, they were not feeling up to battle either. Besides, they were having their own problems with the greed and aggression of the absent nation, the Mohawks. If the Mohawks wanted to take on twelve hundred Christians armed with flintlocks, might the Great

Spirit help them. The Oneidas, the Onondagas, the Cayugas, and the Senecas were not about to.

Hope sprang into the heart of Mathurin Bernier. Perhaps he would face nothing more hostile than the expression on the faces of the priests and nuns who patrolled Ville-Marie. No such luck. Against common sense Salières was ordered to prepare a contingent of soldiers and local militia to join a major assault of more than five hundred troops against the Mohawks in the Hudson River valley in January. Major de La Fredière and Mathurin Bernier were two of the unfortunates whom Salières sent into the Canadian winter with fifty pounds of equipment on their backs.

Except for the officers and the settlers, few were equipped for the blizzards, ice, and sub-zero temperatures they would encounter during the six weeks and hundreds of miles ahead. They lacked heavy clothing, warm bedding, sufficient food, guides, and snowshoes. The glare of the day blinded them; the cold of the night froze their blood. They lost their way in woods and white-outs. They ate bark and sucked on trees for sustenance. They became trapped in four-foot-deep snow on Lake Champlain and Lake George. They starved. They went to sleep in the snow and never awoke.

At last, on February 20, the enemy was engaged: some old Indian women and a young boy cowering in fear in a few huts near Schenectady, the Dutch trading post that had passed into English hands in 1664 and eventually became a city in New York State. The French troops, wrote the historian Jack Verney, "half-crazed by the privations and miseries of the preceding three weeks and lusting for something on which to vent their pent-up rage, overran and ransacked the cabins in a frenzy of willful destruction" that culminated in the slaughter of the women. Their anguish was heard by a band of Mohawks who happened to be at the post. A brief clash ensued, during which Balthazard de La Flotte de La Fredière was shot in the thigh.

"Too bad they didn't shoot him in the nuts," Mathurin Bernier thought.

The English agent in nearby Albany rushed out to arrange a truce (and sell some provisions). The French officers looked at the remains of their army, surveyed the cruelty they had just inflicted, considered the enemy country and the bad weather, and decided to get home a step ahead of the Mohawks and hunger. Fewer than a quarter of the expedition returned to New France alive. Of the four hundred dead, only seven had been victims of the enemy. On March 11 Mathurin limped back into Montreal, slumped down in a chair, and wondered what the hell that had been about.

It had been about intimidation, if anything, and it worked. Throughout the spring and summer of 1666 more Iroquois chieftains – including some Mohawks – passed through Montreal on their way to smoke the pipe with the Marquis de Tracy at Quebec. But a general treaty with the Indians was not yet possible, in part because Tracy was planning a new and more conclusive offensive. In September he sent six hundred French soldiers, six hundred Canadian militia, and a hundred Indian guides on three hundred boats up the Richelieu to Lake Champlain and down into the Mohawk nation.

The rain was uncomfortable, but at least it was not snow. The Marquis de Tracy was dropped into a river by the Swiss soldier who had been carrying him, but a Huron sprang to the rescue. The rations were meager, but the Indians took deer, hare, and chestnuts from the land. At the end of the long march there was no enemy to be found, only four deserted villages stocked with food and supplies. Tracy ordered them set on fire, to handicap the Mohawks and send them a warning, and then the soldiers sang the Te Deum and said Mass. Not as glorious as combat against the infidels, perhaps, but Tracy claimed the region for France by right of conquest anyway. He could have tried to drive the English out of New York; he chose instead to about-face and quick-march north before the first snowfall in November. Bells pealed and bonfires crackled to hail the return of the conquering heroes.

My ancestor was not among them. Mathurin Bernier had been

kept behind by Major de La Fredière, now the military governor of
Montreal. La Fredière had left a chunk of his thigh on the battlefield
at Schenectady and an eye somewhere in Europe; loyal though he
was, he felt he had given enough of himself for the glory of the king.
He would see plenty of action anyway, he figured. There would be
women to conquer.

As a member of La Fredière's staff Mathurin Bernier spent a year
as a servant in the underworld the major created in the holy realm of
Ville-Marie. Young and good-looking, he pimped on command for
his grotesque officer. When a husband got in the way, he delivered the
order that removed the cuckold from town on some flimsy pretext,
or tortured him on the "wooden horse" by hanging a hundred
pounds of rocks on his feet until he surrendered his wife. Mathurin
sold the major's extra rations of brandy and wine on the black
market to the habitants and the natives; he stole weapons and supplies from the military stores; and he flipped the profits from liquor
and other contraband into furs for the major's pension account. All
this was against the law, of course, but La Fredière was the law. He
was able to rule like a despot until some brave citizens finally risked
his wrath and revenge by appealing to Tracy for help. Even then,
because the Marquis de Salières had his own bad-tempered reasons
for defending his nephew, the Devil was not driven from Montreal
until August 1667.

"Eight hundred and eighty-seven days down, two hundred and
eight days to go," Mathurin Bernier said soon after La Fredière had
gone. But as the winter passed into spring and the end of his contract
approached, he began to think of staying on. Peace had finally been
made with the Iroquois, in part because of the peace in Europe, in
part because of the smallpox epidemics and tribal wars that had
weakened the Five Nations. The king was offering cash, land, and a
year's rations to those soldiers who remained in New France, and
Mathurin had learned a great deal about farming and the fur trade
while working with the settlers. He had grown to envy their liberty,

and gradually he became one of more than four hundred soldiers – including half a dozen of my ancestors – who realized he had fallen in love with the space and light of Canada.

These veterans left a greater legacy than their strange victories. They strengthened the colony by their military experience and numbers. They opened new settlements along the St Lawrence and the Richelieu until Canada was, in the words of one Jesuit, "no longer the forbidding and frost-bound land that was formerly painted in so unfavorable colors, but a veritable New France – not only in the salubrity of its climate and fertility of its soil but in the other conveniences of life." The veterans also helped to transform a remote mission station into an important trading center with shops and commercial houses and storage sheds – from Ville-Marie into Montreal, in fact, as if to confirm its secularization. But Mathurin Bernier did not settle down, even after marrying in 1670. Set free, my ancestor became a *coureur de bois*, a runner of the woods, one of the three or four hundred "willful individuals," as the intendant Jean Talon described them, "pursuing careers as bandits."

Heirs to the spirit of Thomas Godefroy, the coureurs de bois went up country to trade furs, for themselves or for their backers, before the Indian canoes departed for Montreal. Gone for months and sometimes years, paddling their burdened birchbark canoes from sunrise to sunset day after day for hundreds and even thousands of miles, shooting wild water or carrying their loads around rapids, pausing only to smoke a pipe of tobacco mixed with the bark of a cherry tree or tell the tale of brave Cadieux's fight against the Iroquois at Seven Falls portage, sneaking home like pirates (in the words of one observer) "to eat, drink, and play all away as long as the goods hold out," they were more like tribesmen than Frenchmen – and so, through their liaisons with Indian women, were many of their children.

"They love to breathe a free air, they are early accustomed to a wandering life," a priest said of them. "It has charms for them, which make them forget past dangers and fatigues, and they place their glory in encountering them often." Once too often, in Mathurin Bernier's case. He died in January 1678, age thirty-two, the father of four, killed by a winter storm and his love of freedom.

The Embezzler, 1681

IN 1672, forty years after the restoration of New France from English hands, the people of Quebec turned out to greet yet another new governor general. Louis de Buade, Comte de Frontenac et de Palluau, was the grandest so far – a godson of the late Louis XIII! a brigadier at twenty-four! a general with the Venetian army against the Turks in Crete! He was to become the greatest *chef* since Samuel de Champlain, but the first impression he gave was of conceit and ostentation in his powdered wig, damask coat, and plumed hat. He seemed taller than he was and older than his fifty years; his long nose and pointed chin seemed refined rather than ugly. His grandeur gave no hint that he was deep in debt from decades of extravagant and dissolute living around the edges of Louis XIV's court.

Zacherie Cloutier was not in the crowd. He had more or less retired from the world since selling La Clouterie in 1670 and moving to his son's home at Château-Richer. Nor was Hélène Desportes, for she was still mourning the death of Marie de l'Incarnation two months earlier. But Louis Rouer de Villeray was front and center, hoping to get back the offices of councilor and tax collector that the previous governor general had taken from him in a dispute; and there too, propped up by his daughter and granddaughter, was Michel Leneuf du Hérisson, with yellowed lace at his throat, red silk stockings, and an otterskin hat. He had been ill, and the trip from Trois-Rivières had not been easy, but the old judge had not spent half his life in Canada without learning the usefulness of flattering the king's agents.

At last, he thought, as he watched Count Frontenac step off the gangplank into the muck of America amid a turmoil of servants and secretaries as cannons and muskets blasted a welcome and twenty guards led the way, at last this hell has received a gentleman worthy of a Leneuf – and he bowed his most elaborate bow.

Frontenac glimpsed a somewhat shabby, pathetic figure, dressed in a style long out of fashion and swaying in the June heat, but he paused only long enough to admire the mouth of the younger of the two women who were trying to keep the comical buzzard from falling face-first into the dirt.

"Arrogant prig!" Michel Leneuf roared at the snub, when the governor general's party had passed safely out of earshot. "Who does he think he is? I happen to know that he doesn't have a bean to his name. That's why he's here, of course, to evade his creditors and replenish his coffers. Well, he's in for a surprise, *mes filles*, if that's his game. This place will bring him down a few pegs, if it doesn't kill him." In fact, it killed Michel Leneuf himself before the end of the year.

Frontenac's obvious desire to feather his own nest was not unusual in New France, of course, but he pursued it with a vigor that threatened the nests of the other vultures. Ignoring the king's neat divisions of power, he barged into the intendant's affairs, trampled over the sovereign council, bullied the local governors, harassed the bishop, and even thumbed his nose at the instructions he received from the king's great minister, Colbert. In particular he ignored Colbert's command to stop the colonists from "roaming about in the woods in the hope of profits, which tends toward the utter ruination of the colony," for Frontenac had adopted Jean Talon's vision of westward expansion for the glory of France and the hope of profits for himself.

77

Sometimes Frontenac behaved so badly that the screams of outrage reached the monarch. "Sire, he has just thrown the governor of Montreal and a priest into jail for no reason. Sire, he has just tried to take over the sovereign council and placed three of its most distinguished members under house arrest. Sire, he has just defied Bishop Laval by allowing the traders to sell brandy to the Indians. Sire, he has just jailed a much-respected councilor without cause. Sire, he continues to disobey Colbert's order not to weaken the colony by extending its trade and defenses to …."

"Monsieur le comte de Frontenac," the king wrote, "I was astounded to learn of all the new disputes and new divisions that have occurred in my province of New France, all the more so since I gave you clearly and firmly to understand, both in your instructions and in all the letters that I have written you in the past years, that your one main purpose must be to maintain unity and tranquillity among all my subjects living in that country. But what astonishes me even more is that in nearly all the strife that you have originated, there is very little justification for all that you have laid claim to."

"Merde!" Frontenac responded, in effect. He dismissed the charges as competitive jealousy. By establishing his own trading posts to the west of Montreal, hiring his own coureurs de bois, and sending his own explorers all the way to the mouth of the Mississippi, he had upset the cosy arrangements of the merchant families and their political agents. Who was this supposedly abused governor of Montreal, for example, but another well-connected soldier with scores of creditors back home and only a few years to make a fortune in the fur business? (Once they sorted out their differences, in fact, the two governors recognized their common purpose and became business partners against the intendant, the council, and the angry citizens of Montreal.) Who were these maltreated stalwarts of the council but hypocrites such as Charles Legardeur, who would give up his opposition to Frontenac for the sake of a job, or Louis Rouer de Villeray, Sevestre's shady son-in-law parading now as the very soul of law and rectitude? Who was this indignant bishop but part of the Jesuit conspiracy to put God and His priests above the king and his agents in New France?

But most of Frontenac's considerable ferocity was saved for Jacques Duchesneau de La Doussinière et d'Ambault, who became intendant in 1675. He was the most stubborn and effective impediment to the governor's rule. He too had friends and relations near the king's ear. He too had the legitimate powers of his office as financial and administrative boss in the colony and influential allies among the traders and the clergy. He even had the mad courage to challenge Frontenac on every issue from the liquor trade with the Indians to the chairmanship of the council.

"All the corporate bodies and nearly all the private individuals who return to this country," the king wrote to Frontenac, "complain of clear-cut cases of ill treatment meted out to them in a manner quite contrary to the spirit of moderation that you should exercise in the maintenance of peace and good order among the people, all as enjoined in my orders and dispatches. My revenue collectors complain that trade is being lost and destroyed by the coureurs de bois, that they receive no protection and that you permit neither the departure of the ships at times when they could leave nor freedom of navigation on the rivers without your permits and passports. The bishop and his clergy, the Jesuit fathers and the sovereign council, and, in one word, all the public bodies and private persons, they all complain."

The seven-year war of feuds and recriminations between governor and intendant often brought the colonial government to a standstill. The vendetta reached a high pitch in early 1681, when a few of the governor's gang got into a street fight with Duchesneau's teenaged son. Though the lad insisted that he had been "singing for his own amusement an air without words" and minding his own business, he was accused of insulting Frontenac and dragged before the governor, who beat the boy with his cane before servants intervened and the boy fled.

Duchesneau *père* and *fils* locked themselves into their house. Bishop Laval traipsed back and forth trying to prevent an armed clash. Frontenac promised to drop the matter if he got an apology, but when the accused was brought before him, he put the boy behind bars.

It was the custom of both men to get at each other through their supporters when they couldn't get at each other directly. That was why the intendant and his friends went after my ancestor Louis Boulduc, the king's attorney at Quebec. The son of an apothecary-herbalist from Paris, Boulduc had come with the Carignan-Salières Regiment in 1665 on the *Aigle d'Or*, the same leaky vessel that had brought Mathurin Bernier. He too had stayed on after three years' service and married one of the young women the king had sent from France to domesticate the warriors. But neither Louis nor his bride (described by one official as "a rather poor piece of goods," though she was the daughter of a Parisian attorney) was made for farming, and after a couple of years they had moved from their grant to Quebec. Somehow Louis had climbed into the great governor's view, proved himself a loyal Frontenac man, and in 1676 had been appointed public prosecutor. Since the courts were seen as a device by which Frontenac might usurp the council's jurisdiction, the new attorney became an object of suspicion, particularly after he charged a woman for speaking badly of Count Frontenac in public.

"Monsieur Boulduc," the intendant wrote in 1680, "is unworthy of his post. He has been accused of extortion, of theft in every house that ever suffered his presence, of continual debauchery and dissipation, and without the protection given him by Monsieur le comte de Frontenac I would have sent him to trial." ("What are we to make of these accusations hurled against your ancestor?" the kind genealogist hastily asks in a note in the Moncel family record given me by my cousin. "Little, in sum, for the passions that divided Quebec into two camps at that time were the cause of many divergencies of opinion and, no doubt, as many blots on truth, if not on charity.")

In January 1681 the council moved against Boulduc and accused him of embezzlement. It was a minor and uncertain matter, but he was ousted from his job pending a sweeping investigation by Louis Rouer de Villeray, no less. Furious, Frontenac responded by questioning Villeray's own honesty and denying him leave to go to France on business. Then he hastened to explain his action to the king before more slanders reached Paris.

"It's been eleven months," Frontenac wrote, "since the king's attorney in the provost court of this town, because he was not agreeable to Monsieur Duchesneau, was forbidden to perform his duties by members of the intendant's cabal because of a simple accusation by a merchant from Bayonne who trades here and who was permitted to return to France two months ago, despite the protests that I made, because they saw that he couldn't prove the things he had claimed. Nevertheless, though the attorney-general didn't have the proof he had hoped for, and asked for an inquiry into the accused's life and habits during the seventeen years he's been in this country as well as the six years since he received his commission as the king's attorney, without complaint or opposition, and heard seventy witnesses without finding any evidence worthy of a charge, that being the case after all the chicaneries that were made to drag out this affair, notwithstanding the large number of requests by the king's attorney for a judgment, the last straw was this request by the Sieur de Villeray for permission to go to France, where he had been just a year ago, which I was obliged to refuse so that the official can have justice as soon as possible."

Justice did not come soon, however, and it may not have come at all. On March 20, 1682, the sovereign council declared Louis Boulduc guilty of embezzlement and banned him from ever holding judicial office. This was another smack at Frontenac, of course, and he could no longer strike back. The king and Colbert had grown weary of the rambling rants that arrived with every boat. Weary of the byzantine intrigues and hysterical quibbles. Weary of trying to figure out who was right and what was going on over there. A few months after the

Boulduc affair, both Frontenac and the intendant Duchesneau were recalled to France.

Louis XIV must have had some regrets during the next few years, for the Atlantic no longer stood between him and the count's moods. Back in France, besieged by his moneylenders once again, Frontenac swung between fury and despair in his demands for a pension or a job. He became a pest, arguing on behalf of lost causes such as Louis Boulduc. In 1685 the ministry of marine conceded my ancestor an income and even mentioned him tentatively to the new authorities in Canada, but Canada did not want the "out-and-out rascal." Soon afterward, Monsieur and Madame Boulduc gave up on the New World. They returned to France, leaving their half-dozen children to the mercy of others and their dubious reputations to the judgment of historians.

What News? 1690

MONTREAL in the 1680s was still a small town of fewer than two thousand people huddled around the wharves at the river's edge. François Lorit, my great-great-great-great-great-great-grand-father, was the sergeant-at-law in the bailiff's court and the local process server. It was a job, like barber or priest, that made him a familiar figure and a bearer of secrets. Everyone knew him. Though many equated the mere sight of him with legal trouble, most accepted that he was simply doing his duty. Damage to his vocal chords – for which he was nicknamed Gargot, a word that described his throaty mumble – made it hard to fear him, and the stammer brought on by his nervousness made it hard to dislike him. Indeed, he owed his profession in part to the compassion aroused by his handicap. It had endeared him to the Jesuits for whom he had gone to work after his arrival in New France in 1664 at the age of eighteen. They had taught him to read and write, then started him off with a grant of land not far from Trois-Rivières. But he was drawn more to words and writs than to wheat and wood, and he proved a better functionary than farmer.

A law-abiding sort, Lorit had journeyed from his farm to Quebec in the fall of 1670 to comply with the intendant's order for the bachelors of the colony to marry the "amenable, hard-working, skilled, and intensely religious" women sent by the shipload for that purpose, totaling more than eight hundred and known as "the king's girls." By the time he arrived, the year's selection of a hundred women had been reduced by half. The officers, the soldiers, the seigneurs, the merchants, and the government men had already taken the best of them, but at least François was ahead of the landless laborers and young riffraff who would get no women at all. He was terrified, and his terror did not help his stammer.

"How much land do you have?" a nun barked at him. "Have you a house and a crop yet? How many cows, how many pigs? Any illness, any dirty habits? Speak up, I haven't got all day, hurry or you'll lose your chance. Are you deaf? Are you an idiot?"

"I-I-I-I-"

"What difference does it make, I suppose, since all men are imbeciles anyway. Oh, there go the bells for lunch. Enough dilly-dallying, there's no perfection this side of heaven. Take that one. Her name is Perrette Parement, she's twenty-four years old, she's an orphan from Troyes, and if you put a little meat on her bones and don't work her too hard, she'll last the winter and make a good mother."

Before François could say anything, he and Perrette had been whisked before a notary to draw up a contract. A few days later they were joined in holy matrimony and sent off with the governor's blessing, fifty livres from the king, and three hundred livres' worth of belongings.

Even this dowry, however, had not been enough to make them prosper on their land. After ten years of struggle, broken by debt, they and their children had drifted into Montreal. There François Lorit discovered his true métier. Being the process server kept him busy. Montreal had come far from its origins as a community of saints. Immediately below the new church of Notre-Dame the taverns were full of drunken farmers, drunken traders, drunken soldiers, and drunken Indians. The streets around the seminary and convent were the muddy arenas of mêlées, duels, murders, and lewdness. The very year the Lorits arrived, the authorities had to cancel the annual two-week fair, where hundreds of Indians and traders met to exchange furs for kettles and muskets, because of the violence, debauchery, and nudity that scandalized the year-round residents. Then there were suits against corrupt officials, campaigns to punish illegal traders, and the never-ending litany of commercial and domestic feuds. "The Canadians are difficult to govern," remarked one official. "They love liberty and have a loathing for authority."

No case brought François more honor or amusement than the case against Pierre Le Moyne d'Iberville, the most famous of the military sons of a wealthy, influential, and ennobled trader and landowner. By 1686, while still in their twenties, Pierre and two of his eleven brothers were already covered in glory for their role in seizing the forts that the English had built on Hudson Bay to compete with the French fur traders to the north and west of New France. When the Le Moyne boys returned triumphant to Montreal, however, Pierre found more than a hero's welcome waiting for him: he found François Lorit stuttering on his doorstep. Iberville blanched as he had not done when faced with eighty-five days of slogging by canoe and snowshoe through the Arctic wilderness or when trapped by himself in Moose Fort with only his sword and gun to protect him from seventeen Englishmen. For the process server was pursuing him on behalf of a young woman whom Pierre had wooed too well. Lured by his promise of marriage, her family argued, she had lost her great virtue and become pregnant. Iberville should either make good his word or be charged with seduction. He denied both the promise and the charge. For almost two years now the affair had been as much the talk of the taverns and washtubs as the latest Iroquois rumor.

"What news, Gargot?" the people of Montreal asked François when they passed him in the market or met him in the tavern.

"H-h-he called her a m-m-money-grubbing little wh-wh-wh-wh-"

"He didn't! Well, he's getting too big for his breeches, if you ask me, like all those Le Moynes. Just because he's governor of three shit-houses up where the polar bears live, that doesn't give him liberty to have his fun and not pay the price like the rest of us. Thank Mary and Joseph that his daddy, may Charles rest in peace, didn't live to know this stain on his great name."

"Better," said another, "that the hussy's father, as upright and valiant a Christian as ever seen in Ville-Marie, died before seeing her disgrace. As if the promise of marriage, not that I believe it for an instant, would excuse such behavior! The girl saw his title, his fortune, and his shapely legs, and the rest was the Devil's play. The family is cursed. Wasn't that new husband of the harlot's sister found guilty of playing billiards on Easter Monday last? I pity the poor baby, I really do."

"What news, Gargot?"

Finally, in October 1688, he had some. The sovereign council had found Iberville guilty as charged and ordered him to support the child until she was fifteen, though he wasn't compelled to marry the girl's mother. Iberville had gone back to slay more Englishmen and capture their furs on Hudson Bay meanwhile, and it was another year before my ancestor had the pleasure of delivering the verdict person-ally to the short, handsome, weather-beaten warrior.

"What did the big hero say, Gargot?"

"N-n-n-nothing." But until his dying day, François remembered the expression in Iberville's eyes. François had experienced his own share of tragedy – corpses ripped apart by the Iroquois, corpses lying in the snow after a duel or fracas, and the thin corpse of his wife, Perrette, who had been taken by the smallpox and measles epidemic that claimed more than fourteen hundred victims a few years before – but Iberville had seen horrors that burned like the glare of sun on ice: men freezing to death in a blizzard, men dying of scurvy or starvation for the sake of his victory, men killing each other for the unique exuberance of the sport. While François had come to love the law as a garrison of civilization in a wilderness of savagery, Iberville had come to regard it as a diversion for soft minds and idle hands. What was this stern judgment from the sovereign council against the mortal judgment of nature, of fate, and of the sword? Iberville listened to the guilty verdict with a strange bemusement and incomprehension. François recognized the look. He had seen it every time he arrested *un sauvage*.

The Iroquois raids on New France had begun again during the 1680s after almost twenty years of relative peace. They had been provoked in large measure by Frontenac's westward expansion, which the Iroquois saw as a new threat to their own territorial and economic security, and by English schemers in New York who saw a new opportunity to smash the overextended defenses of New France. In 1684 twenty-five hundred Iroquois warriors defeated a colonial army of eight hundred men led into their territory by Frontenac's successor, La Barre, and though the king quickly sent another fifteen hundred troops under a more competent governor, the Marquis de Denonville, Canada did not have the military strength to do more than scare the enemy into another shaky peace.

"The habitant trembles as he eats; no one who leaves his house may count on returning; his sowings and reapings are abandoned for the most part," an eighteenth-century historian wrote of this period. "The seigneur sees all his lands pillaged and burnt, nor can he reckon himself safe in his stronghold. The traveler moves but by night. Let anyone walk in the fields, either he is massacred, or he is suddenly carried off to be burnt alive, or he is felled by a crushing blow to be scalped."

The decade ended with a gruesome climax. Just when Denonville thought he was about to secure a treaty, fifteen hundred Iroquois in red-ochre warpaint paddled across the St Lawrence under cover of night and a heavy rain. At dawn on August 5, 1689, they attacked the settlement at Lachine (once the seigneury of the explorer La Salle, now a Montreal suburb) with only their ululations as warning. Families were pulled from their beds. Most of the houses were destroyed by fire. Parents were forced to throw their infants into the flames. Ninety people were taken prisoner, and at least two dozen were massacred on the spot – including my ancestor René Chartier, two of his sons, and his Indian slave. A state of shock compounded the state of siege, but the people of Montreal drew some comfort by burning three Iroquois captives in the marketplace.

In October, François Lorit had good news to pass along in the market and the tavern: Count Frontenac had returned to New France with a new commission as governor general, hundreds more soldiers, and a mandate to take on the Indians and their English allies. He was approaching seventy and not about to change his corrupt or arrogant ways, but the thought of war gave him a discipline and magnanimity often lacking in his first regime. He also had a new strategy: instead of concentrating on the Iroquois, the army would focus its campaign against the English settlers in New York and New England who had been arming the Five Nations and encouraging their assaults on the French. A European war had just broken out between England and France, after James II had been ousted from the British throne by his Protestant and anti-French relative William of Orange. The war in

Europe was Frontenac's excuse to strike south against Boston, Albany, and Manhattan.

Winter prevented Frontenac from launching his first offensive, but in January 1690 he unleashed a guerrilla attack on three English villages. At Schenectady, Pierre Le Moyne d'Iberville, two of his brothers, and a hundred other Canadians screamed as fiercely as their native allies, stormed into the village at dawn, murdered five dozen innocents, led away two dozen prisoners and fifty horses heavy with booty, and left wailing children amid the embers. "The cruelties committed," one observer later said, "no pen can write nor tongue can express." Another witness took a more philosophical approach, commenting that "it is but what our sins and transgressions have deserved."

The raids drew the English out from behind the Iroquois warriors and into an allied expedition by land against Montreal and by sea against Quebec. All summer Montreal prepared itself for the reported invasion from Albany, but it never materialized. It collapsed en route because of smallpox and ineptitude. British sea forces from Boston under Sir William Phips were proceeding up the St Lawrence toward Quebec nevertheless, and Frontenac sped from Montreal to rally his full army against the fleet of thirty-four ships transporting more than two thousand soldiers. If Frontenac were not successful, New France might well fall as it had fallen to the Kirkes seventy years earlier, for though there were more than twelve thousand French in Canada by 1690, there were more than a quarter-million English in America eager to drive them out.

"What news, Gargot?" a voice shouted when François came into a cabaret near Place du Marché (today a tiny square in Old Montreal known as Place Royale). Aux Trois Pigeons was crowded with men drinking eau de vie and gambling at dice or cards with money made out of playing cards stamped as legal tender, but this was not the usual crowd. Many of the coureurs de bois were still in the *pays d'en haut* trading furs, and many of the soldiers had been summoned downriver to defend Quebec. Their regular tables had been taken by settlers who moved behind the town's cedar barricades each night as a precaution against both the Iroquois and the English.

The crowd fell silent. François had just received the first report from Quebec. The English ships were below the town, troops at the ready. An English subaltern had been sent by Phips to inform the French that they had an hour in which to surrender, "your forts and castles undemolished, the king's and other stores unembezzled," before the wrath of Boston came down upon their heads.

This took a while for François to explain, and he was interrupted frequently by cries of "Louder, we can't hear you!" and "Get on with it, you buffoon!" Now another voice shouted, "And what did Monsieur le comte do?"

Standing on a chair, trying to bring Frontenac's age and nobility to the moment, François Lorit said, "The g-g-g-governor was very a-a-a-a-"

" – Amused?"

" – Agitated?"

"Quiet! Let him finish!"

" – Angry, and he t-t-t-told the Englishman, 'I will a-a-a-a-'"

" – Accept?"

" – Attack?"

"Oh, mon Dieu, we'll all be Protestants before we hear the end of this."

"' – Answer your g-g-g-general from the m-m-m-mouths of my cannons!'"

A hurrah went up, and so did François. A couple of men put him on their shoulders, passed him a brandy, and carried him round the room. "The m-m-m-mouths of my cannons!" everyone chanted. "The m-m-m-mouths of my cannons!"

Lost Brothers, 1696

THE DECLARATION of war between England and France in 1689, coupled with the Iroquois raid on Lachine that summer, opened a period of conflict between the English and French colonies in America that lasted, with a short interruption, for the next quarter-century. After Sir William Phips stared into the mouths of Frontenac's cannons and promptly fled, the conflict was rarely between armies marching back and forth to smash each other's forts. Often it was between guerrillas sneaking in and out to shatter each other's nerves. Sometimes the guerrillas were Europeans behaving like marauding Indians. Usually they were Indians sent to do the Europeans' dirty work, incited by New York to capture the fur trade from New France or provoked by New France to terrorize New England.

The French considered an attack on the English of Massachusetts as useful as an attack on the Iroquois in New York. Better, in fact, because the English were more vulnerable and less likely to come back brandishing tomahawks and hollering for scalps. To unsettle the New York settlers and their native alliances, therefore, Frontenac and his successors offered rewards for the ransacking of New England villages and the capture of New England hostages.

On August 5, 1696, while the aging governor general was being carried by armchair into battle against the Onondagas far to the west, a party of Abenakis (allies to the French in what is now Maine and New Brunswick) filed through the woods near Haverhill, a settlement north of Boston on the Merrimac River. They made less noise than deer. They stopped when they saw a clearing through the trees.

From it came sunlight and young voices. Nearer, and they could see the children, four of them, a tall girl and three boys, gathering beans in a field by the side of Hawk's Meadow Brook, teasing and quarreling, impatient for the swim their father had promised after their work. He was there too, reaping hay, his musket on the ground, his back to the painted faces. There were no sounds other than the birds, the brook, the scythe, and the young voices.

And then there were demonic whoops as the Abenakis ran from their hiding place. One grabbed up the girl, almost a woman, who tried to sink her teeth and nails into his damp, hairless skin. Two picked up the smaller boys, who kicked and pummeled and yelled for help. The rest went after the teenaged boy and his father, who were pulled away by hands as strong as a dog's jaw. "Sarah! Sarah!" Jonathan Hains called to his wife, but by the time she came to the door of their house, she heard only the birds and the brook.

That night, when they were finally allowed to rest, Jonathan said to his children, "At least we are together, we can thank God for that." They had been kept on the move for hours, to put distance between the camp and any rescuers who might have followed. Though exhausted, they could not sleep because of fear and shock and cold and hunger. There was already an autumn chill, but spruce boughs were their only bedding. They had been given nothing to eat but corn and acorns.

"Come, children, let us pray as the Lord taught us."

"Our Father," Mary, Thomas, young Jonathan, and Joseph recited with him. Some Abenakis nearby recognized the rhythm of the prayer and began to repeat it too, in French, as they had been taught by the Jesuits who had brought them to Jesus Christ.

But God did not keep the family together for long. When they reached the village of the Penacooks, a tribe living south of Abenaki territory, Jonathan and his eldest boy were traded to Indians from Maine and taken away. Mary and her two other brothers, twelve and seven, were kept among the villagers until the snow fell. Then, with Mary riding on a sled, they were led two hundred miles northward again, over the Green Mountains, across the ice on Lake Champlain, to the fort at Chambly, just east of Montreal. There the Indians sold them to the French, who shipped them to different families to be converted to Catholicism and raised as Canadians.

At nineteen Mary was too old to change her ways or forget her home on Hawk's Meadow Brook. In time her resistance paid off. She was ransomed back to the English for a hundred pounds of tobacco and passed the rest of her life as Mrs John Preston of Andover. But the boys were still impressionable enough to learn the Roman catechism and the French tongue. In May 1710 "Joseph hins at cap Sainct ignace" and "Another Joseph hins, his brother, at coste de beaupré" appeared on the long list of English captives – "all professing the catholic, apostolic, and roman religion" and "desiring to end their days as our subjects" – whom Louis XIV accepted as citizens of France. One of those Josephs, probably young Jonathan, married Marguerite Maroist at L'Ange-Gardien that year and, jettisoning the last of his Anglo-Saxon and Protestant origins, became a Latin lover. My ancestor fathered twenty-one children by four wives.

Decades later, according to one legend, three brothers by the name of Hains arrived in New France from New England in search of their two missing uncles. The brothers were probably the sons of Thomas, the eldest son of Jonathan senior. After Thomas and his father had been taken from Penacook, they had managed one night to undo the willow cords on their wrists and knees and escape into the forest. Lost, they had wandered without food or direction, never daring to stop for more than an hour but growing weaker by the day. Soon Jonathan couldn't continue. "Hide here, Father, rest, and I'll come back for you with help," said Thomas, as determined and optimistic as any sixteen-year-old. By pure luck or divine grace he was true to his promise. One morning, delirious with worry and hunger, he heard a buzzing in his head. It grew louder. He realized it was the sound of a sawmill and followed it into the settlement at Saco. Leading a rescue party back to the hiding place, he shouted, "We're saved, Father, saved!"

Saved only for further trials, it turned out. Less than two years later father and son, working again in the fields near Haverhill, were again set upon by Abenakis. Better dead than another ordeal, Jonathan Hains thought, for his heart had stayed full of morbid hatred since the loss of his other children. He was killed when he put up a struggle, but Thomas was caught, bound, and carried away once more. And once more he escaped, to enjoy a long life and tell his own children about the fate of their grandfather and their lost uncles. He never forgot his lost brothers, never stopped feeling responsible for their well-being or guilty about their misfortune. As he grew older, he became obsessed with knowing what had become of them. When his own sons were men, he commissioned them to go to Canada and bring the hostages home at last.

The sons of Thomas Hains eventually found their uncles, the story goes, by then two elderly habitants named Hens. Neither remembered a word of English or of Calvin. Neither had the slightest interest in uprooting his family to the realm of the heretics. Neither would live to see the day when, by a twist of history to be played out on the Plains of Abraham, their children would become subjects of the English king anyway.

The English Ward, 1707

A T THE AGE of nine Elizabeth Lamax was more plain than pretty. Her auburn hair was dirty; her homespun dress was torn; her freckled face was sullen. Her parents had told her a thousand times not to go wandering with Lydia Drew – "The woods are full of Indians and that girl is a bad influence, she reads poetry!" – but Elizabeth was already in a rebellious phase. She had a juvenile crush on Lydia, who was thirteen years old and did indeed recite Shakespeare, Milton, Marvell, and Donne when she was not gushing about cute Francis Mathes. They liked to lounge beneath the great chestnut near Lydia's grandfather's "garrison," a shack that had been transformed into a tiny fortress. That was where they were on the morning of May 22, 1707.

Elizabeth was the daughter of Deliverance Clark and Nathaniel Lamax (variously written Loomis, Lomax, and Lammos), a Puritan couple who had emigrated from Ipswich, Massachusetts, and settled near Oyster River in present-day New Hampshire. She had been born in May 1698, several months before the natural death of Count Frontenac up in Quebec. By the time she was four England had again gone to war with France, this time over the right of Louis xiv's grandson to succeed to the throne of Spain, and a new governor in New France had revived the terror campaign in New England. "We must keep things astir in the direction of Boston," wrote Philippe de Rigaud de Vaudreuil, who was appointed governor general of New France in 1703, "or else the Abenakis will declare for the English." A year later a French and Indian force descended upon Deerfield just before dawn, smashing the head of two-year-old Mercy Sheldon against a stone and butchering five-year-old Marah Carter because she was too puny a prize.

"Licence my roving hands, and let them go, before, behind, between, above, below," Lydia recited. "O my America! my new-found-land, my kingdom, safliest when with one man mann'd."

"Hearken a moment, I heard something yonder," said Elizabeth. There was only the noise my great-great-great-great-great-great-grandmother herself was making with the wad of spruce gum in her mouth. "If it's my ma or pa, I'm in for another thrashing and more sermons. I hate them. I tell thee, Lydia, when I'm 'with one man mann'd,' I'll be hence faster than a jack rabbit."

An Abenaki warrior may not have been quite the man she had in mind, but that is what she had heard. Elizabeth was not the first person from Oyster River to greet an abduction, frightening as it was, with a sentiment akin to relief. Scores of captives preferred to remain with the Indians, and hundreds chose to stay with the French – some because of the brainwashing, some because of the freedom, some because of the abuse they had received from their zealous fathers and husbands, some because of what a nineteenth-century priest considered "the blessing of being Catholics and the advantage of being Canadians."

Lydia Drew pined after Oyster River and dashed back at the first opportunity to recover her Protestant beliefs and marry Francis Mathes, but Elizabeth Lamax snuggled into the bosom of a family that was much more comfortable and agreeable than her own. She was adopted by Etienne and Elisabeth Rocbert as a companion for their daughter Marie-Elisabeth, then eleven. Though Etienne Rocbert had recently spent time in prison for killing the valet of the governor of Montreal in a street brawl, he was the keeper of the King's Store on Rue Saint-Louis, notable enough and wealthy enough to get the governor to serve as godfather at the baptism of the new English ward. Elizabeth was now Marie-Elisabeth, after her friend and godmother, and the haste with which she assumed the faith and name indicates more than youth or vulnerability: she was free from Nathaniel Lamax and Deliverance Clark forever.

My ancestress also forgot Lydia, who had disappointed her by resisting the very sort of romance they had yearned for under the great chestnut. Instead, she became devoted to Marie-Elisabeth Rocbert. The two girls whiled away the summer days and winter evenings munching bonbons, reading Molière and Racine, strolling up and down the dusty street, or fanning each other with the tails of wild turkeys. They shared the secrets of what to wear and how to fix their hair. From 1712 to 1718 they wept together over the joys and sorrows of Marie-Elisabeth Rocbert's clandestine affair with Claude-Michel Bégon. It was clandestine because she, born in the colony to a glorified shopkeeper, was not judged good enough by his well-regarded, well-connected, and oh-so-important family back in France.

Claude-Michel's father was a colonial pooh-bah who lent his distinguished name to the begonia; his brother became intendant of New France in 1712. Claude-Michel had arrived with him as a young officer. He had lodged with the Rocberts in Montreal and wooed their witty and attractive daughter, who in turn found his blind eye and wounded hands the very definition of gallantry. To the Bégons she was "l'Iroquoise," a Canadian primitive. Soon, through the family's connections, almost everyone of importance was conscripted into preventing their marriage, including the governor and the bishop. Love conquered all, however. At a cost to his career Claude-Michel Bégon married Marie-Elisabeth Rocbert, first *à la gaumine* (by announcing their intention during a Mass) and then officially in December 1718. Marie-Elisabeth Lamax shed many tears at the wedding. She cried for the loss of her sweetest companion and for the happy-ever-after ending.

Three years later she herself married. She and Joseph Parant were blessed with three daughters in rapid succession. But almost as quickly, Marie-Elisabeth Parant began to know the dark side of romance. In 1726 a fourth daughter was born, only to die. A year later her husband was dead, leaving her destitute with three children under nine. She found another man in 1735, but he came too late to breathe spirit back into her. Two years after her second marriage, shortly before her thirty-ninth birthday, Marie-Elisabeth fell mortally ill. Was it the punishment of her parents and her God for her sins? In her fever, did she see their wrath and feel their vengeance? Had she been possessed like the witches of Salem, executed not long before her birth? In her final hour, did she try to recollect a childhood prayer in a long-forgotten language?

Original Sin, 1740

O NCE UPON A TIME a stranger came into a village on the north shore of the Ile d'Orléans, the long island in the middle of the St Lawrence just downriver from Quebec, sometimes called the Isle of Bacchus or the Isle of Sorcerers. He was young, charming, and dressed in a beaver coat as for town. In 1740 the habitants of Sainte-Famille were not used to passing strangers. They suspected that people from town meant trouble, and they resented the temptations of the young men who roved like the coureurs de bois.

"Idleness is the Devil's work," Madame Gagnon thought. She held her tongue, however, when her husband Jean invited the stranger to stay for the wedding of their son, Marc-Antoine, to Madeleine Deblois. What was one more mouth to feed when the whole parish of cousins would be present? Besides, her husband reminded her, it was well to remember the sad old song about the Wandering Jew, who was condemned to travel the earth forever because he had refused to let Jesus Christ rest on His way to Calvary. "Sur le mont du Calvaire," he sang to himself as he went about the chores, "Jésus portait sa croix."

The marriage of Madeleine Deblois and Marc-Antoine Gagnon, my ancestors of seven generations ago, was a union between two pioneer families of local importance. The groom's great-grandfather, Jean Gagnon, had arrived in New France in 1635 and settled below

Quebec at Château-Richer. There his son, also Jean, had known the bride's grandfather, Grégoire Deblois, and around the turn of the eighteenth century both men had moved their wives and children to better land on the island at Sainte-Famille. Their boys grew up together, married girls from nearby farms, and conspired to join their blood by pushing Marc-Antoine toward Madeleine at dances or after church. The families were thus in a mood to be generous to the stranger, particularly since the celebrations fell between the Gagnons' forty-first anniversary and the Mardi Gras *carnaval*.

"Almost the same day, but another century!" Jean Gagnon told his visitor with a slap on the back. He was renowned in the area for his stories and songs, and had a reputation as a healer. "February 16, 1699, the worst snowstorm of the decade. We almost couldn't get to the church at Saint-François – a sign from God is what I said – but the Devil and Anne's father found the way. 'Cause it's the Devil's church, you know. He built it. Ask anyone. One day he came to Saint-François disguised as a big black horse. But the priest recognized him and trapped him by throwing a sacred stole around the horse's neck. Then he put the Devil to work, dragging stones for the new church, with no sleep and nothing to eat, to make him sorry for taking the souls of good Catholics. There was nothing else the Devil could do because the stole was as sacred as the cross. When the church was nearly finished, the priest tied the horse to a tree and went for a rest. A workman saw that the poor beast was thirsty, so he let it loose. The Devil was free again! He gave the church a great kick and vanished into yellow smoke. You can still see the hoof mark on the wall by the door. And he left me with ten kids! I'll be happy when our new church here is finally finished – it's going to be shaped like a cross to keep the Devil away – so we won't have to go to Saint-François any more."

"Stop talking such blasphemy," his wife interrupted, "and fetch some wood. Our guest is shivering. He's still wearing his gloves."

"Shivering from fear, eh? Well, it's true."

"It may be true," said Madame Gagnon, "but it's not lucky to speak of it."

Early on the Monday morning of February 22, 1740, while it was still dark and cold, the stranger joined Marc-Antoine, his family, and their friends as they tramped to the Deblois house to serenade Madeleine with compliments and songs. "A la fontaine m'en allant promener," they sang, "j'ai trouvé l'eau si belle que je m'y suis baigné." They continued on the back of the heavy *berlot*, usually used to carry timber, as the workhorses pulled it along the snow track to Saint-François, eight miles away on the eastern tip of the island, where they would wait for the bridal party to arrive in fast *carrioles* to the jangle of sleighbells. The earth was a blinding white, the sky a brilliant blue, and the crisp air froze their eyelids and mustaches.

At the church the stranger ran his gloves over the deep dent in the foundation stone. He had come from Montreal and Quebec, where he had hobnobbed with judges, officers, and traders in his search for an uncle who had been kidnaped from New England by the Abenakis fifty years earlier. Now he was happy to spend time among people who would leave no record but their births, their marriages, and their deaths. They were the vast majority, of course, those whose lives were a routine of ordinary work and domestic matters. They were also the greatest strength of New France. They cleared the forests and tilled the soil. They harvested the wheat, their principal crop, and milked the cows. They fished the waters and bartered the furs. They built the towns and crafted the tools, withstood the winters and the wars, and raised the families that were the core of the nation. *Les familles-souches*, the founding families, as they are called in Quebec to this day.

Heroes died, but families survived, and their survival became the story of French Canada. Their simple hardships based on the land and the hearth became as legendary as the courage of Champlain or the exploits of Frontenac. Their gaiety, piety, and pride defined an entire people. Their farmhouses, music, and stories described the basic culture. They were the organizing principle of law and society in New France. Between 1700 and 1740 the population of New France trebled to forty-five thousand people, and their children were healthier and lived longer than those in France. (More drowned than died of disease, according to one contemporary report.) The great majority were now Canadiens by birth, not immigrants from France, and only a fifth were townspeople in Quebec or Montreal. The colony was really "one continued village," in the phrase of Pehr Kalm, a Swedish botanist who visited in 1749, "fine houses of stone, large grain-fields, meadows, pastures, woods of deciduous trees, and some churches" strung for two hundred miles along both banks of the St Lawrence, linked less by the remote government or the seigneurial system or even the Roman Catholic Church than by the family networks.

After five generations and one hundred years, the settlers and the soldiers had created a new tribe of habitants. "The ordinary habitants would be scandalized to be called peasants," a French officer remarked in the 1750s. "In fact, they are of better stuff, have more wit, more education, than those of France. This comes from their paying no taxes, that they have the right to hunt and fish, and that they live in a sort of independence." Even many modern French Canadians nourish a nostalgia for their paradise lost. They construct replicas of the stone houses with steeply sloped roofs in modern suburbs and fill their high-rise condos with antique armoires and pine chairs. They join family associations that keep the genealogical records and gather from time to time to celebrate their names.

If New France had a Golden Age, it was the "long peace" between 1713 and 1744. The wars against the Indians had finally ended when the Iroquois, crippled by their casualties in more than seven years of war, gave up the struggle in 1701. The wars against the English colonies were suspended when France and England agreed to peace at Utrecht in 1713. Under the terms of the treaty France lost control of Acadia and Hudson Bay as part of the price of keeping the Bourbons on the throne of Spain, but its American empire still reached diagonally across the continent from Louisbourg on the Atlantic coast, up the St Lawrence, across the Great Lakes, down the Ohio, all the way to Louisiana at the mouth of the Mississippi. Peace in Europe meant that France had money to spend on fortifying its empire against the thirteen colonies, which now numbered almost a million and a half English, and by the 1730s the La Vérendrye family had begun to open up the huge territories west of the Great Lakes to the foothills of the Rockies. The fur trade gradually revived after its collapse from war, corruption, and oversupply at the end of the seventeenth century, and even many farmers supplemented their incomes by voyaging to the west. The colony's chaotic financial affairs were put in better order; Canada began to export wheat, lumber, tobacco, and cod to France and the French West Indies; and the new king, Louis xv, renewed the motherland's interest in developing New France for strategic and commercial reasons by subsidizing the building of ships and the forging of iron. More significantly, two generations of peace had encouraged the growth of the large, stable, and prosperous "village" to which the Gagnons and the Deblois belonged.

No wonder they looked so satisfied during the Mass and the exchange of rings. ("Unfortunately," Kalm noted, "religion seems to consist here only of external observances.") No wonder everyone made so merry when they all returned chez les Deblois. It was a merry time of year to begin with, despite the long nights and the blizzards. The woodcutting was done. The maple sugaring had yet to begin. The daily chores were hardly heavy labor. From Christmas to Ash Wednesday life became as slow as the flies trapped in the houses, as languid as the dogs lying by the fires. It was the season of evening visits, stories, cards, and quadrilles. The wedding, which would be celebrated for three days, was merely a highlight of two months of feasts and dances.

"One can scarcely find in a city in other parts," Pehr Kalm wrote in his diary, "people who treat one with such politeness both in word and deed as is true everywhere in the homes of the peasants in Canada. I traveled in various places during my stay in this country. I frequently happened to take up my abode for several days at the homes of peasants where I had never been before, and who had never heard of nor seen me and to whom I had no letters of introduction. Nevertheless they showed me wherever I came a devotion paid ordinarily only to a native or relative."

My ancestors showed the same to the charming young stranger. He was absorbed into the warmth and the noise of the farmhouse. Too many people were jammed into the two rooms on the ground floor of the two-storey stone house, one the kitchen and sitting area, the other the main bedroom, not four hundred square feet in total. The open fire and adjoining oven were unnecessary for heat. The smoke from the men's clay pipes created a dizzying atmosphere already made dreamy by the strange light coming through the waxed-paper windows. Through the haze, as through an old mirror, the stranger watched Madame Gagnon and the other women preparing the salt bacon, smoked eel, roast mutton, and pickled calves' feet while the Deblois girls loaded the table with pea soups, venison ragoûts, game pies, cheeses, potatoes, apples, nuts, and fresh loaves of oval bread for the wedding breakfast. Jean-Baptiste Deblois had been left a widower in 1728 after his wife died giving birth to their eighth child, who also died after six months. As on this day, everyone helped him to raise his family, but he never stopped missing his wife. Tomorrow, he thought suddenly amid the laughter, tomorrow is the anniversary of her death: how proud she would have been of the little girl, now a bride, who had been named after her.

"All the women in the country, without exception, wear caps of some kind or other," Pehr Kalm observed. "Their jackets are short and so are their skirts, which scarcely reach down to the middle of their legs. They have a silver cross hanging down on the breast. In general they are very industrious. However, I saw some who, like the English women in the colonies, did nothing but prattle all day. When they have anything to do within doors, they commonly sing songs in which the words *amour* and *coeur* are very frequent." They also had a weakness for curling their hair every morning and wearing fashionable dresses on Sundays, he noted; even poor habitants often lived on bread and water because they had sold their produce in town for brandy and fine clothes. "Everywhere the girls were alert and quick in speech and their manner rather impulsive; but according to my judgment and as far as I could observe, they were not as lustful and wanton as foreigners claim the French to be." They could be blunt, however. "One of the first questions they put to a stranger is whether he is married; the next, how he likes the ladies in the country; and the third, whether he will take one home with him."

"Are you married?" Madame Gagnon asked the stranger after she and her husband had served the bride her meal, as was the custom. Before he could answer, the fiddle started and the newlyweds were dragged toward an open space to sing a song and lead the first minuet. Marc-Antoine, twenty-eight years old, already red-faced from sunburn and excitement, already perspiring from the wine and the heat, blushed with shyness.

As for the men, Kalm reported, "The French in Canada in many respects follow the customs of the Indians, with whom they have constant relations. They use the tobacco pipes, shoes, garters, and girdles of the Indians. They follow the Indian way of waging war exactly; they mix the same things with tobacco; they make use of the Indian bark boats and row them in the Indian way; they wrap a square piece of cloth round their feet, instead of stockings, and have adopted many other Indian fashions. The peasants, and especially their wives, wear shoes that consist of a piece of wood hollowed out, and are made almost as slippers. Their boys and the old peasants themselves wear their hair behind in a queue, and most of them wear red woolen caps at home and sometimes on their journeys."

"Are you married?" Madame Gagnon persisted. Instead of answering, the stranger got up and asked her daughter Marguerite to do him the honor of dancing "Tous les bourgeois de Chartres" with him. Normally Marguerite hated dancing, but she accepted because he was a guest, with an amusing way of speaking French and a sophisticated habit of wearing deerskin gloves.

"Foolish child," Madame Gagnon muttered.

Marguerite was no child – she was thirty-seven and still unmarried – but she may have been foolish. She was full of religious sentiments that made her seem rather soft in the head. A saint, the kinder ones called her, but none of the local boys was looking for a saint.

Weddings make the best parties, for happiness is contagious and love unleashes all reserve. The generations mingle. Newcomers are suddenly family. Misers spare no expense, and even pessimists see hope. While the stranger whirled and reeled, he became giddy with the beauty around him: the blush of the girls, the strong hands of the boys, the hair of the children, the faces of the elders, the industry of the mothers and fathers in the prime of life. It was an illusion, of course, which overlooked the squalor, the shabbiness, the hardship, the decay, and all the sufferings of yesterday and tomorrow. But for the present, dancing in this peace and joy with my ancestors, the stranger felt nothing else.

On and on he danced with Marguerite, with fine steps and endless energy, on and on all afternoon and into the night, as Jean Gagnon sang of a mythical kingdom set in the forest primeval, the home of the happy. "There," Longfellow was to describe it in his poem about Evangeline, "in the tranquil evenings of summer, when brightly the sunset lighted the village street and gilded the vanes on the chimneys, matrons and maidens sat in snow-white caps and in kirtles scarlet and blue and green, with distaffs spinning the golden flax for the gossiping looms, whose noisy shuttles within the doors mingled their sounds with the whir of the wheels and the songs of the maidens."

"Come away with me," the stranger whispered in Marguerite's ear when supper was finished and the dancing had resumed. "Come with me to town, *ma jolie*, and I will buy you dresses from Paris and slippers made of gold."

Oh, how she was tempted, for she was foolish and rather tipsy.

He whispered more, she protested less, and they conspired to escape. He had to leave the next day. Tomorrow was too soon for her, but next week would be fine. There was to be a *veillée* at the Gagnons for Mardi Gras. It would be easy to slip away in the darkness when everyone was drunk. They did not dare kiss as they danced – Madame Gagnon had been frowning at them all evening – but they sealed their pact with a squeeze of her waist and a look in his black eyes.

"Mon Dieu," Marguerite laughed, surprised by the lightheadedness that had possessed her. "I don't even know your name."

"George. Like the king of England."

"Un Anglais!"

"From Boston," he said.

"Un protestant!"

"A freethinker, in fact. It is the eighteenth century, my dear, not the Dark Ages."

"You speak like the Devil."

"And you dance like an angel."

In the morning he was gone. All week Marguerite tried to behave normally, which caused everyone to wonder what was the matter with her. She told her secret to no one but her little sister. Whenever she was overcome by doubts or fears, she remembered the way she had felt in his arms. Her family, her home, her friends, her island – they all became more precious because they were about to pass away. They would vanish without farewell, and with them her innocence.

"Why are you crying, Marguerite?" her mother asked one evening as they were weaving by the fire. "Still thinking of your stranger? Forget him. That's what strangers do: they stay for a bit, and then they leave us with our tears. How many times has your father told you about Rose Latulippe, eh? She danced with a stranger too, the Devil himself, and he would have carried her away if the priest hadn't stopped him with a cross."

"Oh, Maman, I'm weary of such fables," said Marguerite. "This is the eighteenth century, not the Dark Ages."

"Who put such nonsense in your head? The Devil is no fable. Better your stranger disappeared too. The day such devils decide to stay is the day we'll have reason to cry."

On the night of Mardi Gras, Marguerite decided it was too risky to take anything with her except her favorite comb and her silver cross. In the years that followed, after her mind had gone peculiar, she often wondered if her cross had kept him away. Perhaps he indeed had been the Devil, and she had been spared by God – but spared only for guilt and despair and milking the cow. She hadn't sinned, the priest told her during her confession on Ash Wednesday, but she hadn't resisted temptation either. He put ashes on her forehead and ordered her to meditate upon Christ's temptations in the wilderness for the forty days of Lent. The songs and the dances stopped. There was only fasting and penance.

Nothing seemed to go well after that. There were serious crop failures throughout New France for the next few years, and famine threatened Sainte-Famille. When the yield improved in 1744, news arrived that England had gone to war again to curb the imperial and commercial strength of France. Trade suffered, invincible Louisbourg fell within a year, and the old threats from the English colonies and the Iroquois nations reappeared. Peace was barely concluded in 1748 before Marguerite's father died; then her mother died. Then Europe and North America began to prepare for a longer and more serious conflict, which would see the Acadians expelled from their villages in the east and Sainte-Famille occupied and finally destroyed by British troops.

"It's all my fault," Marguerite told her confessor again and again in her dementia. "We're all being punished for my weakness."

"It's God's will," he replied. "He crucified His own Son for the sins of the world. But He raised Him from the dead too. Be patient. He's trying us, but He'll lift us into Paradise if we remain faithful. On earth as it is in Heaven. We'll suffer, we'll die, but we'll be reborn."

So Marguerite Gagnon learned to be patient. In 1744, at age forty-three, she married her neighbor, not because she loved him but because his wife had died and left him with seven young children. If her weakness had lost her a place in God's heart, she would try to earn it back by sacrificing her life to the service of others. She worked hard, she never complained, and though her husband was five years her junior, she survived him by eight years through sheer tenacity. She even survived her brother and his wife, whose wedding she could describe in vivid detail to their son and six daughters when she was almost eighty.

"I can go now, I've suffered enough," she declared just before her death in 1783. But suddenly, as if her long-subdued spirit were surging up in one concentrated burst of affirmation before it was extinguished, she beckoned her nephew to approach. "I was only waiting to see how that war down in Boston turned out," she whispered. "I'm glad they've kicked the English king in the backside. We should do the same."

"Tante Marguerite, hush, that is a dangerous thing to say!" He had never known her to have any views, let alone rebellious ones.

"Let them hang me. I'll buy them the rope. This is the eighteenth century, after all, not the Dark Ages."

Abandoned, 1763

B Y T H E 1750s the ambitions of the million and a half English sub-jects in the thirteen American colonies could no longer be contained along the eastern seaboard. Unlike the French, they had been content to settle closely together and develop a strong agricultural

and commercial base, but the pressure for new land and more opportunities had become explosive. In the past, war in North America had
often been an incidental result of war in Europe, fought mostly by
colonial troops for colonial reasons. Now North America was about
to become a central battleground for the clash of European armies
and imperial designs. At stake were the future of the continent and
the fate of the seventy-five thousand Canadiens.

Between 1755 and 1759 some six thousand soldiers were sent from
France to save the American empire of Louis xv, and among them
was my ancestor Charles Leret. As with almost all soldiers at that
time, he was given a nom de guerre, Moncel, probably because he
had an association with the village of that name not far from his
parents' home in Saint-Pierre, in the western province of Lorraine.
For years on official documents he wavered among "Leret," "Ret,"
and "Leret *dit* Moncel"; some of his children never gave up Leret; but
Moncel eventually prevailed. Charles Leret *dit* Moncel set sail from
Brest in the spring of 1755 with the Régiment de la Reine, part of the
six battalions of thirty-six hundred *troupes de terre* under the
command of Baron Dieskau.

The fighting in America had begun a couple of years before
England and France again declared war. In 1754 French and Indian
forces had fought for control of the Ohio Valley against a Virginian
militia led by Major George Washington, who hardly distinguished
himself by murdering ten members of a French delegation in cold
blood and then losing a skirmish at Great Meadows, south of
present-day Pittsburgh. In July 1755 fewer than a thousand French
and Indian allies held the Ohio by routing three times as many
British and colonial soldiers under General Edward Braddock. Two
months later, in September, Baron Dieskau's regiments saw their first
action after rushing to Fort Saint-Frédéric on Lake Champlain to
stop a rumored offensive against Montreal by Colonel William
Johnson's New York militia.

Charles Moncel probably saw nothing more than guard duty, for the great controversy of that expedition concerned how many of his men Dieskau did *not* take into battle. Fifteen hundred accompanied him, along with one thousand Canadiens and five hundred Indians; but most never left the camp at present-day Ticonderoga, New York, not far from where Champlain had fired at the Iroquois more than a hundred and fifty years earlier. Baron Dieskau selected only two hundred soldiers to bolster a raiding party of six hundred settlers and five hundred Indians for a strike against Johnson's weak defense at Fort Edward, north of Albany on the Hudson River. The result was a fiasco. Fort Edward was stronger than reported, and the Indians refused to charge its cannons. A plan to ambush the reinforcements that Johnson was sending to the fort backfired when the militiamen and the Indians charged too soon. After an exhausting cross-country chase – as maladroit as it was frightening – Johnson's men reached his camp, where guns were waiting behind makeshift barricades to blast the French to pieces. Dieskau's men marched straight into death, as they had been trained to do, while the militia and the Indians dodged, shouted, and scurried like the guerrillas they were. The baron himself suffered three leg wounds and a shot in the groin.

"Continuing my march against the battery in the confidence that the Indians would not dare abandon me, seeing me so far advanced," he later explained as a prisoner of war nursing his groin in Bath, England, "I perceived that the Canadians, instead of marching on their side against the entrenchment, were scattering to right and left firing Indian fashion."

The battle was short and changed nothing – Johnson neither retreated to Albany nor advanced to Montreal – but the dispute between the French soldiers and the Canadiens went on for the rest of the war and may have shaped the result. "If only the regiments had been sent against Fort Edward," Charles Moncel sputtered, "we would have crushed it with our skill and our discipline!" To which the militiamen spat, "If only your *maudit* officers had let us fight *la petite guerre* without their stupid etiquettes, we could have done to Johnson what we did to Braddock."

They were still sputtering and spitting the next May when war broke out in Europe. In the same month the Marquis de Montcalm, with two more battalions, arrived in Quebec to take Dieskau's place. Born into a noble family in 1712 and put into military service at the age of nine, the veteran of eleven campaigns across Europe and the survivor of five serious wounds, Montcalm hated being under the thumb of Pierre de Rigaud de Vaudreuil, the first Canadien governor of New France. "In appearance, background, character, and temperament, these two men were very different," the historian W.J. Eccles observed. "Vaudreuil, Canadian born, was a big man, courteous and affable, lacking self-confidence but not given to intrigue, obsessed by a need to issue a constant stream of directives to junior officers and officials, anxious to impress his superiors in the ministry of marine, but always motivated by a genuine concern for the people he governed. To him the French regulars served but one function, the protection of New France from Anglo-American assaults. Montcalm, by contrast, was physically small and rather portly, vivacious, extremely vain, determined to have his own way in all things, critical of everything that did not conform to his preconceived ideas and of anyone who failed to agree with him completely, and possessed of a savage tongue that he could not curb."

He unleashed that tongue soon enough, when Vaudreuil dispatched him and three thousand men to take Fort Oswego on the south shore of Lake Ontario in August 1756. It turned out to be an easy victory, but Montcalm was appalled by the tactics of the fifteen hundred Canadiens. "These militiamen have no discipline," he reported home. "In six months I would make grenadiers of them, but at present I would not rely on them, nor believe what they say of themselves, for they think themselves quite the finest fellows in the world."

Certainly the governor credited their success to the cunning and courage of the settlers, so unlike the caution and convention of the French regiments. Surprise attacks had long been the colony's strategy against its English and Indian enemies, and Vaudreuil had the authority to overrule Montcalm's preference for defensive entrenchment. A year later, in August 1757, he ordered Montcalm to complete Dieskau's aborted task by marching more than twenty-five hundred soldiers, three thousand militia, and two thousand Indians down the western shore of Lake Champlain to capture Fort Edward. The huge army set off, but stopped sixteen miles north of its target to take Fort William Henry, which Johnson had built on the site of his barricades. Though the fort fell within three days, Montcalm refused to push on south, in part because of his timidity, in part because of the chaos that ensued when his own Indians stole hundreds of English prisoners from his protection, killing some.

Vaudreuil cursed Montcalm for being a coward, Montcalm cursed Vaudreuil for being an incompetent, and their curses were heard in every camp across New France all the way to Paris, spreading tension and despair among the tired ranks. Accusations and acrimony swirled around Charles Moncel's ears all winter, along with the usual gripes about the food, the cold, the pay, and the officers. It was hard to know what was worse. The pessimism or the horsemeat? The corruption or the price of rum? The tedium in the garrison or the thought of the next forced march?

The English, down but not out, seemed to get a second wind. In July 1758 they took the crucial Atlantic post at Louisbourg. In August they destroyed Fort Frontenac (now Kingston, Ontario), where Lake Ontario narrows into the St Lawrence River. In November they took Fort Duquesne (near present-day Pittsburgh) in the Ohio Valley. But their major thrust against New France was again blocked near Ticonderoga when a mammoth legion of six thousand British soldiers and nine thousand British colonials, heading north beside Lake Champlain, met Montcalm coming south with only three thousand French troops and a few hundred Canadiens. Though outnumbered five to one, Montcalm's regiment managed to fire European-style into wave after wave of redcoats. They killed nearly two thousand of the enemy and sent the rest fleeing for their lives. This time the French troops had won with little help from the settlers and the natives.

"Vaudreuil kept the Canadians back on purpose," Moncel whispered by the fire late that night in July as he cleaned his Charleville flintlock. "He wanted to see us massacred. Well, screw him, we showed we don't need those madmen."

My ancestor kept his misgivings to himself. He knew he would have been dead if the English had used their cannons against Montcalm's log defense or outflanked it by an easy march through open country. He wondered why Montcalm always pulled back after victories won with so much sweat and blood, and he heard rumors that at least nine French officers had been dismissed after the battle. "One, a knight of Malta and scion of an illustrious family, had been insane for some time and it had become impossible to conceal his condition," Eccles later confirmed; "five others were sent back for displaying a want of courage – or as Montcalm put it, *'pour avoir manqué à la première qualité nécessaire à un soldat et un officier'* – two for stealing from their fellow officers and one for having displayed considerable talent as a forger."

Nevertheless, the victory near Ticonderoga helped to tilt the favor of the French court away from Vaudreuil and toward Montcalm. In October 1758 Montcalm was made military commander in America, above the governor, and with him was promoted a defensive strategy. Instead of scattering their energy and resources on guerrilla campaigns into the Ohio Valley or New York, the French forces were instructed to consolidate their hold along the St Lawrence River. If England massed troops to the south and west, so much the better, for that meant the English would have fewer soldiers and supplies for the war going on in Europe. France had decided that it could not save the barn while its own house was on fire. New France would have to save itself.

By the summer of 1759, predictable consequences ensued. In the west the French had withdrawn from the Ohio and, with the fall of Fort Niagara, had been driven from the Great Lakes. To the south the English army under General Amherst had pushed the French from Ticonderoga and was poised to move north on Lake Champlain. Meanwhile, there had come from the east a British armada of one hundred and sixty-eight ships carrying eighty-five hundred soldiers under the command of a sickly thirty-two-year-old major-general, James Wolfe. A rather neurotic mixture of friendliness and irritability, Wolfe had served in Bavaria, at Culloden, in Belgium, and most recently at Louisbourg, and he had crossed the Atlantic with the words of Grey's elegy heavy in his mind: "The paths of glory lead but to the grave." At the end of June the armada anchored below Quebec, and Wolfe's troops seized Ile d'Orléans. The Gagnons and my other relatives at Sainte-Famille fled into the hills on the mainland.

Montcalm was surprised that the British had been able to navigate so far up the river, but he was no more pessimistic than usual. He had twice as many men, after all; he had an impregnable fortress; he had fresh supplies. Even if he did nothing, winter would assist him. For two months British cannons destroyed the town and British contingents set fire to the villages for miles on both sides of the river, yet Wolfe lost the only major skirmish – not far from where, more than a century earlier, Zacherie Cloutier had tilled his land. By the end of August 1759, dispirited, quarrelsome, and in poor health with rheumatism and dysentery, Wolfe had begun to lose hope of capturing Quebec before winter forced the English fleet to leave for home. "The Marquis de Montcalm is at the head of a great number of bad soldiers," Wolfe wrote to his mother, "and I am at the head of a small number of good ones, that wish for nothing so much as to fight him – but the wary old fellow avoids an action, doubtful of the behavior of his army."

Wolfe's very hopelessness prompted him to carry out the folly that should have led to unmitigated tragedy for Britain and its future in North America. On September 13, in the middle of the night, he sneaked almost forty-five hundred soldiers two and a half miles upriver past Quebec and up the steep, two-hundred-foot cliff at Anse-au-Foulon in the rain. "I don't think we can by any possible means get up here," Wolfe remarked, "but, however, we must use our best endeavour." By dawn they were positioned about half a mile outside the walls of the city on the Plains of Abraham, where Hélène Desportes had played as a girl, ready to awaken the garrison. Astonishingly, no one had challenged them. Montcalm had refused to heed warnings about a possible attack from that direction, mostly because the warnings had come from Vaudreuil.

Now, faced with the bad news, Montcalm made the blunder that would cost him his life and his king an empire. Like Frontenac in 1690 when faced by the armada from Boston under Phips, he should have done nothing. He had the high ground and the numbers, including three thousand men positioned behind the English at Cap Rouge. Time alone would have forced the redcoats from the field. If they had not surrendered, they would have been slaughtered trying to escape down the cliff to their boats. Instead, Montcalm panicked. Without even waiting for his full force to assemble, he decided to charge the English line in columns at ten o'clock in the morning. It was less a battle than a mêlée of confusion, smoke, mud, drums, and volleys as he directed his men to within forty paces of the redcoats, who held their fire despite their casualties until, as Wolfe had ordered, platoon officers gave the command to shoot. That broke the French charge. Then one volley from the entire line and the battle was won. Within half an hour the French and Canadien troops were in flight, pursued by the Highlanders' bayonets, and both Wolfe and Montcalm had been fatally wounded. Only the muskets of the Canadiens on the flanks prevented an immediate capture of the town. Vaudreuil wanted to fight again, but the French officers refused: they had not the stomach for it. They insisted on abandoning the field, retiring upriver to regroup. Seeing that, the commandant of the

Quebec garrison, fearing a massacre of the town's civilian population were it to be taken by storm, rejected an order from Vaudreuil to hold out. Instead, Quebec was surrendered.

To save their own honor, the French officers later persuaded Louis xv – and many historians – that Quebec had fallen not because of Montcalm's errors but because of the incompetence of Vaudreuil and his militiamen. "Four times deservingly victorious," reads the monument to Montcalm that stands today on the Plains of Abraham in Quebec City, "and at last defeated, through no fault of his own."

———————

It was not the fault of Charles Moncel, at least. My ancestor had not been at the Battle of Quebec. The Régiment de la Reine had been left with a couple of other French regiments at Fort de l'Ile aux Noix at the north end of Lake Champlain to await Amherst's invasion from Ticonderoga. "The only satisfaction I can derive from this disaster," Moncel heard Colonel Bourlamaque say about the reports from Quebec, "is not to have been a part of it." All through the winter of 1759–60, Moncel mused upon how history would have been different if he had been at Quebec. He would have been standing guard at the top of the cliff, of course, and he would have alerted Montcalm in the middle of the night. He would have braved the British fire and decimated the British ranks. Why, he personally would have saved North America for the French king and the Roman faith!

"Enough of your fantasies, Moncel," Captain d'Hébécourt barked. "Now you'll have a chance to prove yourself. We've been ordered to join the Chevalier de Lévis and Colonel Bourlamaque to recapture Quebec."

It was April 20, 1760, when the expedition set off from Montreal by boat, to the beat of drums and a chorus of "Le couvre-feu." A week later Moncel and his regiment approached the ruined capital, where some seven thousand British soldiers had passed an especially dreadful winter. Some had died from the cold; some had died from hunger and scurvy. Some had been shot by the locals while trying to fetch wood or food. Barely half were able to muster when the five thousand French soldiers showed up at the gates. Nevertheless, the new British commander, James Murray, repeated Montcalm's mistake, needlessly rushing his men from safety to engage the French at Sainte-Foy. This time it was the French who outflanked the British, turned column into line, and fired with precision. This time it was the redcoats who fled in panic. Indeed, the English would have been trapped and butchered outside the garrison if the Régiment de la Reine had not misread its orders, moved to the wrong position, and missed the fighting altogether.

"Bravo, Moncel! Very courageous of you, and very clever too!"

At least, my ancestor consoled himself, he had done his bit to erase last year's shame. Now he had only to wait with the others for the ships to arrive from France, and Quebec would be French once more. He had no way of knowing that France, weakened by war and heavily in debt, had given up on Canada as a lost cause. Louis xv sent only a token force, too weak even to reach the St Lawrence. The sails that finally came into view in the middle of May were British sails, and the mere sight of them was enough to send Lévis and his regiments scampering back to Montreal. There they faced a three-pronged attack by sixteen thousand redcoats – from Quebec, from Lake Champlain, and from Lake Ontario – which led to the final surrender of Canada to the British in September. Many of the Canadiens had already abandoned the fight to save their farms and families from the systematic campaign of British terrorism. Hundreds of French soldiers had slipped into the villages and forests rather than die for the sake of honor.

Charles Moncel was among them. He had quit more than military life, as it turned out. He had quit his country, his king, and the Old World itself. He had joined that exotic family of men and women, les Canadiens, who found themselves subjects of the British Crown when, in the peace treaty of 1763, France showed itself more interested in safeguarding its European position, its Atlantic fisheries, and its Caribbean sugar islands than in keeping the costly and contentious territory of Canada. He would join the family more formally in 1767 by marrying thirteen-year-old Anne Généreux, the granddaughter of a soldier who had come with the Carignan-Salières Regiment.

There were seventy-five thousand Canadiens by then. (Between the British occupation in 1629 and the Conquest of 1759, no more than thirty thousand French had emigrated to America, but only some ten thousand had stayed on.) Except for the most recent arrivals, they saw themselves as a society as different from France as the thirteen colonies were from England. The difference between the French and the Canadiens had been dramatized by their quarrels during the war. The French had been fighting as Europeans for imperial goals, the Canadiens as North Americans for their homeland.

"If I only dared," Voltaire had written to France's foreign minister in 1760, "I would implore you on my knees to rid France forever of the administration of Canada. By losing Canada, you lose nothing; if you want her restored to you, you restore a perpetual source of war and humiliation – no more." And again, in 1762, the famous philosopher argued that Canada was only "a few arpents of snow not worth a soldier's bones."

Still, the Canadiens had remained loyal to the motherland. It was the motherland that betrayed them – on the battlefield, at the peace talks, and ultimately, twenty years later, with the revolution against the Crown and the Church that severed the colonists' links to the king and bishops of France. For more than a century New France had been left to its own devices every autumn, when the ships departed and all communication ceased. But every spring the ships had returned, with tough soldiers and new economic schemes, with bright administrators and arrogant governors, with ambitious traders and pious clerics, with corrupt officers and the latest fashions. When the ships left for

France this time, leaving my ancestor to watch them go, they never came back. The French Canadian family would have to survive the British Conquest by itself.

Another King and Country, 1783

FOR CAPTAIN John Munro, it had been a good war. A Scotsman, my great-great-great-great-great-grandfather had come to North America to fight the French with the Forty-eighth Regiment in 1756 and been posted at once to Albany. For the next four years he had marched up and down the Hudson River valley in the various British efforts to control Lake Champlain and attack New France. According to family legend he was the Munro in James Fenimore Cooper's *Last of the Mohicans* who surrendered Fort William Henry to Montcalm in 1757; in truth he was part of the "cowardly" force that failed to go to the defense of Lieutenant-Colonel George Munro. In 1758 he fled the fire of Charles Moncel's regiment at Ticonderoga. In 1759, after the fall of Quebec, he retreated with General Amherst's soldiers instead of advancing against Montreal. In 1760, just weeks before the Battle of Sainte-Foy, he was out of the army and safe in the arms of his new bride in Schenectady.

She was Mary Brouwer, the great-granddaughter of a Dutch settler in New Amsterdam (which became New York in 1664) and the granddaughter of an Albany fur trader whose home still stands as the oldest house in Schenectady. John Munro followed his father-in-law into "the Mercantile way of Business." By 1765 he had picked up more than ten thousand acres between the Hudson and the Connecticut in what is now Vermont. He called his estate Foulis, after the ancestral home of his Scottish clan, and he built upon it a "tolerably large house decently furnished" for his wife and seven children, barns for the cows and horses, granaries for the wheat and corn, a sawmill, a grist mill, a small potash works, and "a Genteel sphere of Life."

His happy fortune did not last long. His lands were part of the territory claimed by both New York and New Hampshire. Each colony had been making grants to its own settlers, and the resulting disputes had turned into a small civil war. As a major landowner and local justice of the peace appointed by New York, Captain Munro was at the center of the official campaign against the "Green Mountain Boys," a local gang of farmers under the leadership of Ethan Allen who were determined to defend the New Hampshire grants by violence.

"Every person that pretends to be a friend to this Government are in danger of both Life and property," my ancestor reported to Albany in May 1771. "They assemble themselves together in the night time and throws down all the Yorkers Fences as we are called and Drives the cattle into the Fields and meadows and destroys both Grass and corn, and do every mischief they can think of. Pardon the imperfections of this and the other papers herewith sent you as I am in confusion my House being full of Rioters."

To the Green Mountain Boys, Captain Munro became "a malicious and bloody enemy" and the leader of "a wicked, inhuman, most barbarous, infamous, cruel, villainous, and thievish attack." On New Year's Day 1772 Ethan Allen jumped up at a meeting at the Catamount Tavern in Bennington and vowed, "We shall make a hell of his house and burn him in it!" They tried, but "divine interposition" and a timely yell of the Munro war cry – "Castle Foulis in flames!" – saved Munro's home and family from destruction. Later he wrote, "the rascally Yankees spoiled my best hat and sword coat with their Pumpkin sticks," and they set fire to his potash works. On another occasion one of the Green Mountain Boys "drew his cutlass," according to a history of Vermont, "and striking the pugnacious magistrate over the head felled him to the ground." His assailant was rewarded with one hundred acres "for his valor in cutting the head of Esquire Munro the Yorkite."

"What can a justice do when the whole country combines against him?" Captain Munro lamented soon after his recovery. In 1773 he wrote to the governor of New York to warn that "the mob has broke loose. A messenger brought me word this minute that in a few days the whole of my property would be burnt to ashes."

But his property was spared – and then lost – by a greater conflagration: the American Revolution. While the Green Mountain Boys went on to become rebel heroes in the struggle of the thirteen colonies for independence from England, Captain John Munro, in his own words, "could by no means divest himself of his Allegiance to his King and Country." In 1775 he joined the Royal Highland Emigrants and began rallying men to the Loyalist side. He was captured, released, and captured again. He spent eighteen months confined in one of the sloops that made up "the fleet prison" on the Hudson River near Esopus. His family was told that he had been hanged. He was told that they had been murdered.

"It would almost make a volume to enumerate the many various and difficult hardships your Memorialist and Family have undergone both in Body and Mind," Munro wrote later. He escaped from prison and certain death, sneaked north through wild forests, met up with "Gentleman Johnny" Burgoyne's forces at Ticonderoga, and continued to Montreal. From there he managed to send a message to his wife that he was alive.

During his absence his home was attacked. His family fled with little besides their clothes, a cow, and some silver they had hidden. "Your Dear Children are all well," Mary replied just before leaving Foulis forever; "as for myself I am in a poor state of health and very much distressed. I must leave my house in a very short time, and God knows where I shall get a place to put my head on, for my own relations are my greatest enemy's. I have scarcely a mouthfull of bread for myself or Childer for heavens sake my dear Mr. Munro send me some relief by the first safe hand. Is their no possibility of your sending for us, if their is no method fallen upon we shall all perish, for you can have no idea of our sufferings here, let me once more intreat you to try every method to save your family – my heart is so full it is ready to break – adew my Dearest John may God Almighty bless preserve and protect you, that we may live to see each other is the constant prayers of Your affectionate tho afflicted Wife. p.s. The Childer send love to You."

In great distress the Munro family sought refuge with the Brouwer relatives in Schenectady, "in hopes of meeting Consolation and parental affection, instead of which they could scarce find anything but reproaches and bitter invectives." An old friend hid my ancestress and her young children for a year, however, and one of her rebel relatives managed to secure them a pass to Canada. In the early autumn of 1778 they set off north from Albany into hunger, fatigue, and uncertainty. The route had been the scene of heavy fighting once again. In 1775 the American congress had sent three thousand rebels – including John Munro's nemesis, Ethan Allen – to smash the British forts on Lake Champlain and seize Montreal, which finally fell that November. When Benjamin Franklin himself failed to persuade more than a handful of Canadiens to join the revolution and make Canada the "fourteenth colony" to liberate itself, the Americans pulled back to Ticonderoga. There, in July 1777, they were defeated by General Burgoyne's invading army, which was defeated in turn at Saratoga in October. The fleeing Munro family had to move across a front, therefore, where the combatants were poised to shoot. As it happened, the greatest danger came when, crossing Lake George by boat, they were pursued by a party of Indians.

At last, in late October they arrived at Fort Saint-Jean on the Richelieu River. To their great joy they were greeted by none other than Captain Munro, whom they had not seen in two and a half years. "Tho very sickly the whole Winter," Captain Munro wrote after his reunion with his family, "the Children recovered but Mrs Munro never will from the excessive hardships they underwent."

After arriving in Canada Munro had joined the King's Royal Regiment of New York under Sir John Johnson, whose father had fought against Baron Dieskau's French soldiers twenty years earlier. One of Munro's first assignments was to help settle the hundreds of Loyalist families seeking refuge near Montreal, so he was well placed to find food and quarters for his own, even though the family was "totally destitute" and "confined to Live with my slender income in a very Expensive and Extravagant Country."

In 1780 he was forced to leave them again, to lead one hundred men on a raid into New York. His mission was to draw attention from John Johnson's attack on Oswego and lure recruits to the Loyalist cause. Though he missed the pleasure of murdering his in-laws at Schenectady, he was able to destroy the rebels' houses in Ballston eight miles to the north and capture its militia commander in a midnight foray. According to some American historians, the "notorious" and "brutal Munro" marched his undressed and barefoot prisoners through the night and ordered them slain if the rebels counterattacked. By his own account, however, all but one were saved "with great difficulty from Indian vengeance by Munro's care and vigilance" and delivered to the British camp on Lake Champlain. Instead of being hailed as a hero, he was rebuked for not following up his victory. But, he argued lamely, his men were tired, hungry, and "distressed for everything having wore out all their Shoes, Mockosins, Trowsers, Leggings."

That was my ancestor's last action. In 1781 his detachment was posted to guard the prisoners of war in the compound outside Montreal. Though he was blamed for a remarkable number of escapes, he passed the remainder of the conflict near the bosom of his family. Indeed, he and Mrs Munro produced an eighth child, and their other four sons joined their father as volunteers in the regiment. Hugh, the eldest boy, became a lieutenant at the age of nineteen.

The moment peace came in 1783, with the victory of the American colonists and their allies from France over a debt-laden and war-weary Britain, Captain Munro sent Hugh to the United States to see what property or debts he could collect for the family. Hugh met nothing but "abusive and threatening language" from a gang of former neighbors, who swore that "they would make an Example of him instead of his Father," and narrowly got away with his life. "I must find an Asylum for my numerous family," Captain Munro pleaded to the British authorities in Canada; "the whole of my property is for ever wrested from me." He was fifty-five years old, he added, and "it's a severe Reflection to begin the World again after a painful Experience of Twenty Seven Years of Care and Industry."

Captain Munro was not alone. About forty thousand Loyalists had fled the "American Usurpation." Some went to England, Bermuda, and Nova Scotia; some went to the former French colony of New France. All of them petitioned for compensation for their losses in the form of cash and new land. Like Captain Munro, they added up the value of every burnt barn and stolen cow, gathered witnesses to attest to their honesty and loyalty, submitted bills for their out-of-pocket expenses (not including, in Munro's case, such trifles as "Gills of Rum and Soap from Sutherland the butler" for his men), and often met disappointment. Munro's first request for twelve thousand acres near Montreal was rejected, and he had to spend two years and untold sums in London to obtain a paltry three hundred pounds, about 2 per cent of his estimated sacrifice. When he returned to Canada from England in 1787, however, he and his family were rewarded with large tracts of land up the St Lawrence to the west of Montreal in what is now eastern Ontario.

The province of Ontario had its origins in the five thousand Loyalists such as John Munro who settled in the "western settlements" along the north shore of the river and lakes from Montreal to Detroit. As British subjects they did not want to be subject to the French laws and customs that had been left mostly intact since Wolfe's defeat of Montcalm. Furthermore, as former Americans, they wanted an elected assembly to balance the power of the colonial governor and his appointed council, though they realized the dangers of an assembly in the grip of the French and Catholic majority. As early as 1785, therefore, Captain Munro signed a petition demanding that Canada be carved in two and its western territory given to the English-speaking Protestants. The British authorities moved cautiously, in part not to agitate the French Canadians, in part not to lose control of the colony to the merchants and democrats; but in 1791 Upper Canada and Lower Canada came into being, each with an assembly of limited power, as the forerunners of Ontario and Quebec.

John Munro began to prosper again after that. He was appointed to the new council by Lieutenant-Governor Simcoe, and he reassumed his former glory as a local magistrate. He built another tolerably large house, more barns for more cows and horses, a new sawmill and grist mill, and an even more genteel sphere of life. "Captain Munro conducted me to his house," wrote Patrick Campbell, who traveled through Matilda Township in 1791, "and entertained me with a great deal of politeness, attention, and hospitality."

If there was a cloud in his last years, it seems to have been his son Hugh. It must have been difficult for Hugh, a Loyalist officer in his own right, to live under the roof and work under the scrutiny of a tough old Scot like his father. Whether it was the cause or the result of their tensions, Captain Munro filed a strange petition in 1787. Stating that he had built his house "for the General benefit of the Family" on a lot that had been granted to Hugh, he asked that the fifty acres around the house be put in Mrs Munro's name, in case his son's "having the Whole in his power might prove injurious to all the rest of the Family." Ten years later he filed another petition, requesting the land to which his wife and children were entitled because he was a councilor; but Hugh was not listed among his children. Finally, in his last will, Captain Munro left Hugh nothing.

A classic tale of father versus son, perhaps, but I detect another element, one that was to recur more than a hundred years later when Edith Brady decided to marry my grandfather Moncel. While in Montreal, either as a soldier or as a vendor of lumber and wheat, Hugh Munro saw much of a comely young woman named Angélique Larocque. According to another faulty legend, she was related directly to Jean-François La Rocque de Roberval, an impoverished nobleman who had explored the St Lawrence with Jacques Cartier in 1542. In reality, Larocque was Angélique's husband's name. He had been the first of his kin to bring it to New France, where he had established himself as a successful merchant in the prosperous village of L'Assomption northeast of Montreal and its first representative in the assembly of Lower Canada. He had died shortly after being elected, in 1792, leaving his young widow with two small boys.

If Angélique was not a La Rocque de Roberval, she was a Leroux d'Esneval – and therefore, goes the family gossip, a direct descendant of the twelfth-century French king Louis the Fat. Her father had come to New France in the 1740s as a soldier, before he too became a successful merchant in L'Assomption and died in 1792, but her mother's line went all the way back to Zacherie Cloutier's neighbors at Beauport in the 1640s. Her brother, Laurent Leroux, was a famous fur trader for the North West Company, the first white man to explore Great Slave Lake, the father of four girls by an Ojibwa "wife" in the North, a justice of the peace, captain of the militia, member of the assembly, autodidact, and yet another L'Assomption merchant who made a fortune in grain, hardware, potash, and real estate.

Angélique moved through the most sophisticated circles of commerce and politics, made up of practical French Canadians who were ready (even anxious) to deal and connect with their new rulers. No doubt she had been introduced to the sweet lieutenant with the sad eyes in 1784, while the Munro family were living in L'Assomption and awaiting their future. His reserve did not intimidate her for a minute: she saw it as proof of his infatuation, and so charmingly British! She never forgot it. Her first husband was less than a year in his grave when she and Hugh were married on May 4, 1793, in Montreal's Anglican Christ Church.

Captain Munro was not fooled by the Protestant church. Its rector was an old Frenchman whose English was incomprehensible; its building had been used as a Jesuit chapel; and, as a Presbyterian elder, John Munro saw little difference between the Church of England and the Church of Rome. Whatever the formalities, Hugh had been tempted by the Scarlet Woman, who would inevitably take his soul for sinful favors and burden him with scores of Romish children. Hadn't this trollop, still in widow's weeds, already brought him two such boys? May God forgive Hugh, because his father would not.

"It's not just a betrayal of me!" the captain shouted at his long-suffering wife, in a complaint that would be echoed in certain Protestant households of Upper Canada and Ontario for more than a hundred years. "It's a betrayal of the whole clan of Munro! We didn't whip the Stuarts at Culloden and slay Montcalm on the Plains of Abraham in order to breed a bunch of French-speaking, Latin-mumbling incense-sniffers! We'll have nothing more to do with him!"

So Hugh sold his land in Upper Canada to his brother Henry and moved to his new and more tolerant family in Lower Canada, at first at L'Assomption, where he took over Laroque's business until selling it to Angélique's brother, and then at Saint-Esprit north of Montreal. There Hugh became known as Hugues Munro, a justice of the peace and retired officer living on half-pay. There he and Angélique raised their five children, of whom four survive in the records with French Canadian names and French Canadian spouses. And there the Loyalist soldier from Vermont and Upper Canada became a Roman Catholic, so that he could be buried with his wife. My great-great-great-great grandfather, the eldest son of a Scottish Presbyterian soldier, had become, through love, a Canadien.

Reign of Terror, 1802

WHEN CAPTAIN John Munro died in 1800, he could not have guessed that his position as paterfamilias would soon pass to a French Canadian Catholic. Indeed, given his strong prejudices, it may have been his death that freed his youngest daughter, Charlotte, not yet thirty but already the widow of a British officer, to marry Michel-Eustache-Gaspard-Alain Chartier de Lotbinière on November 15, 1802. Fifty-four years old, seigneur of Lotbinière and Rigaud and Vaudreuil, former speaker of the legislative assembly of Lower Canada, member of the legislative council, Alain de Lotbinière became by virtue of his age, wealth, and influence the effective head of Captain Munro's family – or, more accurately, of the half who followed Hugh's example, married French Canadians, and moved back to Lower Canada.

The Lotbinières were related to some of the great names of France and, in the words of one historian, "of all the families who made their home in New France they were of the most ancient lineage." The first to Canada had arrived in 1651 with Governor Lauson, a relation, and he had become an important magistrate, the host of the colony's first ball, the father of a judge who wrote atrocious poetry, and the patriarch of a series of distinguished officials, soldiers, and seigneurs, of whom Alain was the latest. But Alain drew as much satisfaction from his alliance with the Munro clan, though it had little of his pedigree and less of his cash, as he had from his first marriage to Marie-Josephte Godefroy de Tonnancour, of the rich and noble fur-trading family in Trois-Rivières, who had died childless three years earlier.

Charlotte Munro represented a personal and political triumph.

Forty years before the wedding Lotbinière had stared into the face of ruin, humiliation, and exile. As an eleven-year-old cadet he had fought in the service of his cousin Vaudreuil on the Plains of Abraham; a year later, following the capitulation of Montreal, he had left Canada with his father, a military engineer and seigneur, for France. They were part of a wave of French officials, soldiers, merchants, and seigneurs who chose to abandon the occupied colony to save their professional and economic links with the motherland – a wave some historians have exaggerated into a "decapitation" of New France's commercial and social elites that rendered permanent damage to the prosperity of French Canadians under English rule. But France proved a foreign and unwelcoming realm for purebred Canadiens such as the Lotbinières. By the end of 1763 father and son had returned home.

Not that there hadn't been troubles in New France. The long and brutal war had devastated the colony. The situation was "shocking to Humanity," according to one British officer, whose soldiers had been inspired by "Benevolence and charity" to share a portion of their provisions with the hungry and homeless. The last French administration had deliberately created famine and need among the habitants for its own profit and flooded the economy with paper money whose worthlessness broke many merchants. The invading British forces had destroyed more than a thousand farms and laid waste fields and villages from the Ile d'Orléans to Montreal. Worse, perhaps, had been the fear of deportation, the fate of ten thousand Acadians a few years earlier, and uncertainty about the future of the Roman Catholic faith, the French language, and the seigneurial customs at the hands of the conquerors.

Still, it was in everyone's interest "to resurrect from the ashes the sad remains of the fruit of their labours," as one report phrased it; and, despite the memories of the British army's terrorist tactics, French and English set to work "in perfect harmony and good humour." The Lotbinières even saw opportunities under the new regime now that the corrupt and incompetent officials had returned to France, and had began buying up seigneuries from departing friends and relations. More problematic, however, was the political response to the Conquest. Merchants from Britain and the American colonies wanted to take control of Canada as quickly as possible, and they benefited from the English law that prohibited Roman Catholics from holding public office. In 1763 London proclaimed its desire to make the new province of Quebec attractive to even more British merchants and immigrants by turning it into an English-speaking, Protestant outpost subject to English laws and an English assembly. At the same time it set up new authorities over the Atlantic fisheries and western territories, reducing the old empire of New France to the St Lawrence Valley.

The proclamation may have made sense on paper and in the fantasies of colonial bureaucrats across the sea, but it was nonsense to the first governors commissioned to implement it. Often bilingual and aristocratic soldiers, they identified at once with the refined manners, military backgrounds, rural pursuits, and monarchical views of the seigneurs, whom they considered trustworthy agents who could mediate between the victors and the vanquished. In contrast, their own English-speaking merchants struck them as greedy, unruly, and "Licentious Fanaticks." And so the seigneurs, ironically, acquired a power under the British that they had never really had under the French, when their title as feudal lord had been mainly ceremonial.

"I will with Joy undertake anything to distress & reduce to reason my Royal Master's Enemies," James Murray, the first British governor general, wrote to his superiors in 1764, "but I cannot be the Instrument of destroying, perhaps, the best and bravest Race on this Globe, a Race that have already got the better of every National Antipathy to their Conquerors, and could they be indulged with a very few Privileges, which the laws of England do not allow to Catholics at home, must in a very short time become the most faithful & useful Set of Men in this American Empire."

Murray's attitude soon caused his dismissal, but the same mixture of practicality and prejudice moved his successor Guy Carleton toward the same affinity with the seigneurs, and even with the Catholic clergy, who were preaching obedience in order to protect their own position. "The better Sort of Canadians fear nothing more than popular Assemblies," Carleton wrote in 1768, "which, they conceive, tend only to render the People refractory and insolent." The seigneurs wanted power for themselves, however, and when London realized after ten years that its post-Conquest strategy had been a disaster for Canada's fur trade and a delusion considering the vast numerical superiority of French Canadians, it reversed direction.

The Quebec Act of 1774 re-established the French civil law known as the Coutume de Paris, the old western boundaries, the Roman Catholic Church, and the rule by governor and appointed council, on which Catholics could serve. The new government was, ironically, more aristocratic and theocratic than that of New France. "A new principle of empire was laid down when it was conceded that the French Canadians could be British without becoming English," the historian Mason Wade remarked, and "in the virtual establishment of Catholicism in Canada, there was an anticipation of that ending of the old religious hatreds which did not come in England itself until the Reform Bill of 1829."

The English merchants were unhappy about the loss of English laws and the promised assembly; the American colonists were unhappy about the loss of the western lands and the Protestant hold; but Alain de Lotbinière's father was unhappy too. Having overextended himself financially with his land purchases and been forced to sell or give most of his properties to his son, he had been pressing for a prominent place in the government of Quebec through a seigneurial assembly. When that failed to materialize, he lost his faith in the British authorities and retired once more to France. There, and later in Boston, he agitated to help the Americans in their revolution against the English king, not as a democrat or a republican but with the hope that France might regain Canada during the rebellion and he might regain his lands and authority.

Alain, meanwhile, had fought alongside the British against the American rebels who invaded Montreal in 1775. Though many prominent merchants and most habitants were vaguely sympathetic to the Americans or else indifferent to the outcome, Alain responded to Guy Carleton's cry for help and spent two years as a prisoner of war in the United States. "I am destined to live with the English, my welfare is in their command, I depend entirely upon them," he explained to his father, who was to die alone and impoverished in New York after fleeing the French Revolution. "Consequently, my policy is to adapt myself to circumstances."

Or, as an American observer put it somewhat bitterly in 1775, "The French of Canada constitute the sort of people who know no other way of procuring riches and honor than in becoming sycophants of the Court; and since the introduction of French laws will give positions to the petty French nobility, they crowd around the governor."

Whether for principle or profit, Alain de Lotbinière adapted himself to circumstances, which had started to change rapidly after the American Revolution. The coming of the Loyalists into Quebec had increased the number and significance of the English merchants, who were already growing wealthy from furs and commerce, and lent weight to their demand for an elected assembly. That demand was heard by the more open-minded politicians in London, who were anxious to avoid the pressure for "no taxation without representation" that had just cost Britain its other American colonies. So, in 1791, an assembly was granted, but only on condition that Quebec be carved into two parts – Upper and Lower Canada – to prevent most of the Loyalists (including Captain John Munro) from being subjected to a French Canadian majority, and only with the governor and council still in place to control the democratic urges of the masses. Though Alain de Lotbinière had always opposed the idea of an assembly, he ran in the first election in 1792 and won.

Soon afterward he delivered a famous speech in defense of bilingualism. "Since the majority of our constituents are placed in a special situation," he argued, "we are obliged to depart from the ordinary rules and forced to ask for the use of a language which is not that of the Empire. But, being as fair to others as we hope they will be to us, we should not want our language eventually to banish that of His Majesty's other subjects."

That spirit of pragmatism and fair play served him well. In 1794 he was elected speaker of the assembly, and in 1796 he was appointed to the legislative council. His marriage to Charlotte Munro was both a symbol and a celebration of his accommodation with the British rulers, therefore, and the wedding party at his manor house west of Montreal on the Ottawa River was a merry mélange of French speeches and English songs, of Scottish reels and French Canadian jigs.

By coincidence, his success and happiness marked a decade of relative prosperity and peace in Lower Canada. After the Conquest and the American Revolution, no one had wanted to get involved in the horrors of the French Revolution and the Napoleonic wars. After the famines and the commercial readjustments, there had been a sudden boom in agriculture and the fur trade. After the constitutional confusion and political quarrels, the assembly and council had provided a modus vivendi in which the English merchants and Canadian seigneurs could meet and compete – though the deal had been built on an injustice, the 6 per cent of Lower Canada's population who were English-speaking receiving a third of the assembly seats and half the places on the council. That was to change within the next decade, however, and my cousin Alain de Lotbinière would have to pay for his compromises and rewards.

Nothing seemed to go as well after 1802. A deep recession hit, and unlike the regular downturns, it was rooted in the structural problems underlying Lower Canada's two basic products: wheat and furs. Poor harvests, lower exports, exhausted soil, and the outmoded agricultural methods of the habitants haunted the first; higher costs, smaller markets, tougher competition, and the cumulative impact of Britain's concession of Canada's territories southwest of the Great Lakes to the United States in 1783 undermined the second. Everyone felt the effects, but not everyone agreed on the solutions. The result was the start of a political brawl between the British governors, the English-speaking merchants, and their French Canadian allies on the one hand, and a new generation of French-speaking professionals in control of the assembly on the other.

These French-speaking professionals, well educated but not well paid, socially ambitious but not removed from their rural origins, had risen to power during the 1790s by getting themselves elected to the new assembly and learning how to manipulate its procedures to serve themselves and their people. They were fervent democrats when asserting the rights of the elected majority over the authority of the governor and his appointed executive; but their goals were neither democratic nor reformist.

"This bourgeoisie," the historian Fernand Ouellet concluded, "dreamed of a society centred around the St Lawrence Lowlands, devoted to agriculture, enclosed by the seigneury and by the Coutume de Paris, but directed by them. They thus resumed contact with certain ideals of New France, even beyond the developments of the last half of the eighteenth century. It was for a society, longed for before, freed from the grip of the fur trade, and firmly guaranteed of moral and social stability. It was a reaction against all the uncertainties of the beginning of the nineteenth century. It was not the fur trade alone which was the object of the liberal professionals' aversion, but commercial capitalism as a whole."

The English merchants had expected that the assembly would be their vehicle for the money, laws, and fundamental reforms necessary to advance commercial capitalism, canals, and their own interests in

Lower Canada. Finding themselves in the minority, however, they set aside their democratic rhetoric and sought the support of their old foes – the governor, the seigneurs, and the Catholic Church – against the "backward" peasants and their "upstart" representatives. Though the governor's clique did include some French Canadians – Alain de Lotbinière for one – the struggle between the governor and the assembly became almost immediately a nationalist struggle between the English and the French, beneath which stirred a struggle for public capital, public jobs, public contracts, public lands, public education, public policies, and a definition of the public good.

"What remains to be done?" the *Quebec Mercury*, the voice of the English merchants, thundered in 1806. "Withdraw these privileges which are represented as being too few but are in reality too many, and which the conquered enjoy too liberally, and take measures to ensure that the administration of public business takes place in English and by Englishmen, or men with English principles. This would be the first and most efficacious step towards the Anglicization of the Province."

The struggle flared up in 1808 around Alain de Lotbinière's former brother-in-law. Pierre-Amable De Bonne was a vain seigneur, a controversial theater producer, a lazy judge, a notorious philanderer, and the unofficial leader of the governor's French Canadian faction in the assembly. More a defender of seigneurial power than an advocate of British commerce, he nevertheless hated the nationalist professionals who had formed themselves into the Parti Canadien. They in turn hated him for being a *vendu,* a sellout or quisling.

Partly to oust De Bonne, partly to affirm the impartiality of the bench, the nationalists passed a bill forbidding judges to be members of the assembly, but the council (after a strong speech by Lotbinière, who defended De Bonne despite the man's miserable treatment of his sister) overturned it. In 1809 they tried to pass it again. The governor, Sir James Craig, no supporter of democracy or of French Canadians or of Roman Catholics, was so angry that he stormed into the assembly, dismissed it, and forced a general election, in which he himself campaigned against the Parti Canadien. Though the sexual and financial morals of De Bonne were major issues in *Le Canadien* and other newspapers, De Bonne won again – but so did his enemies, who now simply barred him from taking his seat. In a fury Governor Craig again dismissed the assembly and ordered new elections. This time he also closed *Le Canadien* for its "wicked, seditious, and traitorous writings" and jailed three prominent leaders of the Parti Canadien without trial. This "reign of terror," as it became known among Quebec nationalists, did not produce its intended effect: De Bonne lost his nomination as a candidate; the prisoners won their ridings.

"It really, my Lord, appears to me an absurdity," Craig wrote to the colonial secretary in London to justify his actions with rumors of rebellion and massacre, "that the Interests of certainly not an unimportant Colony, involving in them those also of no inconsiderable portion of the Commercial concerns of the British Empire, should be in the hands of six petty shopkeepers, a Blacksmith, a Miller, and fifteen ignorant peasants who form part of our present House."

Whatever London thought, it was no time to upset French Canadians. England was still at war against Napoleon, and it would soon be at war against the United States because of a series of commercial conflicts and diplomatic quarrels. Despite Craig's contention that most French Canadians were infected with an attachment to France and a keenness for American democracy, more French Canadians rushed to defend British North America against the American invaders during the War of 1812 than at the time of the American Revolution. Alain de Lotbinière, sixty-four years old and the father of three daughters, led his Vaudreuil militia to the defense of the British monarch; the Catholic bishops called for their followers to show loyalty and gratitude to the king who had spared their faith from the ravages of the French Revolution; thousands of habitants rallied for the sake of their homeland as militiamen or regulars in the first French Canadian regiment in the British army; and even the assembly suspended its quarrels to vote money and support for the preservation of Lower Canada's language, religion, and way of life.

When international peace came, however, the domestic conflicts resumed. They were based on too many profound contradictions about politics and the economy to be appeased by a moment of military glory or a couple of conciliatory governors like Sir George Prevost and Sir John Coape Sherbrooke. Thus, in 1818 Sherbrooke's gentle ways were replaced by the tough stance of the Duke of Richmond and Lennox, a noted soldier and sportsman, who took the side of the English merchants against the assembly and the Parti Canadien. More alarmingly, he seemed to warm to Craig's old point of view that Upper and Lower Canada should be rejoined to break the hold of the French Canadian nationalists on the assembly, suppress the French language, and facilitate economic expansion.

The duke's behavior was a popular topic at the reception Alain de Lotbinière, now seventy, hosted at his elegant new townhouse on Rue de Saint-Sacrement in Old Montreal in February 1819. It was to celebrate the marriage of his wife's niece and godchild, my ancestress Charlotte, the daughter of Hugh and Angélique Munro, to Dr Joseph Leduc. Lotbinière's silver hair was thinner, his quick wit slower, but his eyes still glittered beneath his arching brows and high forehead, and his voice still blended eloquence with kindness. His personality attracted people as he sat in his favorite armchair by the fire in the drawing room, watching the younger ones dancing and remembering some of the same faces at his own wedding almost twenty years earlier. Summoning the bride and groom, he gave them a wonderful present – he had arranged for Joseph to become the doctor on the seigneury at Vaudreuil – and then he returned to his argument with Hugh's stepson, François-Antoine Larocque.

"You're playing with fire," Lotbinière warned him when the thirty-four-year-old businessman expressed sympathy for the Parti

Canadien. "The rabble always begins by demanding bread and justice and always ends by getting guillotines and tyrants."

"With all due respect, sir," Larocque replied, "it is to prevent tyranny that we must control the governors. I need hardly remind you that it was your friend Craig who jailed people without trial and closed down a legitimate newspaper."

"But the rule of law had to be maintained, my dear boy. Those sowers of sedition had to be stopped. People were afraid, it was a volatile situation. Craig had to restore some sense of order. We'll talk more about this, but now isn't the time. I've been ill and I'm tired. All I'll say now is, listen to the other side. I worry, my lad, that you don't always do that."

Poor Lotbinière was to die within three years, leaving his estates to his daughters. One married a Montreal merchant named Harwood; another married the son of an American senator whom Alain had met when he was a prisoner of war in Pennsylvania; and the third married a Swiss Protestant who was killed in the service of the British army during the Indian Mutiny at Lucknow. Ironically, therefore, while Hugh Munro's descendants became predominantly French, Alain de Lotbinière's became predominantly English. To his political enemies, that was no surprise. It was the obvious outcome of flirting with the English. Power on the council and many of the old seigneuries passed from the distinguished families of New France to the wealthier, English-speaking businessmen; the seigneurial regime itself began to collapse. As the tensions mounted between the French Canadian nationalists in charge of the assembly and the commercial leaders who wanted to "unfrenchify" Lower Canada, the middle path that my kin Lotbinière had represented became harder and harder to sustain.

The Price of Dissent, 1836

FRANÇOIS-ANTOINE LAROCQUE was a not a typical supporter of the Parti Canadien. After his father's death and his mother's remarriage to my ancestor Hugh Munro, he had been sent to school in the United States, where he became more fluent in English than in French. Through his uncle's connections with the fur trade, he had worked while still a teenager in the western wilds of present-day Manitoba as a clerk for the XY Company and the North West Company, whose owners were mostly British. Then, with the decline and fall of the fur companies, he had returned to Lower Canada to go into business with his uncle at L'Assomption and in Montreal. His career had suffered an interruption between 1812 and 1814, when he fought for the British against the Americans and was taken captive to Cincinnati for six months, but by the time of his quarrel with Alain de Lotbinière at the wedding in 1819, Larocque had married the daughter of a prosperous merchant and joined his uncle as one of the very few French Canadian directors and shareholders of the newly created Bank of Montreal.

Everything, in other words, pointed to his being a partisan of the so-called English party around the governor, the merchants, the council, and Lotbinière. In fact his sympathies lay with the Parti Canadien, even as it opposed the business class's attempts to transform the Canadian economy into a modern commercial and capitalist component of the British Empire. The Parti Canadien condemned the greed and vices of the fur trade, which in the words of *Le Canadien* "destroys the industriousness and morals of the countryside, which should be the true source of our riches," and "takes away the strong backs necessary for agriculture." It attacked banking in general, and the Bank of Montreal in particular, as evils introduced by the British merchants to rob the French Canadian people. But Larocque remained loyal to its democratic principles and nationalist sentiments, even when the Parti Canadien challenged his own interests and became more radical in its means, perhaps because he had been educated in the United States and influenced by British parliamentary liberalism, perhaps because he had always felt himself an outsider in the Munro family and English business community.

Though the French Canadian professionals had secured more financial authority for the assembly and impeded the idea of a union with Upper Canada, they grew more aggressive during the 1820s. In part they were responding to the rise of nationalist liberation movements in Italy, Greece, Brazil, and Bolivia. In part they were responding to the growing impatience of the merchants and capitalists, who were frustrated to the point of rage by the tactics of the assembly. In part they were responding to their own sorry conditions. The agricultural crisis worsened as production, prices, and exports fell. The good land could no longer support the habitant population, which therefore saw an economic as well as a cultural threat in the influx of hundreds of thousands of British and American emigrants, who were moving into the fertile valleys of the Eastern Townships and making Montreal 60 per cent English-speaking by 1841. The professions themselves were producing more lawyers, notaries, and doctors than the society could employ, pushing more of them into politics and increasing the importance of seizing control of the government for the sake of patronage and favoritism. All that was needed to make these conditions explosive was an explosive leader.

That leader emerged in the charismatic person of Louis-Joseph Papineau, seigneur and democrat, lawyer and demagogue, reformer and traditionalist, anglophile and nationalist, whose very complexity made him the perfect *chef* of his movement. "In him," Fernand

Ouellet wrote, "French Canadian opposition, with all that implied, found a leader, and nationalism a symbol. His eloquence, which could dazzle the semi-rural members of the House of Assembly, his idealism, his instinctive hatred of the capitalist –'those individuals gorged with gold' – a doctrinaire spirit, an obstinacy which knew no limits, as well as a number of engaging qualities, all these made him the man of the times."

Under Papineau, the Parti Canadien became the Parti Patriote, and its rhetoric went from reform to revolution. It started to lose the support of those reformers, including many English-speaking members, who preferred gradual political and economic progress for French Canadians to Papineau's inflammatory and often inconsistent speeches. Among the disillusioned moderates was Dominique Mondelet, a young lawyer who had married Harriet Munro, my ancestor Hugh's niece. In 1831 Mondelet was elected to the assembly on a platform of judicial, agricultural, and educational reforms, but a year later the *patriotes* conspired to have him expelled on a technicality. His real offense had been to oppose their virulence, which had already led to violence in a Montreal by-election and, increasingly, to talk of an independent republic for French Canadians.

Still François-Antoine Larocque did not pull away from the party's extremism. After the death of Hugh Munro from an inflammation of the breast in 1825, his stepson seemed to be drawn back to his French side. Among his business contacts was Joseph Masson, a carpenter's son who had become a partner with a Scottish merchant, traded woolens and textiles for potash and wheat, and built a fortune upon shipping, gas light, banks, and land. Masson had also been a director of the Bank of Montreal and was related to Larocque through his wife. When Larocque's wholesale business ran into trouble in the late 1820s, Masson invited him into a new partnership, with little money down and all the prospects in the world. Two years later, however, the company was dissolved, for Larocque had had a nobler vision: he wanted to put together a company of French

Canadian businessmen to counter the commercial power of British capitalists.

"There are some," one such capitalist said of the French Canadians in 1828, "who are engaged in the lower branches of commerce; they run stores and small shops in the country, half-inns and half-stores, but generally they are not business people, and of those who are engaged in business few have managed to make a mark or amass much property."

The French Canadians bore some of the responsibility. Their educated sons tended to go into the priesthood or the professions. They had little experience with free-market capitalism and little regard for corporate concentration. Those who had made money in furs or farming were often unwilling to risk it in timber or railways. But much of the explanation for the commercial inferiority of French Canadians lay in the advantages the British merchants enjoyed in terms of capital, contacts, and contracts. From the time of the Conquest the French Canadians lost more and more control over their economy. When they were not pushed from it, they increasingly withdrew from it, as from something dark, dangerous, and foreign.

"Here, then, is our position," said a correspondent in *Le Canadien*. "The government does all it can to frustrate our industry and then tells us: you are not industrious. It seizes assets intended for the schools, discourages education, and then tells us: you are ignorant. It refuses us the posts of honor and profit and then says: you have no wealth, no status. The press it controls, along with all who benefit from this state of affairs, take up the chorus: you are lazy, you know nothing, you are poor, you are unimportant. Injustice has all too unfortunately bred this very result, which they now seize upon to humiliate us. We stand convicted of lack of industry and want of knowledge, as if the crime and shame were not upon those who are their cause."

To combat that injustice, François-Antoine Larocque launched

Larocque, Bernard et Compagnie – "The Great Concern" – in 1832. He could hardly have chosen a worse moment. For the next few years crop failures created famines and crippled the entire economy. A massive flood of poor immigrants from the British Isles – more than fifty thousand in 1832 alone – added to the strain, bringing cholera epidemics and demographic pressures that some nationalists interpreted as a deliberate strategy by the British to eradicate the Canadiens. In 1834, therefore, despite another round of conciliatory overtures from London and the governors, Papineau raised the heat by publishing the Ninety-two Resolutions, a comprehensive manifesto of grievances and demands. Though many of them were reasonable democratic measures and overwhelmingly popular with French Canadians, Papineau's heroic attitude left little room for negotiation. When the British government rejected the package, Papineau issued a call to arms.

"If the liaison with the mother country could bring good fortune to the colony," he declared, "if it could bring prosperity, it would be right to continue a liaison that nevertheless ought inevitably to cease in time. But such refusals have shown that a kind of loyalty is demanded that would require the renunciation of the good fortune of Canadians in favor of the fallacy, pride, and greed of the civil servants in the mother country and in the colony. Loyalty thus understood has received its death blow."

The colony's British defenses were put on alert. The British merchants armed themselves. Young *patriotes* formed the Fils de la Liberté, the Sons of Liberty, as a fighting force, and in November 1837, the two sides clashed in Montreal. For all his passionate speeches (which sounded to the *Gazette* like those of "a well-drugged Malay running amuck"), Papineau himself was reluctant to fight. Swept along by the history he was creating, he barely saw action at Saint-Denis before fleeing in disguise to safety in the United States. Within three weeks the British soldiers routed the ill-prepared and badly led mobs at Saint-Charles on the Richelieu and Saint-Eustache

north of Montreal. Except for a couple of futile efforts the following
year by the hotter heads who had run south of the border, the nationalist uprising was crushed.

———————

In the aftermath it was no surprise to find Dominique Mondelet
acting as prosecutor against some of the rebels who were sentenced
to hang. Three of Hugh Munro's other French-speaking nephews by
marriage, however, found themselves in prison charged with treason
for having supported the revolt. On April 11, 1838, they were joined
behind bars by their wives' cousin, Uncle Hugh's distinguished
stepson, François-Antoine Larocque. Though he had not taken part
in the fighting, he had supported the Fils de la Liberté and dis-
tributed what the authorities considered an inflammatory pamphlet.
It was, in fact, a reprint from an issue of the *Westminster Review*, the
most prestigious liberal journal in London. The Canadian situation,
it argued, was "a contest of races; that being a conquered people, they
cherish the feelings of a conquered people, and have made an
attempt to shake off their conquerors; is this treason? Is it not the
conduct with which, when other parties are concerned, Englishmen
have been called upon to sympathize, and to subscribe their money,
and to proclaim their admiration of the sufferers and their abhor-
rence of the conqueror to every region of the earth?"

Larocque soon learned the price of dissent. A month later his
company fulfilled the expectations of Joseph Masson, who had been
sympathetic to its purpose but leery of its practicality, by going
bankrupt. Then, while Larocque was out of prison on bail, the British
authorities replaced the assembly with an emergency council and
recruited to it his best friend Jules-Maurice Quesnel and his Munro
cousin Dominique Mondelet. Disgusted, Larocque gave up the world
of commerce and public affairs shortly afterwards, though he was
only fifty-seven years old.

The special council barely had time to meet before it was suspended by the new governor, the Earl of Durham, a progressive aristocrat who had been sent to investigate the problems in Canada and advise London on their solution. "I expected to find a contest between a government and a people," Durham wrote in his famous report of 1839. "I found two nations warring in the bosom of a single state. I found a struggle, not of principles, but of races." Divided by language, religion, education, traditions, ambitions, and pride, French and English had come to regard each other with what Durham bluntly called hatred, though his description was based on his limited visit at a time of heightened passions. The French, he wrote, "brood in sullen silence over the memory of their fallen countrymen, of their burnt villages, of their ruined property, of their extinguished ascendancy, and of their humbled nationality. To the Government and the English they ascribe these wrongs, and nourish against both an indiscriminating and eternal animosity. Nor have the English inhabitants forgotten in their triumph the terror with which they suddenly saw themselves surrounded by an insurgent majority."

If that was Canada's problem, what was the solution? Dismissing Britain's earlier efforts to buy peace with the French Canadians as a "vain endeavour," Durham had "no doubt of the national character which must be given to Lower Canada; it must be that of the British Empire; that of the majority of British America; that of the great race which must, in the lapse of no long period of time, be predominant over the whole North American continent. Without effecting the change so rapidly or roughly as to shock the feelings and trample on the welfare of the existing generation, it must henceforth be the first and steady purpose of the British Government to establish an English population, with English laws and language, in this province, and to trust its government to none but a decidedly English legislature."

Assimilation wouldn't be a punishment, Durham argued, so much as a gift. It would rid the French Canadian professionals of the language and customs that had confined them to "a hopeless inferiority," and it would elevate the humbler classes from their "poverty and dependence." "In these circumstances," he wrote, "I should indeed be surprised if the more reflecting part of the French Canadians entertain at present any hope of continuing to preserve their nationality. Much as they struggle against it, it is obvious that the process of assimilation to English habits is already commencing. The English language is gaining ground, as the language of the rich and of the employers of labour naturally will."

Seeing no other solution to forty years of parliamentary conflict, the British government in 1840 acted on Durham's recommendation and resurrected the old idea of reuniting Lower and Upper Canada. Though the population of Lower Canada was about 50 per cent greater than that of Upper Canada, each was given forty-two seats in the new assembly. English was made the only official language.

"God in His mercy has left hope to the oppressed," wrote a moderate French Canadian at the time, "and it is all that remains to us." Thousands of French Canadians protested the Act of Union, but most fell into the "sullen silence" that Durham had noted. "It was impossible to arouse either the town or the countryside," a *patriote* remembered, "so discouraged were they by events." Many simply minded their own business; many "sought distraction and amusement" in parties and dances; many turned to the conservative Catholic revival being promoted by the fiery new bishop of Montreal, Ignace Bourget, who was building up the political and social authority of the Church (with the blessing of the English governors) to a degree seldom enjoyed by the bishops of the Old Regime.

This was the period when the French Canadians turned inward upon their river valley, their agricultural vocation, and their religious obedience in a way they had not when the Canadiens of New France had ranged the continent, engaged in the fur trade, and showed themselves (in the words of one intendant) "no better educated in our religion than the Indians." This, too, was when they fell far behind the English in commerce, feared for the loss of their customs and language among the tens of thousands of British immigrants, and gained a nationalist aversion to their conquerors that had not been apparent in the first decades after the Conquest. This was when the Saint-Jean-Baptiste Society was founded to defend and glorify the traditions of the French Canadian people; this was when the Church preached about the messianic role of French Canadians to safeguard the most conservative values of Rome in North America. This was when the idea of an independent nation took root.

François-Antoine Larocque was not untypical, then, in his reaction to the failure of the rebellion. "Concerned only with his eternal salvation," his biographer noted, he retired to a hospice run by the Grey Nuns at Saint-Hyacinthe "and spent the last years of his life in retreat and study."

———

Fifty years earlier Larocque had ridden out from Fort Assiniboine on a June morning in the company of Charles Mackenzie, his heart heavy with the dangers ahead but his spirits soon made cheerful by the freedom and adventure of the open country. Like the coureurs de bois of old, he had headed west in pursuit of skins and robes, and roamed beyond the Missouri among the Mandans, the Big Bellys, and the Crows of the Yellowstone River. He had fired at Assiniboines who tried to steal his horses, hunted buffalo and elk "in amazing numbers," built rafts to cross the rain-swollen rivers, withstood hurricanes and heat waves, seen deer and bear and bustards and fowl, and been so ill that he hardly had the strength to stay in his saddle. He had watched two thousand Rocky Mountain Indians approach the Mandan camp to trade robes and leggings for corn and tobacco, admired the agility and dignity of the six hundred warriors who thundered through the village with a pageantry of beaded apparel and painted shields and feathered lances. He had bestowed axes, knives, rings, awls, ivory combs, tobacco, cock feathers, beads, vermilion, and a thousand rounds of ammunition upon their chiefs, smoked the pipe with them, and told them through signs and interpreters that if they behaved well toward him and killed beavers and bears for him, the chief of the white people would make them his children, give them weapons, and supply all their wants. He had witnessed a war dance at Large Horn River, shuddered with horror when two captives were ripped to pieces with his knives, heard the drums and rattles of the scalp dance night after night, and shared the great feasts at which the braves recounted their deeds. Then, after loading up his bounty of one hundred and twenty-two beaver pelts and four bearskins, he had taken leave of his friends with the promise that he would return the next year to the mountain called Amanchabe Chije, where he would light four fires on four successive days so that they would know it was him, come in peace again.

Two chiefs had accompanied him for the first eight miles of his journey home. They had smoked a parting pipe with him, embraced him, and made him swear that he had told them no false words. Finally, they had followed him for another mile, crying and calling his name, moving more and more slowly until their cries faded into the sunlit grasslands. Till next year, he had promised, till next year on Amanchabe Chije. "Certainly I had no intention of breaking my oath," Larocque wrote in his report. But he had not known that his world was about to become smaller – an office in Montreal, a jail cell, a spartan room at the Hôtel Dieu – or that he and his people would withdraw from the western plains and run no longer in the woods.

"Amanchabe Chije, Amanchabe Chije," the nuns used to hear the feeble-minded old man mutter. How sweet, they thought: he's trying to repeat "Hail Mary, full of grace."

Dominion, 1867

IN 1867 my great-great grandfather Louis-Gonzague Fauteux was a well-to-do merchant with an office on Rue Saint-François-Xavier in Old Montreal and a home on Rue de La Gauchetière. "He went *fifteen* times by sailing ship across the Atlantic on business!" his daughters boasted whenever they wore the gold and turquoise jewelry he had brought them from Europe. It became a symbol of what he had achieved by work and enterprise, for he had been born in a village on the north shore of the St Lawrence toward Trois-Riviéres. His father, his grandfather, his great-grandfather, and his great-great-grandfather had all been named Pierre Fauteux after the first Fauteux to come to New France, from Normandy around 1666, and his older brother Pierre had married Laurent Leroux's granddaughter in 1842. Through that connection Louis had met and wed my ancestress Hermine Leduc, Hugh Munro's granddaughter, who had given him an entrée to the Lotbinière clan and to Alfred Larocque, François-Antoine's son and second president of the City and District Savings Bank, which had been founded in 1846 at the instigation of Bishop Bourget as a vehicle to provide capital to French Canadians and encourage savings among them.

Louis Fauteux never held public office, but he represents an important political movement. That movement explains how French Canadians survived more than twenty-five years under the Act of Union and finally overthrew it. Its heroes were two men of my great-great-grandfather's generation, Louis-Hippolyte La Fontaine and George-Etienne Cartier. Both had been born in the countryside in the early part of the nineteenth century; both had become brilliant students at the Collège de Montréal; both had money, Cartier by birth and La Fontaine by marriage; both had successful law practices; and both had begun their political careers as rebels with Louis-Joseph Papineau, La Fontaine writing virulent pamphlets and dressing like a habitant, Cartier composing patriotic songs and joining the Fils de la Liberté. In 1838 their radical nationalism had landed La Fontaine in jail and Cartier in exile, though neither had committed a crime that could not be excused by the end of the year. Then they broke with most of the *patriotes* and many of the moderates. Instead of merely opposing the Act of Union, they determined to manipulate it.

"I saw," La Fontaine later explained, "that this measure enclosed in itself the means by which the people could obtain that control upon the Government to which they have a just claim." If the French Canadian moderates of Lower Canada were to join with the English Canadian reformers of Upper Canada in an alliance that placed democratic ideas above language or culture, he realized, they would be in charge of the new joint assembly. Together they could break the power of the British governor and his yes men by making certain that the government always acted according to the wishes of the elected majority. Once that had been achieved, French Canadians would be able to legislate on their own behalf.

It took a decade of parliamentary maneuvers and electoral setbacks, but it happened just so. La Fontaine found his Upper Canadian counterpart in Robert Baldwin, an exceptionally honest, principled, and fair-minded lawyer from York, as Toronto was then known, who was as committed to justice for French Canadians as he was to democracy for his own people. (He even sent his children to French schools to make them bilingual.) So successful were they in putting their ideological goals ahead of their ethnic differences that La Fontaine was elected in York and Baldwin in Rimouski. Their strategy depended on winning a reform majority, of course. That meant turning the French Canadians' fear of the union – as a trap to assimilate them – into hope. If they united behind him, La Fontaine promised them their survival as a people and the repeal of "the cruel injustice of that part of the Act of Union which aims to proscribe the mother tongue of half the population of Canada." Not only did La Fontaine become identified with the protection of the French language; he managed to associate his success with the traditionalist interests of the Roman Catholic Church – quite a trick for an anticlerical progressive!

In 1847 La Fontaine and Baldwin won most of the seats in both parts of the union, and then were fortunate enough to confront a governor general who was sympathetic to their democratic goals. Lord Elgin, though a Tory and a peer, had imbibed the more liberal views of his wife's father, the late Lord Durham, and her uncle Lord Grey, now the colonial secretary in the British Cabinet. When La Fontaine and Baldwin formed the government, therefore, Elgin behaved as their servant rather than their master. In January 1849 he opened the parliamentary session with a speech in French as well as English. In April he gave his approval to a controversial bill that would compensate Lower Canadians who had suffered financial losses during the rebellion.

"The Union has completely failed in its purpose," thundered the leader of the English-speaking merchants in the assembly. "It was enacted with the sole motive of reducing the French Canadians under English domination. And the contrary effect has resulted! Those that were to be crushed, dominate!"

On the streets of Montreal gangs of English gentlemen and anti-Catholic Orangemen pelted Elgin with eggs and rocks. At night fifteen hundred of them attacked the assembly, dissolved "this French House," and burned its building to ashes. They smashed La Fontaine's home, threatened to assassinate him, and ran riot through the town for days before the soldiers were able to stop them with bayonets. When all their protests failed, three hundred and twenty-five prominent English Canadian citizens signed a manifesto calling for the colony's immediate annexation to the United States. Most of them were respectable businessmen and loyal imperialists, but they saw Elgin's capitulation as the latest in a series of economic and political betrayals by London. Their welfare was being sacrificed on the altar of free trade and British new industry.

"To us," Lord Grey confided to Lord Elgin, "except the loss of prestige (no slight one I admit) the loss of Canada would be the loss of little but a source of heavy expense and great anxiety." If that indifferent attitude was enough to turn avid monarchists into rabid republicans, it also threw them into an alliance of convenience with their worst enemies, the extreme French Canadian nationalists, including Louis-Joseph Papineau, now back from exile. He and his supporters had co-signed the Annexation Manifesto as a way of breaking from the British Empire and breathing the fresh air of North American democracy.

Many nationalists still had not accepted the Act of Union despite La Fontaine's achievements. Indeed, his achievements ironically gave a new energy to French Canadian nationalism. Once La Fontaine wrested power from the British governor and the English-speaking Tories, he obtained significant control over government jobs, government contracts, and government industrial policy. That helped to create a modern class of French Canadians — including my ancestor Louis Fauteux — linked to politics and business while allied to the Church hierarchy and the English reformers. This class replaced the seigneurs, who had become socially and economically powerless, and the nationalist professionals, who had been deflated and discredited by the fiasco of their rebellion, as the political leadership of French Canada. Moderate by nature and realistic by experience, this new class preferred to co-operate with the English rather than fight them. It recognized the necessity and inevitability of industries, banks, canals, railways, and other basic innovations to combat the perennial crises of poverty and unemployment; and however patriotic in its own purposes, it accepted the advantages of the British Empire, the British parliamentary system, and even the British monarchy.

Its very accomplishments, however, created a class of young and educated dissidents who felt excluded from the rewards of power. They were Papineau's "other children," as it were, who still rejected the path of commerce and conciliation for an agrarian, anticlerical, and republican nationalism – a kind of pastoral and French-speaking United States – which was why some of them supported annexation to the English-speaking and mercenary Americans. Their isolationist and obstructionist tactics, their feuds with the businessmen and the bishops kept them from power and patronage, but *les rouges* (the reds, as they came to be called) represented an underground force that would eventually have its day in the sun.

When illness and fatigue compelled La Fontaine to retire from politics in 1851, his disciple George-Etienne Cartier took over as head of *les bleus*, the blues. Cartier soon saw that his natural English-speaking allies were no longer the Upper Canadian reformers, for when the English population of the united Canadas surpassed the French during the 1850s, it was they who now raised the cry of "No French domination!" and demanded more assembly seats for the English in the name of democracy. Cartier sought his alliances among the moderate English-speaking merchants and industrialists, therefore, and his English counterpart – his Baldwin, so to speak – turned out to be a sly, wry, and often inebriated Tory immigrant from Scotland, John A. Macdonald. Macdonald had been among those who had screamed at Lord Elgin for sacrificing English interests to the French in 1849, but like many Tories he had been lulled by prosperity and practical politics into dealing with the French Canadians – especially ones like Cartier, who, despite his *patriote* past, had been named for a British king and employed as a lawyer by British railway financiers.

Macdonald and Cartier formed their first government in 1857. Though they survived in office for most of the next five years, Cartier soon realized that the political system itself was in deep trouble. There were so many strong and divergent factions in the assembly – *bleus* and Tories, reformers and *rouges*, moderates and radicals – that weak and unstable coalition governments were the norm. The reformers' demand for "representation by population," which would greatly reduce French Canada's clout, could neither be suppressed forever nor granted easily. The custom of governing according to a "double majority," in which both English and French Canadians shared power in practice, had led to paralysis and confusion. Then, to the political chaos, economic pressures were added. Prosperity depended upon trade. Trade depended upon railways. Railways depended upon capital. Capital depended upon revenue and debt that were beyond the capacity of the small and separate British colonies of North America. Britain itself had become increasingly anxious for its colonies to relieve its own burdens, and wanted to strengthen the colonies against the ambitions of the United States.

Cartier's solution was a federation of the colonies into a single, semi-autonomous country with a central government based on "rep by pop" for general matters, provincial governments with their own authority over local matters, and links to Britain in defense, foreign policy, justice, and the monarchy. It took almost ten years, three major conferences, an extraordinary coalition of old foes in the assembly, and the push of Britain's colonial office and Britain's banks, but in 1867 the British Parliament passed the British North America Act and created Canada.

The BNA Act served as Canada's constitution. It set up the country's institutions, established their rules, and divided money and power between the central government in Ottawa and the provincial governments in Ontario, Quebec, Nova Scotia, and New Brunswick. (They were joined by Prince Edward Island, Manitoba, and British Columbia by 1873; Saskatchewan and Alberta were created as provinces in 1905; and Newfoundland only entered in 1949.) The thorniest debates among the politicians, then as now, involved that division of money and power. The horrendous example of the American Civil War, plus basic economics, had caused Macdonald and Cartier to dream of a more centralized union, but finally they had to accept a federation, primarily because of the fear among French Canadians that their language, laws, and traditions would be swept aside by the English-speaking, Protestant majority of a unified state.

"I am strong in the belief that we have hit upon the happy medium in these resolutions," said the first prime minister of Canada, John A. Macdonald, "and that we have formed a scheme of government which unites the advantages of both, giving us the strength of a legislative union with protection to local interests."

To which Cartier added, "I do not fear the rights of Lower Canada will in any way be placed in peril by the project of Confederation, even though in a general legislature the French Canadians will have a smaller number of representatives than all other nationalities combined." There were legal, moral, and political safeguards to prevent the tyranny of the majority, he argued, and Quebec would control the special concerns of French Canadians in the fields of civil law, education, social policy, and faith.

For years the debates raged across Quebec about whether Cartier was right or wrong. Louis Fauteux used to hear them whenever he and his wife Hermine attended a family wedding or New Year's Day gathering, for two of her Lotbinière cousins were well-known advocates of opposing views. Both Antoine Chartier de Lotbinière Harwood and Henri Joly de Lotbinière were grandsons of Alain and Charlotte, and both had been members of the assembly that had argued about the federation proposals in 1865. Harwood was a *bleu*, however, and Joly was a *rouge*.

"The federal union is our only escape from the slough of status quo in which the wheels of government are stuck fast," Harwood liked to pontificate while standing in the center of attention, brandy in hand. He had a weakness for overblown rhetoric, references to the Greeks and Romans, economic statistics about capital stock and wool prices, and plain good sense. "Progress and prosperity dictate that we cannot separate Upper and Lower Canada again, and a legislative union would be unjust. So a federation it must be."

"But a federation is doomed to failure without a strong central government," Joly always countered, "and that would make it a legislative union, which, as you say, dear cousin, would be unjust. The sympathies of the majority in the federal Parliament will always be against us, and the harmony that has existed between English and French – not intimacy, perhaps, but not hostility either – will be upset. Now Cartier has crushed the weak, cajoled the strong, deceived the credulous, bought up the venal, and exalted the ambitious so that we must give up our nationality and adopt a new one, greater and nobler than our own, we are told. But then it will no longer be our own. Strongly entrenched in our citadel, we are advised to raze its walls in order to secure our safety. I ask you this, Harwood: have you and your friends taken as great precautions to preserve intact the interests of nearly a million French Canadians as you would have taken in making an agreement for the sale of a farm or even the purchase of a horse?"

"But our language, our rights, and our privileges are guaranteed to us," Harwood replied, as the heat rose to his face and Louis Fauteux nodded vigorously by his side, "more guaranteed, I assure you, than they would be if we were absorbed into the United States, which is the only real alternative to a Canadian federation. Hasn't the English element been a majority in the assembly for twenty-five years, yet haven't we the honor to address each other across the floor in French? Why then should the English in a federal Parliament seek to destroy French Canadian nationality? What interest could they serve in doing so?"

"Self-interest," Joly snapped. "There are too many points on which French and English disagree to allow of our living long together in peace, in spite of any sincere wish to do so. Mark my words, Harwood, some day or other a judgment will be given by the federal Parliament, in which the English will have a majority and from which the French Canadians cannot hope for justice. Then the two nationalities will collide."

"On the contrary, Henri, some day or other the Good Genius who rules over our destiny will cry aloud, with one foot on the shores of the Pacific and the other on the shores of the Atlantic, 'All this is ours! This wealth, those far fields, those pretty hamlets, those factories, those canals and railways, those vast cities in which thousands of people enjoy the fruits of their toil and live without fear under the English flag, all belong to us!'"

"Humbug!" Joly shouted as he stormed away. "We mustn't allow ourselves to be dazzled by the ambition of becoming all at once a great people."

Confederation was not put to the people, but Cartier rallied the support of the business elites, the Catholic bishops, and a slight majority of French Canada's representatives in the assembly. (After the fact, in the autumn of 1867, the vast majority of Quebec's sixty-five members in the new House of Commons were elected as supporters of Cartier's Canada.) Joly's prophecy was not wrong, however. Whenever something dramatic reminded French Canadians that they were a minority in Ottawa – when Protestant bigots forced the hanging of a French-speaking, Catholic Métis in 1885 for leading a rebellion in the west, or when British imperialists imposed compulsory military service during the First World War, or when a unilingual Conservative from Saskatchewan became prime minister in 1957 with almost no votes from Quebec, or when the government of Canada instituted a fundamental constitutional reform in 1982 against the wishes of the government of Quebec – the "two national-ities" would indeed collide, and the federation of 1867 would again be called into question.

That was later. For the moment, there was general celebration. Thus, after supper on July 1, 1867, Louis-Gonzague Fauteux accom-panied his wife and their three daughters by two-horse carriage from their home on Rue de La Gauchetière to the McTavish reservoir, a large oval tank set on the lower slope of Mount Royal just above the fields of McGill University. The reservoir was distant enough to seem out in the country and high enough to offer relief from the evening heat. Crowds were laboring in the twilight up the dirt lanes from Sherbrooke Street, drawn like the Fauteux family by the promise of a spectacular fireworks display, brought at great expense from Boston, no less. It was to be the grand finale to a day of trumpets, parades, speeches, marching bands, and lacrosse tournaments organized to welcome the birth of a new nation, Canada.

"When your grandchildren ask you what we did under the Act of Union," Monsieur Fauteux said to his wife Hermine and to *petite* Hermine, Alphonsine, and Eugénie during the drive, puffing on his after-dinner cigar, "you can reply as did Monsieur le comte de Sieyès when he was asked what he had done during the French Revolution. 'J'ai vécu,' he said. 'I survived.'"

A House on Sherbrooke Street, 1913

GUILLAUME NAPOLEON MONCEL had had better days. Sometime in the afternoon of Thursday, March 5, 1913, for no apparent reason, crowds had gathered outside the thirteen branches of the Montreal City and District Savings Bank, of which he was a director, and clamored for their money. My great-grandfather and other respectable businessmen had tried to restore confidence and calm by moving among the depositors and assuring them that the bank was in sound shape – which was true – but to no avail. By the time he walked from his office on St James Street to his home on Sherbrooke

Street – the long, uphill hike was a self-inflicted trial for Guillaume, who was overweight and almost seventy – he was tired, frustrated, and depressed.

His home, the western half of a nineteenth-century stone mansion in the Second Empire style, was his refuge and his pride. It represented the distance he had come from his childhood in Griffintown, the notorious shantytown between the river and the railway tracks, where he had been born the ninth of eleven children and third son of an illiterate shoemaker named Pierre Moncel (sometimes Moncell, sometimes Monsel, and sometimes even Leuré as a variation on the original name of Pierre's grandfather Charles Leret, the soldier who had come to New France shortly before the British Conquest). "I didn't have any food when I was a boy," Guillaume used to admonish his children when he saw their meals going to waste at the table. "We lived on the wild turnips we found in the woods."

My great-grandfather had picked up some education from the priests, some English from the Irish kids, and gone to work sweeping floors in a bank. Then, blessed with a good brain and formidable ambition, according to his obituary in *La Presse*, "he had dedicated himself to business at an early age and succeeded." He was listed as a clerk when he was twenty-seven, and his prospects were solid enough for him to ask for the hand of Alphonsine Fauteux, Louis's second daughter. They were married at Notre-Dame on January 10, 1871, fifty-one years to the day after Guillaume's own parents were married in the same church. There was an awkward moment when the elder Moncel could not sign the register because he had never learned to write his own name; Louis Fauteux wrote his with a quick and fancy flourish.

"Compared to the Fauteux, the Moncels weren't much," said a distant cousin from my great-grandmother's side. "The Fauteux were related to the royalty of France and to the Munros. I was always told that Guillaume Moncel grew up in Rue Fauteux, which honored one of our family, though it's disgraceful that our name was given to that dirty little lane! The Fauteux are buried with the high-class families, but the Moncels are up in the back and beyond with the other *nouveaux riches*."

Whatever Guillaume's own skills in finance, his career had not been hindered by his father-in-law's connections to the Massons, the Munros, and the Larocques. Joseph Masson's surviving children had remained influential in business and politics. Hugh Munro's great-nephew, Henri Joly de Lotbinière, had become Liberal premier of Quebec in 1878. François-Antoine Larocque's son Alfred, after serving two terms as president of the City and District Savings Bank, had remained associated with it until his death in 1890, and the president of the bank at the time of the panic in March 1913 was related to the Larocques by marriage.

With help like that, Guillaume Moncel had been appointed in due course to the board of the bank for which he had once swept floors. He became the administrative executor of the Masson estate, a governor of Notre-Dame Hospital and warden of Notre-Dame Church, and an esteemed member of the Chamber of Commerce and Board of Trade. Eventually, too, his eldest son, Guillaume, inherited his job running the financial affairs of the Masson family, and his second son, Charles, became assistant general manager of the City and District. Business, after all, like politics, had been seen by the French Canadians as a family affair ever since the days of Michel Leneuf and Charles Sevestre in New France.

In the 1890s, by another stroke of good fortune, the gardens of my great-grandfather's previous home on Sherbrooke Street, near Rue Saint-Denis, had been expropriated by the city to create St Louis Square – there are now ice-skaters in winter and drug addicts in summer where my grandfather René kept foxes and geese as a boy – and the compensation made Guillaume Moncel truly wealthy. He moved to the grander house to the west, where he ruled in 1913 like a pasha over his wife, her widowed sister, the sister's daughter and granddaughter, a housekeeper, a parlor maid, and a cook.

They all knew his routines. Every weekday morning he walked to work; every weekday noon he came home and undid the benefits of his walks by enjoying a huge lunch. (Though he never owned a car or a country place because he thought they were extravagances, he never skimped on fine food and decent wines. On Saturdays he liked to go to Dionne's to select personally the best cuts of meat.) Every weekday afternoon he went back to the office; every weekday evening he returned at 5:45. The maid always opened the door for him and took his wet umbrella or mink-lined overcoat. Then a bell rang to remind everyone to change and wash up, and at 6:15 a gong summoned the family to supper in the dining room, a cluttered and rather gloomy Victorian tomb with lace curtains, florid damask on the walls, a sketch of Madame Moncel as a young girl, an allegorical print of a woman wielding a knife over a terrified child, a huge mirror, and a heavy sideboard heaped with Chinese vases, bronze nymphs, silver candlesticks, family photographs, and a clock. Guillaume said little. Most nights, as soon as supper was over, the women indulged their passion for cards while he retreated into his study with the French and English newspapers and an expensive cigar.

On Sundays, though he was not an especially religious man, he led his household to church at Notre-Dame. Then some or all of the five Moncel children came with their families for a long, formal lunch. (Two other children had died in their youth, a boy who was killed by a freak fall in a haystack and a girl who succumbed to pneumonia.) Sunday afternoons were for music. My great-grandfather himself was a musician with enough talent to have played the cello with the McGill String Quartet. Sometimes he put on concerts, with his son Charles and daughter-in-law Adrienne on the violin and his wife or young Guillaume at the piano. On Sunday evenings he liked to sit in the living room and listen to Verdi and Mozart on the gramophone for an hour.

This sedate and civilized regime was disrupted for a couple of days following the run on Guillaume's bank in 1913. It had not been the first in his experience. There had been one in August 1879, when the City Bank was confused with the shaky Consolidated Bank. There had been another in October 1897, when the collapse of a bank in Spain triggered doubts about the City and District Savings because a French newspaper had reported *Espagne,* Spain, as *Epargne,* Savings. Now, from dawn on Friday till noon Saturday, Guillaume Moncel sought to allay the fears of the people who had lined up to withdraw their money. Moving slowly, speaking quietly, putting forward his own reputation for honesty and prudence, with his bright eyes and portly authority, he went up and down the line, pausing only to encourage the harassed clerks or consult with his fellow directors.

At last, after forty-eight hours of turmoil, its cause was discovered. On Thursday morning a well-known playboy had approached the cashier at the Windsor Hotel to cash a check for fifty dollars. He was even better known for his debts than for his idleness. The cashier, wishing neither to offend nor anger him, had pleaded a lack of cash and invited him to return later, then promptly sent a bellboy with the check to the nearest City and District to see if the account was good. "No funds," the bank reported. On the way back to the hotel, the bellboy was puzzled. "Imagine a bank that can't fork out fifty dollars," he thought, and, remembering that his brother had a deposit there, telephoned him the dire news, which soon spread throughout Montreal.

"Please, God, spare me the idiots," I imagine my great-grandfather praying on his knees at Notre-Dame the next day, "and I'll take care of the crooks myself."

———————

Guillaume Moncel's heyday coincided with the heyday of the British Empire and Montreal. Confederation had opened up the resources and markets of a vast Dominion. Politics had built a transcontinental railway and tariff walls behind which Canadian industries could flourish. Immigration from Europe and the farms had created cheap labor and greater demand. Capital had concentrated power in a few urban centers and a small business elite. Montreal became the largest and most industrialized of those centers, and though it was 55 per cent French-speaking by 1881, its business elite worked in English. A handful of French Canadian millionaires settled profitably among the railway lords and corporate knights who were building their palaces in the Square Mile, but there was much less financial dealing or social contact between the two societies than there had been early in the nineteenth century. Where once the Scots and French Canadians had toiled side by side in the fur trade, got drunk together at the monthly meetings of the Beaver Club, and intermarried, their descendants had moved increasingly into separate worlds.

Within the French Canadian world there arose a parallel elite. It made its fortune in its own industries, shops, and services – whether shoe factories or department stores or savings and loan co-operatives – and it created its own *haut monde* along Sherbrooke Street to the east of the Square Mile and, eventually, in Outremont, on the north slope of Mount Royal. Seldom as rich or powerful as the renowned families of British Montreal, the French Canadian gentry nevertheless had its own aristocratic pretensions and grand style. Whenever they could, these families dusted off fancy titles and seigneurial connections from the Old Regime, and they filled their houses and their wardrobes according to Paris fashion. Some became anglophiles and agents for the English, but many remained in the shadow establishment that was French in language, Catholic in religion, still connected to the land and the past, and often *bleu* in politics. As often happens, too much power had tended to make the *bleus* more reactionary in their policies and more traditionalist in their outlook with each passing decade. Their expedient alliances with the imperialist tycoons and Roman Catholic bishops behind the Conservative Party nurtured a self-destructive schizophrenia that pitted Anglo-Saxon commerce against French Canadian conservatism.

Guillaume Moncel, however, was more *rouge* than *bleu*. Cosmopolitan enough to enjoy a large library and frequent trips to Europe, open-minded enough to be curious about other religions, he saw himself as a progressive. By the end of the nineteenth century, moreover, being "red" did not necessarily mean being radical or nationalist. The shift had been made, for the most part, by my great-grandfather's friend Wilfrid Laurier, the charming and eloquent lawyer who became leader of the federal Liberal Party in 1887 and the first French-speaking prime minister of Canada in 1896. Like other *rouges*, Laurier had opposed the federation of 1867 and the authoritarianism of the bishops, but he had reconciled his liberalism to both by dropping the anti-English, anti-business, and anticlerical ideology of the *rouge* movement.

"Gentlemen," Laurier had declared in a famous speech in 1877 in defense of British institutions and modern principles, "when in that last battle, which is recalled by the monument to Wolfe and Montcalm, the hail of bullets was spreading death in the ranks of the French army; when the old heroes, who had so often been victorious, at last saw victory escaping them; when, stretched on the ground, feeling their blood trickling out and their life ebbing away, they saw, as the consequence of their defeat, Quebec in the hands of the enemy and the country lost forever, their final thoughts must doubtless have concerned their children, those they were leaving without protection and without defense; no doubt they saw them persecuted, enslaved, humiliated, and then, one may believe, they breathed their last breath in a cry of despair. But if Heaven had lifted the veil of the future from their dying eyes; if, before they closed forever, Heaven had allowed their gaze to penetrate the unknown; if they could have seen their children free and happy, striding with head held high in every walk of life; if they could have seen the first pew in the old cathedral, which used to be occupied by the French governors, now taken by a French governor; if they could have seen the church steeples rising in every valley from the shores of the Gaspé to the prairies of the Red River; if they could have seen this old flag, which reminds us of the finest of their victories, triumphantly shown in all our public ceremonies; if they could have seen, finally, our free institutions – is one not allowed to believe that their last breath expired in a murmur of gratitude to Heaven, and that they died consoled?"

It was the old pragmatic argument of La Fontaine and Cartier. Laurier was able to appropriate it from the *bleus* by the happenstance of three deaths. The demise of George-Etienne Cartier in 1873 had left a vacuum in the French Canadian leadership of the Conservative Party, allowing Laurier to emerge as the best defender of his people in Ottawa. The hanging in 1885 of Louis Riel, the French-speaking Métis who had led two popular rebellions in the west, had shocked most French Canadians, including their clergy, as a vindictive attack from the Conservatives' anti-French and anti-Catholic wing. Finally, John A. Macdonald's death in 1891 had produced no heir who could match the appeal of either the Grand Old Man himself or Laurier. As a result, Quebec had voted as a bloc for one of its own, and English Canada had gone along for the sake of change.

If Laurier's triumph proved that French Canadians could be powerful within the system, it also proved that they were still a minority in Ottawa. Laurier often had to compromise the best interests of his language and his religion to stay in office, for the English-speaking majority was as vigilant against Romish plots and disloyalty to the Empire as Captain John Munro had been. Laurier gave up the right of Roman Catholics to have their own schools in Manitoba, Alberta, and Saskatchewan, for example; he lent assistance to Britain during the Boer War, which many French Canadians dismissed as a jingoistic adventure; he offered to build a Canadian navy that would be at Britain's beck and call. While most French Canadians were isolationists, Laurier supported Canada's entry into the First World War. When he regained the esteem of Quebec in the 1917 election by opposing compulsory military service, it cost him the rest of the country.

Laurier's predicament gave vitality and reason to those French

Canadians, both *bleus* and *rouges*, who had reacted to the deaths of Cartier, Riel, and Macdonald by returning to nationalism. Instead of compromising for power in Ottawa, they sought to consolidate power in the only place where they were a majority: Quebec. Every effort in English Canada to prevent French Catholics from establishing themselves outside Quebec justified establishing themselves inside Quebec. Each concession by Laurier fueled their arguments.

In 1887, on the ticket of ethnic solidarity and provincial rights, the Parti National had become the government of Quebec under Honoré Mercier (another of my "cousins," I learned, through my great-great-great-great-great-great-great-grandfather Jean Mercier). His victory was the political expression of a cultural movement that was alive in newspapers, novels, histories, poems, manifestoes, and sermons of French Quebec. "God planted in the heart of every French Canadian patriot a flower of hope," Jules-Paul Tardivel wrote in his 1895 novel, *Pour la patrie.* "It is the aspiration to establish, on the banks of the St Lawrence, a New France whose mission will be to continue in this American land the work of Christian civilization that Old France carried out with such glory during the long centuries."

———————

What bothered my great-grandfather about French Canadian nationalism, no doubt, was its continued bias against industrialization and capitalism. Language and culture remained tied to spiritual concerns and agricultural pursuits. The Church – through its power over the schools, the unions, the savings banks, and the social agencies – still promoted the belief that farming in the subarctic hinterland was worthier than laboring in the godless city. Nationalist politicians and intellectuals associated the survival of the French language, the Catholic faith, and the French Canadian family with the land. They harked back to a mythological New France where pious and heroic peasants lived free from foreign influences.

"The life of a people, like the life of man, is in the soil," Guillaume Moncel had heard a priest preach from the pulpit of Notre-Dame on Saint-Jean-Baptiste Day in 1870. "French Canadians, if you do not preserve and fertilize your lands, if you lose the use of them, if you cease to be proprietors, if you have territory no longer, you are no longer a people, you become outcasts. For the soil, that is our homeland. Preserve, defend our nationality by the only means you have, the conservation and culture of your fields."

More than thirty years later, in 1902, yet another priest had delivered the same message on Saint-Jean-Baptiste Day. "Our mission is less to handle capital than to stimulate ideas," he said, "less to light the furnaces of factories than to maintain and spread the glowing fires of religion and thought."

Their vision was mostly a fantasy. Industrialization had come to Quebec by 1850; the rural population had outgrown the arable land, and an increasing number of its sons and daughters had been forced to leave the family farm to seek work elsewhere. Almost half of Quebeckers were living in cities, and more than a half-million French Canadians had emigrated from Quebec between 1840 and 1920 to find jobs in the factories of New England or on the farms of western Canada. (By contrast, no more than fifty thousand had been lured to the boondocks of Quebec by the nationalist appeals of the Church and the traditionalists.) Meanwhile, a quarter of the province – and 40 per cent of Montreal – was not of French Canadian stock and included Jews and Italians as well as English and Irish. Yet the dream of a French Canadian society centered in Quebec sustained Honoré Mercier's nationalism through the conservative regime of Maurice Duplessis in the 1950s to the Quiet Revolution of Jean Lesage in the 1960s to the separatist option of René Lévesque in the 1970s.

If Montreal and rural Quebec after the First World War bore less and less resemblance to what they had been before it, so too had Guillaume Moncel's life changed. He became more prosperous as manufacturing and banking boomed, but wealth did not bring him comfort for the premature death of his dear wife in 1915 or console him when his sister-in-law died two years later. He gave up the big house on Sherbrooke Street, gave up the parties at which Wilfrid Laurier had danced, gave up the cello recitals in the drawing room on Sundays, and lived with his niece and great-niece in a townhouse owned by the Masson family on Prince Arthur Street, just east of McGill University and – I later discovered to my surprise – not three doors from the grotty apartment I inhabited as a student.

There he held to his regular routines, walking back and forth from his office in every sort of weather, going to Dionne's on Saturdays and Notre-Dame on Sundays, greeting his children and grandchildren for six-course lunches, and listening to Mozart in the evenings. In his seventies he became gruffer and more silent. He spent almost every evening by himself, reading in the sanctuary that was his second-floor library, then retiring early to his adjoining bedroom. And then, one bleak morning in November 1923, he was borne away by a procession of business leaders and dignitaries to enjoy eternal rest from his worries and labors. He was lowered into the cold earth of Notre-Dame-des-Neiges, Our Lady of the Snows, and there he was reunited with Alphonsine beneath the tall pink column he had chosen as their monument.

Napoléon's Fall, 1942

IN THE YEAR after my great-grandfather's death his eldest child – christened Alphonsine, after her mother, but always known as Ninette – found herself sitting on a camel near Cairo, staring from under a wide white bonnet at a pyramid. She, her husband Napoléon Tétrault, and their daughter Jeanne were on a six-month tour of Europe and North Africa. It was not the type of extravagance of which Ninette's father would have approved, but he had learned to hold his tongue about his son-in-law's spendthrift ways and had died not long before he could have had the satisfaction of saying, "I told you so."

For the most part, however, Guillaume had liked Napoléon Tétrault's vivacious personality and respected what my great-uncle had accomplished as a businessman. Indeed, everyone seemed to like and respect him. He had been born in 1869 in Chatham in the southwest corner of Ontario, not far from Detroit, the son of a shoe merchant and alderman. No one knows how his French-speaking parents had come to settle there, but at the age of twenty "Nap" reversed direction by moving to Montreal to make his fortune. He did so by making shoes, one of the few industries dominated by French Canadians. Thanks to his connections with the Conservative government that had ousted Wilfrid Laurier's Liberals in Ottawa in 1911, he picked up the major contracts to manufacture boots for the Canadian and French armies during the First World War, and Tétrault Shoe became one of the largest shoe companies in Canada. Napoléon became a millionaire.

Unlike his prudent father-in-law Moncel, he behaved like one. He moved from the French part of Sherbrooke Street to a mansion set in a magnificent garden high on the slope of Westmount – just beside the Bronfman estate that I used to pass on every trip from and to the Circle – and he lived in the grandest style. He pounded out tunes on the piano at parties; he gambled till dawn at the Club Saint-Denis; he loved excellent wine and beautiful objects. He impressed the doormen with his big tips, and he impressed his grandchildren by igniting a mouthful of brandy and breathing fire.

"He liked the good life," Jeanne said with a small smile when I visited her in her room, decorated with Canadian landscapes and some gilded Louis xv pieces her father had given her, at the Résidence Monaco – "The Ideal Life Style for Senior Citizens" – on a suburban street overlooking the Montreal airport. Born in 1902, she was the eldest living grandchild of Guillaume Moncel and the only surviving child of Napoléon Tétrault. Her perfect elegance, formal manners, and alert warmth reminded me of my grandfather, her Uncle René. "My father had an office in Paris, and just after the war he took us there for a year. We had a big apartment near the Parc Monceau. In the summer we rented a house by the sea in Normandy, near the casinos at Houlgate." She went and fetched a photograph album. It guarded Proustian memories of girls on horseback in the Bois de Boulogne and mustachioed aristocrats overdressed in the heat. "We had a wonderful time," she said simply.

Shortly before the Great Crash, however, her father's disastrous speculations in the French franc and his reckless habits ruined him, and he was forced to sell Tétrault Shoe. Down he went, from the huge house on Belvedere Road to a series of apartments in lower Westmount and Outremont, from the bombast and glamor of the Roaring Twenties to a domesticated existence with his wife and two of their daughters, Hortense and Marcelle, the one a plain-looking girl whose husband abandoned her when the money was gone, the other an artistic paranoid who rarely left her room.

His story may not have been typical, but Nap Tétrault was neither the first nor the last French Canadian entrepreneur to rise in a protected industry with government assistance and fall through a combination of high living and bad judgment. The Leneufs and Legardeurs, for example, had been the earliest of a long line of traders and merchants who built considerable fortunes in New France with the help of government regulations, then frittered away their capital on aristocratic pretensions or lost it in grandiose speculations; and Robert Campeau, a Franco-Ontarian like Nap, who developed a real-estate empire on government contracts and threw it away on fancy châteaux and megalomaniac takeovers in the American retail industry, was

169

merely the latest. "One never sees rich people in Canada," an observer wrote in 1744, "and that is a great pity; because people here like to display their wealth and almost no one likes to save. They eat well if at the same time they can afford fine clothes; otherwise they cut back on food in order to be well dressed. Everything here is on the generous side, and in both sexes one sees the finest blood in the world; lively spirits and gentle and pleasant manners are common to all."

Remarkably few of the French Canadian elite who had lived along Sherbrooke Street with Guillaume Moncel before the First World War were still financial dynasties by the time of the Second World War. Some had been, by nature, high-stakes players who had broken from the norm because of their love for individualistic risk-taking and been humbled by defeat. Some had been, by definition, *nouveaux riches* who had neither the experience nor the capacity for self-abnegation to hoard for the lean years or future generations. Some had been more Latin than Norman, more pleasure-bent (as my Grandfather Moncel had called bow-legged women) than priest-ridden, and known that life is short, eternity long, and money made for good food, fine dress, big parties, beautiful objects, and fleeting happiness. Some had been proof of the negative consequences of founding a business class on patronage and protection. But the main factor behind the decline of the French Canadian families was structural: by the 1920s, power and capital had become concentrated in the hands of the English-speaking tycoons of Montreal's Square Mile.

Controlling the biggest banks, the biggest trust companies, the biggest insurance companies, and the biggest brokerage houses, the anglos had been able to create monopolies and conglomerates that owned much of Canada. It was easy for them to pick up successful French Canadian enterprises in their own backyard, as it were, and tempting for the French Canadian entrepreneurs to sell out. Those entrepreneurs became marginal or regional businessmen as a result, and because they tended to move their funds into the stock market, commerce, or real estate, they were especially vulnerable to the ravages of the Crash and the Great Depression. At the same time, because Montreal and the industrial towns of Quebec had been filling up with cheap French Canadian labor from the farms, class as much as language and religion increasingly separated English from French. In novels as well as political tracts, English Quebeckers were the rich owners on the hill, French Quebeckers the poor laborers in the slums.

"Around us came strangers whom we were pleased to call the barbarians," Louis Hémon wrote in his 1924 novel, *Maria Chapdelaine.* "They took almost all the power; they acquired almost all the money." True, to a degree, though Hémon skipped over the impact of Quebec's nationalist thinkers, who still strove to keep French Canadians pious, illiterate, and rural. His own heroine, most significantly, rejects the suitor who holds out promises of wealth in the United States. Instead she chooses the local farm boy, who offers family, tradition, and the survival of the community.

These class tensions only exacerbated the old political, religious, and linguistic tensions. In 1914 Médéric Martin had shattered the tradition of alternating between French and English mayors of Montreal by appealing to the interests of the French-speaking, working-class majority against the interests of the plutocrats of the Square Mile. More significantly, in 1917 battles had erupted in the streets of Montreal over the issue of compulsory military service for the horrendous conflict in Europe. Most French Quebeckers were opposed to fighting England's war; most English Quebeckers saw that opposition as treason. The two sides had started to take a long, hard look at one another, in short, and neither side trusted what it saw.

In this context, Napoléon Tétrault's death in 1942 marked the end of a late nineteenth-century truce. "This genial French Canadian gentleman was a credit to his race and his passing removes one of the most colourful figures in the Canadian shoe industry," *Shoe and Leather Journal* noted at the time. "He worked hard in his day and when the time came for him to enjoy life he drank of the cup to the full. He probably experienced more ups and downs in his long career than most, but he was not one to complain and his remarkable vitality stood him in good stead when the road was rough." To which a certain Warren T. Fegan added, in his own tribute, "Any faults he may have had, any mistakes he may have made, sprang directly from his abounding liberality. We shall not soon see his like again."

Not for about fifty years, as it turned out, when Montreal was suddenly – and unexpectedly – full of his like.

Call of the Race, 1960

NAPOLEON and Ninette Tétrault had two sons, Albert and Arthur, who were as different in style as the ant and the grasshopper, as different in pace as the tortoise and the hare. They were different in politics, too, for Albert remained a Canadian federalist while Arthur became a Quebec nationalist.

Arthur, the younger, was more like his father. Fun and charming, he had inherited Napoléon's ability to make money in the shoe industry and spend it on the finer things of life. His particular passions were art, Paris, and women, all of which he indulged as a young man at the Sorbonne soon after the Great War. There he flirted with the Communist Party and married a beautiful young student who, soon after he brought her to Montreal, was paid to return to France because her background had not met his family's standards. In time he married twice again, but connubial bliss was not his destiny, and both wives died relatively young of alcohol-related causes.

He was more successful as a businessman, shunning the prepared path into Tétrault Shoe to create his own shoe companies, which did well enough to permit him to reverse his father's bad fortune and land once more in a house in upper Westmount. But for Arthur money was less an end in itself than a means to pursue his more artistic pleasures. He decorated his home in the avant-garde fashions of New York and Paris, with Art Deco mirrors, an enormous round bed, and nude nymphs; he commissioned design students to make dining-room chairs out of cowhide from his factories; he demonstrated an excellent eye for contemporary painting and became an early patron of Quebec artists such as Paul-Emile Borduas and Marc-Aurèle Fortin. Ultimately, when his businesses, under the management of his son Marc, began to falter in the 1960s with the lifting of the protective tariffs on shoes, he was able to maintain his annual sojourns in Paris by selling off his collection piece by piece. In the 1960s, too, his cultural connections and nonconformist traits made him sympathetic to the emotional and radical appeal of Quebec nationalism.

"He was a wise man," said his youngest daughter Danielle, "if wisdom means being open-minded and young in spirit. He certainly wasn't your orthodox businessman. He liked the company of artists and young people, and they liked talking with him. There were no taboo subjects at the dinner table. Though he was a Liberal most of his life, he believed in encouraging Quebec's nationalist movements, sometimes with a check, sometimes as a necessary evil, in order to allow French Canadians to advance their rights. Eventually he became more and more nationalistic himself, and the Tétrault family divided – like the Quebec family – into the nationalists and the anglicized."

———————

Arthur's brother was more Moncel than Tétrault. Albert's inheritance had been his mother's silent fortitude and traditional sense of duty. Like Hélène Desportes in the early days of New France, Ninette Tétrault had never been known to break down or complain about her misfortunes – not when she lost three sons to childhood illnesses, not when Hortense's marriage failed, not when Marcelle's psychological problems became apparent, not when Napoléon lost his money, not when Jeanne's husband, Tony Vanier, died of cancer and left his widow with two small girls, not when Arthur showed up with his unacceptable bride. When Napoléon died, Ninette got into their bed and listened to the bells of Saint-Viateur-d'Outremont toll at his funeral because she thought it was a woman's duty to cry alone.

Through her Albert had also imbibed Guillaume Moncel's taste for serious toil, his financial prudence, his progressive attitude, and his love of reading in his private library. More correct and respectful than Arthur, he had gone into the management of Tétrault Shoe as soon as he left school, and he basically ran the Montreal office when his father was in France. Instead of picking up models in Paris or riding camels in Egypt, he applied himself to shoe styles and profit margins. Even after the family lost the company, Albert stayed on as an employee, and since he had no pension, he remained in harness until he dropped dead while shaving one morning in 1963 at the age of seventy. "I remember him after the Crash and during the Depression," said Jacqueline Ouimet, the eldest of his six children, "in his library at night, standing to stay awake, trying to figure out ways to save the company."

Napoléon may have fallen from the Olympian heights of Belvedere Road, but Albert was able to sustain a genteel existence for himself. His wife, Paule, was very much a *grande dame* who dedicated much of her life to bridge and the symphony. Though gossips whispered that her father had been a policeman, her mother had remarried well and lived in the Ritz, and her half-sister was a famous beauty for whom the Prince of Wales had a passion on his trips to Montreal in the 1920s. Paule presided over an attractive townhouse filled with dark Victorian furniture on McGregor Avenue, at the edge of the old Square Mile, with a cook, a maid, a nanny, and (in better times) a chauffeur, and there she held fashionable parties for her card-playing friends and musical celebrities.

"She was witty and intelligent, schooled in France, an extrovert," said her son Claude, a fit and distinguished-looking septuagenarian who is sometimes mistaken for Pierre Trudeau because of his high cheekbones and elegant manner. "My mother had a good time. She never got out of bed before ten, always had her own maid, and she would have spent her life in high society if Dad had been more that kind. He was quieter, less artistic, more intellectual, and he was bloody tired from work. Arthur was more flamboyant and entrepreneurial than Dad, and he probably made – and lost – more money than Dad, who was on salary. But Dad was just as ambitious, especially for his sons. 'A Tétrault always leads!' he used to tell us."

Educated by the priests at Mont-Saint-Louis, where my grandfather Moncel also studied, Albert came to question both the utility of a Catholic education and the validity of the Church's truth; and like his Uncle René he saw that the obvious path to success in Montreal in those days ran through the right schools, the right clubs, and the right firms of the anglo establishment. He just had to look around him. Who lived in the Square Mile and Westmount? Who ran the banks and the major corporations? Who owned the utilities and the department stores? Who financed the mines and the factories? Who controlled the Board of Trade and the Stock Exchange?

Most French Canadians could not dream of rising as high as foreman without giving up their language and faith, and even the wealthiest were not often welcomed as business partners by the anglo elite or served in French by the Bell operator. "In Cantonville's major industries the English hold all positions of great authority and perform all functions requiring advanced technical training," Everett Hughes, an American sociologist, reported in his classic study of a Quebec industrial town in the 1930s. Though the English made up less than 7 per cent of the workforce, he found them "in the majority in the middle and minor executive positions, numerous among the clerical workers and skilled mechanics, less so among skilled operating hands, and hard to find among the semiskilled and unskilled help."

As a result, whether in Montreal or in the mill towns built by British and American capital, English-speaking Quebeckers earned more and controlled more than the French Canadians among whom they lived. Usually they lived apart, in local Westmounts that reflected their higher income and status, with their own schools, churches, and clubs. Their exclusivity proclaimed their superiority. In Grand'mère, for example, the managers and engineers of Laurentide Paper inhabited large homes set among the pines overlooking the St Maurice River up on "English Hill." They prayed at the charming Anglican church at the foot of the hill; they danced at the attractive lodge whose walls were decorated with fox-hunting prints and sporting trophies; they golfed on the private course where, the workers joked, French Canadians were only allowed to play after dark. In style and atmosphere that corner of Grand'mère resembled every other corner of the British Empire in the highlands of Kenya, New Zealand, or India.

It was obvious, therefore, why Albert Tétrault was determined to send his four sons to the elite schools of English Montreal, though he could hardly afford the fees at times. They all began at Selwyn House School, founded in 1908 by a group of Montreal tycoons to give their sons a proper British education, where my grandfather sent my Uncle Robert and my parents sent me. Like us, they all ended up at McGill. At the same time, since proper girls were not supposed to work in those days, he allowed his two daughters to be taught by French-speaking nuns.

"He was modern and anticlerical in his thinking. His church was the Sunday *New York Times*," said Claude, whose own faith had been strengthened recently by his miraculous recovery from an inoperable cancer. "He knew English well – his own father had come from

Ontario, remember – and much of his business, whether selling shoes in Toronto or looking at the fashions in New York, was done in English. But at home he spoke French, unless we had English guests, and he mostly read French books. Because of school, however, the boys became more comfortable with English – our friends on the street were English, too, and even our nanny was English – so we tended to speak English among ourselves and French to our parents and our sisters. People sometimes found the mealtime conversations a little confusing."

The Tétrault boys were pulled into the mentality as well as the language of their schools. Claude served with the Canadian army during the Second World War and worked as a corporate lawyer, first with an American multinational, then with Alcan, the aluminum giant. Robert joined the British navy and worked as an engineer in Calgary before his death. The twins, Jacques and André, became a lawyer and a stockbroker respectively with prestigious anglo firms. All four married English-speaking women and raised English-speaking children in English-speaking neighborhoods – while their sisters married French-speaking men and raised French-speaking children – and though the three brothers who remained in Montreal recovered a working knowledge of French, none would call himself perfectly bilingual. When I asked Jacques, now a senior partner at McCarthy Tétrault, the largest law firm in Canada, if he is considered a prominent French Canadian lawyer, he said, "No, I suppose they think of me as some sort of hybrid."

Their father and their milieu also ensured that all of them would be Liberals, at the federal and provincial level, for Albert Tétrault and most English Quebeckers shared an admiration for the pro-business government of Louis St Laurent in Ottawa in the 1950s and a distrust of the autocratic regime of Maurice Duplessis in Quebec City. In

Albert Tétrault's case, at least, the distrust was closer to aversion: he *despised* Maurice Duplessis.

Duplessis had ruled the province since 1936, except for the war years, in the style of Huey Long or Benito Mussolini. Charming and corrupt, courteous and crude, clever and conniving, Duplessis was a right-wing demagogue with a genius for rewarding his friends and thrashing his enemies. Both were selected by a single criterion: their enthusiasm for his remaining in power. Though something of a libertine in the privacy of the Ritz, where his pious rural constituents were not likely to catch him, he allied himself with the Roman Catholic bishops against liberalism and loose morals. Though forever battling Ottawa for more money and power in the name of French Canadian autonomy, he plotted with Westmount businessmen and American corporations to exchange land, resources, and union-busting for campaign contributions and personal gifts. Quebec made economic progress during the 1950s, but that period became known as "la Grande Noirceur," the Great Darkness, because the mines, mills, roads, schools, and dams were built under the shadow of repression, ignominy, and injustice. So powerful were Duplessis's allies, so pervasive was his party machine, so entrenched was his mystique as *le chef*, the leader, that death alone was able to defeat him. By a strange synchronicity, he died in September 1959, exactly two hundred years after the battle at which French Canada had fallen to the British Empire.

"C'est le temps que ça change!" shouted the handsome young leader of the provincial Liberal Party, Jean Lesage, formerly a Cabinet minister with the federal Liberal Party in Ottawa. "It's time for a change!"

In 1960, and more resoundingly in 1962, the people agreed, and the Lesage government let loose a host of political, social, economic, and cultural forces so potent that their impact became known as the Quiet Revolution. Like the rivers of northern Quebec before the great hydroelectric dams, these forces had been present before 1960, but as diffuse and untapped energy. A new generation of French Canadians had come of age by the Second World War, better educated, better traveled, with broader philosophies and higher ambitions, only to be denied political expression by Duplessis, economic expression by the English elite, and cultural expression by the clergy.

"We are the settlers who, ever since 1760, have been trapped in the fortress of fear – that old refuge of the vanquished – and there abandoned," howled Paul-Emile Borduas and fifteen other Quebec artists in their 1948 manifesto, *Refus global.* "Our leaders set sail to sell themselves to the highest bidder, a practice they have continued to follow at every opportunity. We are a small people sheltering under the wing of the clergy – the only remaining repository of faith, knowledge, truth, and national wealth; isolated from the universal progress of thought with all its pitfalls and perils, and raised (since complete ignorance was impossible) on well-meaning but grossly distorted accounts of the great historical facts."

Such dissidents conspired on the edges of the society or in the cellars of the established institutions: liberal Catholics in the universities and youth movements, union leaders and radical artists, pamphleteers and journalists, and businessmen such as Arthur and Albert Tétrault in the traditional industries or small towns. From time to time their ideas percolated up into the mass consciousness – in 1942 as the platform of the Bloc Populaire, in 1949 as a violent strike against the asbestos industry, in 1956 as a television program called "Point de Mire," in 1960 as a scathing denunciation of Catholic education by "Brother Anonymous" – but they lacked cohesion and power until Lesage's victory.

Lesage let loose more than liberalism. He let loose a modern kind of nationalism, neither traditionalist nor preoccupied with culture but progressive and directed toward business. "Maîtres chez nous!" was his rallying cry during the 1962 election, "Masters in our own house!" and he made clear what masters and whose house by denouncing the "economic colonialism" of Quebec and promising to nationalize the English-owned power companies. The power companies were to French Canadians what the Suez Canal was to the Egyptians or the oil fields were to the Iranians: a symbol as much as a source of wealth. Whether they were connected to some ancient French Canadian romance about Laurentian rivers or simply crucial to every industry and household, the power companies became the prime example of "Anglais" exploitation until Hydro-Québec became the primary model of "Québécois" achievement. One of the most popular nationalist anthems of the 1960s was "Le Manic," a song in praise of a dam.

The Raj had always been more an economic elite than a political elite in Quebec. French Canadians had held the majority in an elected assembly since 1792. They had been powerful players in the government of Canada since 1867, producing three prime ministers and numerous Cabinet ministers. They had controlled the province of Quebec, too, though often they had not developed its apparatus or tested its muscle. The Quiet Revolution promised to do precisely that. Industrialization, urbanization, and communication had produced the makings of a modern, pragmatic, and French-speaking middle class, hungry for the material benefits and self-fulfillment of postwar America. Their way had been impeded, however, by the Catholic institutions of French Quebec and the imperial remnants of English Montreal. Even into the 1950s, the usual choice had been whether to lower your ambition or lose your culture. Now, after 1960, a third choice became possible, as it had not been for Albert Tétrault: to expand both your ambition and your culture by doing away with the Catholic institutions *and* the imperial remnants.

On the one hand, the Lesage government took the schools, the hospitals, and the welfare agencies from the Church and reoriented them toward economic progress and social planning. On the other, it took the hydro companies, the finance department, and the public contracts from the English-speaking elite and opened them to French-speaking professionals and entrepreneurs. Then it set up a multitude of government agencies and programs tailored to assist French-speaking businesses with loans, grants, purchases, and development strategies.

―――――――――

If Albert Tétrault's goal had been that of his Uncle René, to purge his children of any trace of a French accent for the sake of their advancement, his pride in his sons' achievements would have been complete. But unlike my grandfather, Albert remained rooted in French Canada and the French language. While he deplored the authoritarian grip of Maurice Duplessis and anticommercial influence of the Roman Catholic Church on his people, he also deplored the arrogant colonialism of the anglo network in Montreal, best expressed perhaps by the decision taken in 1955 by Canadian National Railways, a Montreal-based company owned by the federal government, to name its enormous new hotel in the center of the second-largest French-speaking city in the world in honor of Queen Elizabeth II, despite official protests and despite a petition signed by more than two hundred thousand French Canadians. Seven years later, adding insult to injury, the Scottish-born president of the CNR declared that he still could not find a French Canadian competent to serve as one of his vice-presidents. Indeed, it was to save his sons from such obstacles that Albert had insisted they go to Selwyn House and join the Winter Club. Inadvertently, however, as both Claude and Jacques said in separate conversations, he created "Frankenstein's monster," for in his dying days Albert Tétrault heard what the nationalist historian Lionel Groulx termed the "call of the race."

"He wanted us to succeed in a big way," said Claude, "but he probably regretted that we had to succeed by becoming English. In his own quiet way, he was a French Canadian nationalist, though never a separatist. He lived just long enough to see the beginnings of the Quiet Revolution, and he was all for it. He was a Lesage Liberal, and he was even in favor of the nationalization of the hydro companies. My brothers and I used to have great arguments with him about it at Sunday lunch, because we were against it for sound economic reasons. Let's face it, we were anglicized – but Dad himself had sent us down that path."

After twelve generations and more than three centuries, this particular line of Zacherie Cloutier's family set off down a new path. After Hélène Desportes had withstood the English occupation in 1630, after François Lorit had reported on Frontenac's repulsion of the English invaders in 1690, after Jonathan Hains had refused to return to his English family in 1710, after Charles Leret *dit* Moncel had defeated the English army at the Battle of Sainte-Foy, after Hugh Munro had raised his children to be French, after François-Antoine Larocque had gone to jail for the liberty of French Canadians, after Louis Fauteux had defended the federation of 1867 as the best guarantor of French Canadian survival, after Guillaume Moncel had worked from poverty to wealth in French, and after Nap Tétrault had returned to Montreal from Ontario, a branch of the family tree was transplanted in the thirteenth generation into English Quebec.

Two branches, in fact: Albert Tétrault's, and my own.

FAMILY REUNION

"The family is but the nation in the seed, writ small,
and the nation is the family writ large."

— Louis-François Laflèche
Grand Vicar of Trois-Rivières
(1866)

Shaken, But Proud, 1963

SHORTLY AFTER three o'clock in the morning on Friday, May 18, 1963, five bombs exploded in various boxes of the Royal Mail on the tranquil streets of Westmount. They were powerful enough to shatter the windows of nearby homes and awaken the families high up on the Circle.

Another ten bombs were discovered during the course of the day. One of them detonated in the face of the army sergeant who had been trying to defuse it. "It is like clearing a captured city of bombs during wartime," said the mayor of Westmount as he led a gallant band of municipal employees toward a suspicious-looking object behind a hedge on Shorncliffe Avenue. The danger was evident, the tension surreal, but when the package was found to contain two cheese sandwiches, His Worship dismissed any hint of personal bravery by asking, with perfect cool, "Anybody hungry?" The boys of Selwyn House School were sent home under police protection; the girls at Miss Edgar's and Miss Cramp's, including my younger sister, were evacuated in orderly fashion after an anonymous caller reported that a bomb had been planted in the school.

"Shaken, But Proud," was how the next day's newspaper described Westmount. These were not the first bombings – a night watchman had been killed outside an army recruiting center less than a month before – but they were the closest, on familiar corners, and more were expected at any moment. For this was the holiday weekend to celebrate the birthdays of Queen Victoria and Queen Elizabeth II, an obvious target for French Canadian extremists. The police had already warned the avid monarchists of Westmount not to confuse matters by igniting fireworks and twenty-one-gun salutes.

This "insolent terrorism," as the *Gazette* termed it, was the work of the Front de Libération du Québec, the FLQ, a clandestine gang of workers and intellectuals inspired by the revolutions in Algeria, Cuba, and Vietnam to build an independent and Marxist Quebec. The FLQ may have been only a hotheaded few, but their bombs dramatized the ideas and emotions that had been swirling through Quebec for several years. Many commentators even noted a general sense of solidarity with these courageous, though misguided children who loved the cause of French Canadians with too much passion.

The Quiet Revolution had been particularly quiet in this part of Quebec: it was some time before its implications really disturbed Westmount. Indeed, Westmount had helped to bring about change by voting for the Liberals as the party of economic progress and clean government. Whenever Jean Lesage was pointed out to me in the Palm Court at the Ritz or the Beaver Club in the Queen Elizabeth Hotel, he looked more like a drunken matinée idol than a Colonel Nasser, and I gathered that he had not been ungenerous toward the shareholders of the companies Hydro-Québec had absorbed. Westmount still dominated the city, the province, and a remarkable amount of the country. Its politicians still wielded extra clout in Ottawa and Quebec City. Its lawyers still gained advantage from being trained in both English common law and the French civil code. Its doctors and engineers still enjoyed the benefits of McGill

University and a prosperous community. Its downtown merchants and movie houses still catered almost exclusively to English customers. Discreet money still spoke louder than French slogans.

If the heirs of the Square Mile had felt any change in the air by 1963, it had blown not west from Quebec City but north from the United States, on the waves of American television and American investment. Aided by mass advertising and mass distribution, things American began to replace things British in Westmount. The lyrics of Elvis Presley's "Blue Suede Shoes" joined Kipling's "If" in my memory bank. Robin Hood was overtaken by Davy Crockett. Even the royal family was challenged by the Kennedys, the Kramdens, and the Cleavers. London began to seem old, drab, and far away. New York City rose up, with bright lights and giddy heights, just a hop away by airplane. It offered the theaters on Broadway, the shops on Fifth Avenue, and the money managers on Wall Street.

This shift mattered little to most French Canadians. Yankee supervisors en route between branchplants were no better than Scottish merchants from the time of the Conquest or Jewish industrialists on the run from Russia: they were all damned English. The FLQ theorists did not stop there. They included among the "parasitic classes" the old *vendu* businessmen – like Albert Tétrault and my own grandfather – and the new Quebec technocrats behind the Quiet Revolution. The first bombs of the "total revolution" may have gone off in Westmount, but the message was also intended for the politicians, the priests, and the parents of French Canada.

"Our childhood: there indeed is where it all begins," Pierre Maheu wrote in *Parti pris*, the intellectual and artistic organ of the FLQ, shortly after the bombings, "so much so that to speak of it properly one would have to speak of everything at once, for childhood was our first contact with the alienation that an alienated society imposed on us. The family incarnated the society for us; the family, that all-important institution, foundation stone of our society, primary cell of the Church – primary place of the fucking up of things, for our parents and hence for us. The French Canadian people, dispossessed of their chief political institutions, had undertaken a kind of cultural retreat into a family that became the main social institution; this retreat had taken place under the aegis of the curés, who also profited from the political void and replaced all social ethic with a morality of fear."

Pierre Vallières, the FLQ's most articulate ideologue, made the thought more specific in his book *White Niggers of America*. "My parents lived in continual fear of *tomorrow*, that is, of possible unemployment, possible illness, possible hunger and want. They could never escape from that fear by allowing themselves to forget their cares once in a while, to let go a little, to have a bit of diversion. No. They had to *economize*. Economize on everything, even affection."

―――――――――――

"Mother," a ten-year-old wrote, "you ought not to leave me alone at this boarding school. If I am left here long, I am afraid I shall become very bad. I am writing to you in the library, where it is cold. I wish I were at home with you."

I did not write that letter, but I could have, for at the age of nine I had been sent into the countryside to Bishop's College School. The boy was, in fact, a character called Tête Blanche in the novel of the same name, which I read when it first appeared in English in 1961. Its author was Marie-Claire Blais, a young French Canadian who had yet to produce her best-known works or be celebrated by the American critic Edmund Wilson. I had discovered it through a rather eccentric teacher, recently arrived from Wales via Oxford University, who literally flung it at me one day saying, "Bloody Canadians, always looking to bloody England for what's good – you even get your jackets shipped over, I can tell by the piping on your lapels, waste of bloody money if you ask me, but I suppose your parents can afford it – well, here, read this: it's as good as anything coming out of England, and it's written by a bloody Frog."

It was my first French Canadian novel, and it stirred deep emotions, in part because I could identify with Tête Blanche, in part because his mother dies shortly after he is sent away. Worse than banishment from the Circle, worse than the strict discipline and the brutal prefects, worse than the atrocious food and the retired colonels trying to expunge the least trace of American television with the same fervor some of the same masters had brought to turning my uncle Robert Guillaume Napoléon Moncel into an Anglican soldier-gentleman, worst of all was the persistent fear that I would never see my parents again.

During the Cuban missile crisis of 1962, when the Bomb was expected to drop on New York or Washington at any moment, my friends and I had spent hours speculating on whether we would be able to reach Montreal before the cloud of nuclear fallout. Usually the fear was that illness or accident would kill my father, my mother, or both. It intensified with my anticipation of seeing them, just before I went home for a holiday or they came to the school for a visit – as they were supposed to do for the Victoria Day track and field events in May 1963.

My terror was all the greater, therefore, when reports of the Westmount bombs reached me between breakfast and chapel on Friday morning – much as the news from Lucknow and Mafeking must have penetrated the thick walls of this imperial outpost – and the hymn-book trembled in my hands when we sang, "I will not cease from Mental Fight, nor shall my Sword sleep in my hand, till we have built Jerusalem, in England's green and pleasant land."

My parents arrived safely, of course, and they were full of reassurances that everything was all right. I sensed, however, that nothing would be quite right again. For years I would not be able to walk past a mailbox without wincing. As the FLQ had supposed, it required a few bombs to blast the reality of French Canadian nationalism into the consciousness of English Quebec. For the first time I felt the sting of grievance and hatred. The families cheering at the edge of the playing fields, the Old Boys perching on their shooting sticks with hip flasks in their tweed suits, the mothers yelling hello to each other with their Labradors straining at the leash: they were no longer ordinary people; they were agents of colonial oppression. A bit dramatic, perhaps, but I was going through a bout of adolescent angst in which a satiric remark about white flannel trousers in Eliot's "The Love Song of J. Alfred Prufrock" had been enough to plunge me into despair about having to wear white flannel trousers at cricket.

"Mama," Tête Blanche wrote after a weekend with his parents, "it is not very pleasant to find yourself back at boarding school on Monday. But I understand more and more that this is my kingdom. There is something about Father's house that frightens me. I can't explain why."

The True Father, 1968

AT THE Saint-Jean-Baptiste parade of 1968 riot police wounded more than a hundred nationalist demonstrators and arrested another three hundred – but the image most people retained was of a single man. He was in the center of the official reviewing stand on Sherbrooke Street. Rocks and bottles were hurtling toward him. The other dignitaries had fled, overturning their chairs, covering their heads with their arms, leaving him dramatically exposed. He stayed in his seat and waved away the security men who were trying to shield him. He seemed furious that they were blocking his view of the floats.

It was Canada's first vivid glimpse of the nerve of its new leader,

Pierre Elliott Trudeau, and of his determination to confront Quebec nationalism. Less than three months earlier, in April 1968, while the cities of the United States burned in grief for Martin Luther King, Trudeau had been elected leader of the federal Liberal Party and prime minister. No one was more surprised than himself. He had only been a member of Parliament since 1965 and a Cabinet minister for a year, and his taste for beautiful women, fast cars, and casual clothes was considered unorthodox, to say the least. But a mania erupted around his complex personality – part Catholic intellectual, part international adventurer, part Peter Pan, part Wizard of Oz – and it was fired by the news clips of his courage at the parade. The next day he led the Liberals to an impressive victory in the federal election, winning almost all the votes in Quebec.

Two ambitions had drawn him to exchange his privacy and freedom for power. "One was to make sure that Quebec wouldn't leave Canada through separatism," he said, "and the other was to make sure that Canada wouldn't shove Quebec out through narrow-mindedness."

As a young man studying at Harvard and the London School of Economics, or traveling through Europe in the 1930s and Asia in the 1940s, Trudeau had developed a lasting horror of ethnocentric nationalism. "A state that defined its function essentially in terms of ethnic attributes would inevitably become chauvinistic and intolerant," he argued, "for it would seek the advancement of one people, one colour, one religion, or one language above the welfare of every individual citizen." However indignant he was about the social and economic injustices committed by English Canadian nationalism, he resented the presumption that French Canadians needed a separate nation or special powers to improve their circumstances. Instead, he argued, they should use the powers that Canada already offered them at both the federal and provincial levels.

"To sum it up," he had written in 1962, "Anglo-Canadians have been strong by virtue only of our weakness. This is true not only at

Ottawa, but even at Quebec, a veritable charnel-house where half our rights have been wasted by decay and decrepitude and the rest devoured by the maggots of political cynicism and the pestilence of corruption."

The Quiet Revolution had begun to strengthen the government in Quebec City, but its successes only weakened the central government and further undermined the French Canadians in Ottawa. Canada's major symbols, from the official flag to the royal coat of arms on the mailboxes, were still British. The working language of the public service was overwhelmingly English; French-speaking bureaucrats held few important posts and earned less than their English-speaking counterparts; most federal services, down to the welfare checks, were delivered in English only. If French Canadians could not play the game in Ottawa, let alone control it, they preferred to move the game to Quebec City. Even Jean Lesage had called his demands for special powers and a greater share of the total taxation revenues "probably the last chance" for the unity of Canada.

So Trudeau had gone to work in Ottawa as a counterbalance, to help bring his people and their language to real influence over the entire country. The bureaucratic and economic reforms initiated by his predecessor, Lester Pearson, a former diplomat who had won the Nobel Peace Prize for his work in the Middle East, were the equivalent of the civil-rights movement in the United States, and they shaped the very definition of Canada. There was even a new flag to replace the Union Jack. Trudeau's own priority as prime minister was to establish bilingualism in all the national services and agencies so that French-speaking Canadians – in or out of Quebec – could feel at home with their federal government. "Once you have done that," he said in 1968, "Quebec cannot say that it alone speaks for French Canadians."

But in the same year, as an equal and opposite reaction to Pierre Trudeau, René Lévesque rose up to create the Parti Québécois out of a variety of marginal independence groups. Its birth had been helped when Charles de Gaulle, the French president, yelled "Vive le Québec libre!" from the balcony of city hall in Montreal during the 1967 world's fair, but its life was due to its popular leader. Lévesque was a clever, disheveled, chain-smoking populist who had been famous as host of the news program "Point de Mire" on television and lionized as minister of natural resources, responsible for the nationalization of the hydro companies, under Jean Lesage. Wounded by childhood experiences of name-calling and exploitation in the English enclave of New Carlisle in the Gaspé, insulted as a journalist by the anglos who dominated Ottawa, and outraged as a provincial Cabinet minister by the smugness of the Montreal business elite (whom he compared to the British in Egypt and Rhodesia), he had been edging toward separatism for years. When he could not convince the provincial Liberals to move with him, he left them and founded the Parti Québécois in 1968.

For Lévesque, Quebec was the only effective jurisdiction in which French Canadians formed a majority, and its nationalism was a progressive and tolerant force. The French Canadians outside Quebec were rapidly going the way of the Cajuns in Louisiana; the English elite inside Quebec were not about to throw open the doors of their boardrooms graciously; and, unless the tail wagged the dog, Ottawa would remain an English town. Instead, Lévesque proposed an economic association between two independent countries, based on rational negotiations and common interests.

"We are Québécois," he declared. "What that means first and foremost – and if need be, all that it means – is that we are attached to this one corner of the earth where we can be completely ourselves: this Quebec, the only place where we have the unmistakable feeling that 'here we can be really at home.'"

Lévesque had been assisted in the preparation of his ideas by a gawky young economist named Robert Bourassa. Bourassa worried about the economic risks of independence, however, so he stayed with the Liberal Party of Quebec (which Lesage had severed from the

193

Liberal Party of Canada) when Lévesque left. Indeed, in 1970 he became its leader and premier of Quebec. Twenty years later Bourassa still has the appearance and personality of Mr Rogers, the ever-so-nice but oh-so-dull children's television host: each hides his intelligence behind an accountant's monotone, each exhibits an obsession with personal neatness that borders on the neurotic, each has a decency that looks like weakness, and each seems to believe that his neighborhood is the center of the world.

Bourassa was the natural heir of the Quiet Revolution. Educated at Oxford and Harvard as well as the Université de Montréal, experienced in public finance in Ottawa and Quebec City, related by marriage to a well-known family of French Canadian industrialists yet ambitious for himself, he emerged in 1970 as the very epitome of the new Quebec technocracy: well trained, pragmatic, and preoccupied with economic progress. At one level progress entailed the continuing modernization of Quebec by its government. At another it entailed continual demands for power and money from Ottawa. Bourassa called it "profitable federalism." He remained a federalist, yet he made clear that his commitment to Canada depended on the bottom line. Patriotism had no place on the balance sheet.

For Bourassa, Quebec's demands for power and money stemmed from Quebec's special responsibilities as the only "homeland" of a French-speaking majority in North America. It wasn't a province like the other nine provinces of Canada, went the argument: Canada itself had been founded on a deal between two peoples, one English-speaking, the other French-speaking, with Quebec as the historical guardian of the language, religion, and collective rights of French Canadians. Quebec, therefore, deserved a "special status" in the form of additional powers under the constitution. "One doesn't have to be a prophet to foresee that among the options available to it, Quebec will choose a special status," Bourassa had said in 1967, "in keeping with its own characteristic traits, within a renewed Canadian federation."

"A woollier concept would be hard to imagine," Pierre Trudeau said of a special status for Quebec. "How can a constitution be devised to give Quebec greater powers than other provinces, without reducing Quebec's power in Ottawa? How can citizens of other provinces be made to accept the fact that they would have less power over Quebec at the federal level than Quebec would have over them?" Trudeau saw special status as an immature wish to have one's cake and eat it too. Its obvious result would be the independence of Quebec, as French Quebeckers lost clout in Ottawa and abandoned it for Quebec City. "Masters in our own house we must be," he countered, "but our house is the whole of Canada."

René Lévesque disagreed with Trudeau, of course; he also disagreed with Bourassa. Special status would merely worsen the "madhouse" that was Canada. "In effect the result would be a strange kind of arrangement where one would try to make *two* governments live together, each almost exactly as powerful and even as *central* as the other," he argued. "Such a project put forward by Quebec would deserve the slightly contemptuous smile that is reserved for those who want both liberty and a kind of all-risk insurance against liberty."

Three men, three parties, three options. All were in position by the fall of 1970 to set the political agenda of Canada for the next fifteen years – and beyond. Like Frontenac fighting Duchesneau over New France's expansion to the west, like Vaudreuil fighting Montcalm over the Canadiens' military tactics, like Papineau fighting with La Fontaine over an accommodation with the English in 1840, like Laurier fighting with Mercier over the strategy for French Canadian survival, the quarrels among Trudeau, Lévesque, and Bourassa were rooted more in the domestic squabbles of French Quebec than in the national issues of the whole society. The three men were brothers in the same family, so to speak. They had been allied against Duplessis. They had shared many friends and associations. Each had lost his father at an early age. Now they were struggling among themselves for the empty seat at the head of the family table and control of the inheritance.

Canada was caught up in their struggle, but English Canadians felt confused, uncomfortable, and powerless. The fate of the country was no longer a matter of debates in the House of Commons and decisions by the Cabinet. It was a question of waiting for the day when the Quebec family made up its mind about its true father.

Simple Convictions, 1970

A T FOUR O'CLOCK on the morning of October 16, 1970, Canada fell under wartime law to deal with an "apprehended insurrection." A few hours later, on my way from Ottawa to spend Thanksgiving weekend in the Eastern Townships, I passed convoys of dark green trucks, full of men and supplies, rolling into Quebec from Ontario. Armored vehicles surrounded by troops in combat gear were posted at the main intersections and bridges in Montreal. The atmosphere was thick with tension and fear.

Eleven days earlier a cell of the Front de Libération du Québec had kidnaped James Cross, the British trade commissioner in Montreal, and threatened to execute him unless Ottawa and Quebec acceded to a list of demands. Both governments refused to negotiate with terrorists. Another FLQ cell responded on October 10 by kidnaping the Quebec minister of labour, Pierre Laporte. Unlike Cross, he was part of "the family," a popular and powerful Liberal politician who had crusaded as a journalist against Maurice Duplessis's corruption in the 1950s. His abduction turned an isolated incident, not much worse than the scores of bombings and holdups to which Quebeckers had become accustomed during the previous decade, into the specter of a ruthless conspiracy to bring down the democratic government of Quebec.

As deadlines came and went, as students and union officials rallied in support of the FLQ, Premier Robert Bourassa barricaded himself in a suite at the Queen Elizabeth Hotel and Mayor Jean Drapeau shook with fear for his life. The Montreal police were exhausted and calling for help. Everyone was expecting other cells to strike soon. There were rumors that the FLQ had enough machine guns and dynamite to launch an urban guerrilla war. Pressed by Bourassa and Drapeau, Prime Minister Trudeau resorted to the toughest defense at hand, the War Measures Act, which gave the army and police extraordinary powers by suspending basic civil rights. During the night more than four hundred and fifty people had been taken from their beds to jail – community workers and union organizers, singers and poets, students and journalists, members of the Parti Québécois who had campaigned against Bourassa a few months earlier, and members of the party campaigning against Drapeau in the upcoming municipal election. In almost every case their worst offense was to have been a Quebec nationalist.

"Even the hint of a theory that I was just waiting for an occasion to sock it to the separatists is completely wrong," Trudeau later protested. He had been appalled by the crumbling support for a democratically elected government among many prominent opinion-makers, by their willingness to release convicted criminals to satisfy the FLQ, and by the bumbling inefficiency of the police forces. "They weren't prepared to deal with terrorists in our midst, children of French Canadian families, some of which were respectable. The whole series of bombings and arsenal raids were made by children of people we knew."

In fact, those children were revolting against Robert Bourassa and René Lévesque as much as against Pierre Trudeau, and it was in everyone's interest to put a stop to the damage the kids were doing to the family. "You've got to hand it to them, they're courageous, those guys," Lévesque had said at the time of the bombings in Westmount in 1963; but when they kidnaped his old friend Laporte, he was quick to distance the independence movement from their radical and violent goals. In fact, the kidnapings cost the FLQ any sympathy it might have had among ordinary Quebeckers and finished it as a political force.

Family tensions were not limited to French Quebec in those days: the National Guard had killed four students on the campus of Kent State University just six months earlier. In my own family, my father and I had almost come to blows about a massive demonstration by French Canadian nationalists against the privileges and English character of McGill University. I did not agree with their views, but I thought the Montreal police had overreacted by attacking them with clubs and horses. My father thought that a heresy. We had to bring in an arbiter to put us back on speaking terms.

The arbiter had been Frank Scott, a former law dean, no less. By luck Frank had become my mentor when I was at McGill; he and his wife Marian had become like grandparents to me after the deaths of my own. In their modest brick house at the bottom of Westmount and at their cottage in the Eastern Townships, they had introduced me to another sort of wealth, based upon intelligent friends, frequent laughter, lethal martinis, sagging shelves of books, Marian's paintings, and big ideas. We talked about the principles of politics and the philosophies of law, the structure of poetry and the source of art. We talked about current events and world history. Mostly, we talked about Quebec. Such were the tensions in those days, however, that I had started quarreling with him too.

F.R. Scott was the same age as the century. Victoria had still ruled over her vast empire when he was born in Quebec City, the son of a high-church Anglican rector, and he grew up enacting scenes from G.A. Henty's *With Wolfe at Quebec* on the Plains of Abraham and pelting snowballs at the French gangs. He went as a Rhodes scholar to Oxford, where the Fabians and modern poetry radicalized his

Christian beliefs, and became a man of many parts: a patrician Westmounter who was a founder of Canada's socialist party, a professor of law at McGill who was a major poet, a rigid academic who was an impish satirist, an intimidating foe who was a gregarious madcap.

Both politics and poetry had led him into French Canada along paths rarely traveled by English Quebeckers of his generation. His love for the Laurentian landscape was unmatched, and his hatred for Duplessis's authoritarianism unmitigated. He campaigned for democracy and social justice among the workers and farmers of Quebec. He led a twelve-year suit on behalf of the Jehovah's Witnesses against Duplessis himself all the way to the Supreme Court, and won. He wrote essays to alert English Canadians to the economic and cultural needs of French Canada, and he served as a member of the Royal Commission on Bilingualism and Biculturalism to make French Canadians more sensitive to the history and ways of English Canada. He was one of the first to translate the important French-language poets into English.

> Fear of the police
> Fear of arrests
> Made me afraid of permissions
> But even more of the unknown
> And of the freedom that led to it

– was how he translated part of "State of Siege" by Pierre Trottier –

> Authority had surrounded me
> Had beamed on me its searchlights
> Which relentlessly pinned me against the wall
> Of the priestless prison of my conscience.

Yet he could never support Quebec nationalism. Any nationalist demonstration in the 1960s brought back to him the mob that had marched through Montreal in 1936 to wreck a public forum of delegates from the Spanish Republican government. Frank had viewed the Spanish Civil War as an epic battle between democracy and fascism, and with his friend Norman Bethune (the Montreal doctor whom Mao later canonized as a hero of the Communist revolution in China) he had helped to organize the forum in support of the Republican cause. Quebec's political and religious leaders, however, generally favored Franco's fascists, who carried the standards of Rome against the legions of Communism. "The grand theories of liberty, of equality, of fraternity are worth nothing," Premier Duplessis told a huge rally the day after the Spanish delegates were driven off the stage by the anti-Communist demonstration of students and nationalists. "Those that count are the three theological virtues: faith, charity, and hope."

For at least twenty-five years Frank had worried about an embryonic fascism in Quebec's traditionalist and Catholic nationalism. He had seen it in the blue shirts and anti-Semitism of Quebec's National Social Christian Party, in the hysterical denunciations of socialist atheism by Quebec's leading bishops, and in Duplessis's bullies. If any major reform of the constitution was needed, he came to believe, it should take the form of a bill of rights that protected all individuals and minorities from the tyranny of dictators and mobs. Those rights would include protection for the French and English languages. "What can touch the soul more deeply," he used to ask, "than the language we learn at our mother's breast?" Thus, he supported Quebec's promotion of the French language, until it clashed with his lifetime desire to build a bilingual Canada. He took offense, for example, if the signs in his bank wished him "Joyeux Noël" but not "Merry Christmas" – "It's creeping unilingualism!" – and he joined legal battles to defend the constitutional rights of Quebec's Protestant school system.

If Frank Scott sounded like Pierre Elliott Trudeau, it was because

Trudeau prided himself on being a protégé of Frank Scott. So did many of the senior civil servants, Supreme Court judges, constitutional academics, and Quebec politicians who had passed through Frank's lectures at the McGill law school – including two of the Tétrault brothers. Trudeau once introduced Frank to Queen Elizabeth by saying, only partly in jest, "This is the man who taught me everything I know about the constitution." Together they had fought for civil rights and the union movement against Duplessis. They had journeyed down the Mackenzie River in the Northwest Territories and argued for hours at parties on Clarke Avenue. Quebec independence would become unnecessary, both men agreed, if political reform and guaranteed rights finally allowed French Canadians to find justice and power in both Quebec City and Ottawa.

In those days I thought that special status was a reasonable concession to the reality of Quebec, and I was not wise enough to appreciate how Frank's position differed from the prejudice I was tired of reading in the *Gazette*. If Quebec had to promote the French language, I had written him a month before the FLQ kidnapings, "the *political* action of restricting the freedom of a minority is often the result of that minority's allowing itself to appear an outside, alien, and threatening force at a critical period of history." (Coming upon that sentence seventeen years later in a biography of Scott, I blushed with shame, for I recognized it as the essential argument on which the Nazis justified their persecution of the Jews.) "You often," I continued, with all the authority of a graduate student, "in discussing this issue, seem defensive, petty, and unsympathetic."

I had not heard from him since.

———————

I was expecting to see Frank and Marian that night in North Hatley, a pretty resort village on Lake Massawippi about fifteen miles from where I had been to school. Normally I would have stayed with the

Scotts, but I had come with a friend and we stayed nearby. Among our hosts' other houseguests was Paul Chamberland, a well-known Quebec poet who had been invited to read from his work at a convocation at Bishop's University in Lennoxville.

Chamberland was a small, slender, youthful man. His childlike manner, brown leather cords, and straight yellow hair that flowed from his bald pate to his shoulders gave him the look of a medieval page. Neither his quiet voice nor his bright eyes nor his delicate features hinted that he had been one of the major polemicists on behalf of the FLQ at the time of the Westmount bombings. Inspired by the rhetoric of Walt Whitman and Allen Ginsberg, his long, incantational poems in *Parti pris* had been hymns to rage and violent revolution. "I am a man ashamed to be a man," he wrote in "The Posterhanger Howls," as translated by Malcolm Reid:

> I am a man from whom manhood is kept
> I am a man attacked through his compatriots and who will never
>   perform for other men an act with any sense until he has
>   effaced at last the infamy it is to be a French Canadian.

By 1970, though, Chamberland had been reborn into cosmic consciousness. Sex and nature had replaced weapons and power. Or so the distinguished English professors of Bishop's University had thought when they invited him to address their students, by chance on the day when many of his friends were in prison under the War Measures Act. The gasp was audible when Chamberland began by declaring himself a member of the FLQ, an illegal organization since dawn that morning. The governors of the university squirmed in their seats, as if worrying whether they too could be arrested for associating with this criminal, and a few of them eyed his shoulder-bag as if it might be carrying a bomb.

But Chamberland's FLQ was no longer the Front de Libération du Québec: it was "Faire l'amour au Québec," Free Love Quebec:

Free ChiLdren of Kébek

Join together against foolishness and hatred.
And against the arrogance and hard-heartedness
    of all those obsessed with power, all
    the big and little riffraff, wherever
    you may find them

– he chanted –

    To the masked comrades I say:
    Don't be a revolution behind.

The next morning, my friends and I went for a walk with him. It was an especially beautiful day, warm for October and radiant with autumn leaves, which made it harder to accept that Paul would probably be in jail by nightfall. He had already heard that the police were awaiting his return to Montreal that afternoon, but he did not seem to care. We walked up the dirt road past the Hatley Inn and came to the plain white farmhouse that belonged to Pauline Julien, the singer, and Gérald Godin, the poet. Both were dedicated nationalists, and both had been taken in the night. Chamberland went up to one of their apple trees. "I'll bring these to Pauline and Gérald," he said, and picked two apples.

As Paul Chamberland was leaving North Hatley, Frank Scott arrived. Frank had been delayed in Montreal by a series of calls from the prime minister's advisers, the Quebec minister of justice, and the FLQ's lawyer, all seeking help from their former teacher. He invited us to dinner.

"The rule of law has to be maintained," he insisted over the meal.

"Democracy has to be able to protect itself. These hooligans are holding up *our* government, threatening *our* civil rights. They have to be stopped. And so do the hotheads who are encouraging them. People are afraid, the situation is volatile, and the War Measures Act is the only instrument we've got, however clumsy, to restore some sense of order."

He was so adamant there seemed little point in arguing. Even Marian seemed unwilling to challenge him. Though delicate and kindly, she seldom hesitated to pit her heart against his logic. "She's an FLQ cell of her own," Frank used to joke. As a white-haired grand-mother she had carried pickets in demonstrations against nuclear weapons and the Vietnam war, and her antipathy toward any form of colonialism made her open-minded about Quebec independence, through violence if necessary. She never minded whether she was cutting her own throat.

Marian's father, Robert John Dale, had been a well-to-do British emigrant who established an insurance business in Montreal at the turn of the century. Marian had grown up in a large house in the Square Mile with servants and a French governess. "The sun never sets on the British Empire," she said as a girl, spinning the globe in her nursery, and every summer she went "home" to England with her parents. But she was sensitive and rebellious, with a longing to be an artist and a sharp eye for injustice. If Frank's childhood memory was of the French-speaking gang that threatened to beat him up on his way home from school, Marian's was of the French Canadian servant who came from a large family in the shantytown near the Dales' summer house at Dorval. She had been bothered when Mar-guerite was told to call her "Miss Marian," even though they were the same age; and she had felt worse when Marguerite was informed, upon her marriage to a chauffeur at another house, that she would not be able to have children while "in service" to her new employer.

"It's an unfair world," Marian had been told when she first protested, "but there's nothing we can do but enjoy it." Marian never accepted that, though few people have savored the joys of the world more deeply. I could see how upset she was at Frank's arguments by her pallor and her very silence.

After dinner Frank took me aside and said, "I want to speak to you, in private." I had forgotten about my letter to him, but I knew he was going to mention it now. For the first time I experienced what his students must have felt when he summoned them to discuss a thesis: the stern eye, the professorial tone. We sat in a corner of the living room. "I got your letter. We'll talk about it someday, but this is not the time. I've been ill and I'm very tired. All I want to say is, listen to the other side. I worry, my boy, I worry that you don't always listen to the other side."

Poor Frank, he did look tired. So I held my tongue and did not protest that I felt baffled by all the sides I heard shouting around me. Westmount would have pegged Paul Chamberland, if it had known of him, as an FLQ fanatic. The FLQ would have pegged Marian Scott, if it had known of her, as a Westmount matron. And what of Frank himself? Westmount knew him as an old socialist who had been told he could not get a mention in the *Gazette* unless he raped a girl on the corner of Peel and St Catherine. The FLQ held him up as proof that the anglo, however genial and well intentioned, will always be a traitor to Quebec.

I no longer had the comfort of simple convictions. Simple convictions had caused four hundred and sixty-five innocent people to be jailed so that a couple of dozen criminals could be found. Simple convictions had twisted the chain around Pierre Laporte's neck and strangled him to death in the name of the Quebec people. Simple convictions had set me against my father and against Frank Scott. Simple convictions had cost Frank many of his French Canadian friends and much of his hard-earned reputation in the progressive circles of Quebec. Suddenly I felt profoundly tired myself, and I longed to be in a place where families did not have to quarrel about political principles and friends could talk of poetry once more.

Frank never gave up, though the last years of his life were marked by a sense of defeat and sorrow at the passing of his Canada. He once described to me a dream that had caused him to awake weeping with happiness: he and a nebulous figure symbolizing French Canada met on a white plain and were reconciled at last by a handshake. When he died, he was more alone than ever on that white plain, but his heart was still true to French Canada and to the vision of humanity that had made him a great man.

The Path Not Taken, 1976

GUY PRUD'HOMME and I were born in the same year, 1948. Cousins, we had grown up not far from each other in the same city. His grandmother Cocoune, the youngest child of Guillaume and Alphonsine Moncel, was my mother's godmother, and his father Maurice had been my mother's playmate when they were children at family reunions. Yet, sequestered in our different districts and different languages, Guy and I had never met – or even heard of one another.

Guy was my alter ego, the path not taken, what I might have become if my grandfather and my mother had remained in the French Canadian fold. We had begun at the same place, our great-grandfather's house on Sherbrooke Street at the start of the twentieth century, and we had evolved into complete strangers. When René Moncel married Edith Brady and moved toward Westmount, Cocoune Moncel married Hector Prud'homme and moved toward Outremont. Hector's father, who had lived just two doors away from

Guillaume Moncel, had founded a successful hardware business; Hector and his brothers had continued the trade. All of Hector's four sons except poor Jacques, who was born handicapped and died young, had been forced (as one of them put it) "to count goddamn screws," though Roger had dreamed of becoming a diplomat, André had wanted to be an artist, and Maurice had gone off to serve with the Canadian army during the Second World War. For Hector Prud'homme had believed above all in the authority of the father and the religion of hard work. Tall, loud, portly, well dressed and perfectly bald, he had exuded a competence and confidence that took charge of the world. After his death Cocoune, a gentle soul who seemed lost in a permanent haze of cigarette smoke and terrified by a game of bridge, had to be rescued from a hotel in the Laurentians because she did not know how to write a check for the bill.

Maurice, their eldest son, had been content enough in the family business until it was sold in 1970, perhaps because he was by nature a happy-go-lucky fellow with an unsophisticated style and a jovial manner, perhaps because he was simply happy to be alive. He had been severely wounded while overseas and marked forever by the horrors of war. Once home, he only wanted to settle down with his bride Renée in the bungalow they built near his parents' home in Outremont. There they raised their three sons and one daughter.

Guy was the first born to Renée and Maurice, beating out his twin Robert by a few minutes. When I was with the British teachers at Selwyn House and Bishop's College School, Guy was with the Catholic clergy at Mont-Jésus-Marie and Académie Saint-Germain. When I was at McGill, Guy was at Collège Jean-de-Brébeuf. When I was studying politics in Ottawa, Guy was studying law at the Université de Sherbrooke. We were like cultural mirrors of each other: when we were children and our parents wanted to say something privately in front of us, mine said it in high-school French and his said it in English.

"Sometimes my parents used to speak English at supper, to teach us, but it seemed sort of ridiculous, so I didn't really speak English until I was eight," he recalled. "Then they sent me and my brother Robert, who now lives in Vancouver, to Powter's camp for the month of August. There were only four French Canadians among a hundred and thirty English kids. I had never been away from home before, and I had never really known any English kids, except one at school and a few on the street who spoke French all the time, so I cried my eyes out the first two nights. I didn't know what was going on for days. Eventually I found the fun, and I went back every summer for ten years. There was a certain amount of 'fucking Frog' and 'French peasouper,' but I got along well and even won the best counselor award in 1967. I gave a big speech about how everyone should be bilingual."

Our paths, we discovered, had crossed indirectly in a few places: watching Pépinot and Capucine on TV in 1953, following the Canadiens to five straight Stanley Cup victories between 1956 and 1960, and attending the huge demonstration that took place at the gates of McGill on March 28, 1969 – though I had been a mere observer, on the steps of an old Square Mile home with Frank and Marian Scott – as five thousand nationalists chanted "McGill français!" and lobbed rocks and Molotov cocktails into the campus until they were dispersed by the charge of a riot squad on motorcycles and a phalanx of well-armed policemen in visored helmets.

"I can't even remember what it was about," Guy confessed. "To make McGill more French, or to get more money for the French universities, or something like that. I was pushed into it by some friends at school because I had a motorcycle to escort the marchers. I wasn't much of a nationalist in the 1960s. Brébeuf was a very conservative school run by the Jesuits, and most of the boys were *les snobs* from the elite families, though I did have René Lévesque's son in my class. I remember the death of Duplessis, I knew about Lesage and the Quiet Revolution, but there wasn't much political interest until the bombs started going off. In fact, there had been a guy in my class named

Corbo, a small kid from Town of Mount Royal, who was later killed planting a bomb somewhere. That got everyone talking."

Ironically, I was more of a Quebec nationalist than Guy in those days. The Prud'hommes had always been ardent Liberals. Duplessis's government had boycotted their hardware business, it was said, because of their Liberal connections. Maurice, in particular, having risked his life for the defense of Canada, had no patience with either the anti-French prejudice of the federal Conservatives or the anti-federalist biases of the Quebec nationalists; nor had Renée, the daughter of an open-minded notary who, like Albert Tétrault, had hated the narrowness of Duplessis and the Church and sent her to school in English as a result. While I disagreed with Trudeau's hard line against special status, therefore, Guy worked to make Trudeau leader of the Liberal Party and prime minister of Canada in 1968. While I opposed the imposition of the War Measures Act during the FLQ crisis of 1970, Guy supported it. While I witnessed the election of René Lévesque and the Parti Québécois on November 15, 1976, with a kind of detachment – by demonstrating the flexibility of Canadian federalism and subjecting the idealism of the nationalists to the reality of governing, I imagined, the very triumph of the PQ might break the momentum toward independence – Guy wept.

"It was a partisan thing," he explained. "I had campaigned for Bourassa's Liberals in 1970 and 1973 and I had gone all out, day and night, during the campaign of 1976. I wasn't traumatized by the threat of separation, but I was exhausted and disappointed. There was a practical side too: I was working at the time at Geoffrion, Prud'homme, the law firm founded by my great-uncle Alex, a big Liberal, and we had a lot of Liberal government work. The defeat jeopardized that, of course, and I soon found myself out of a job."

Lévesque's success was less the triumph of nationalism than the disgrace of Robert Bourassa. Those Quebeckers who did not hate Bourassa thought him ridiculous. (Once I saw him enter a Montreal bar, no doubt thinking himself the leader stooping to conquer the hearts of his people; he was greeted by so many derisive hoots that he ducked out the door at once.) Trudeau thought him a coward, Lévesque thought him a *vendu*, the English thought him a hypocrite, the unions thought him a pawn of business, and almost everyone thought him "Bou-Bou" the incompetent. He had spent more and more time hiding in his well-guarded bunker trying to avoid any decisions lest the strain muss his perfect hair. Lévesque, by contrast, seemed open, affable, and heedless of vanity except for the futile and endearing gesture of covering his baldness with a few gray strands.

The Parti Québécois had been able to rouse the people around one nationalist issue: the survival of the French language. With the collapse of the Roman Catholic Church as a force in Quebec in the 1960s, the French language had become the sacred heart of Quebec's identity. In practical terms the English language remained the most obvious impediment to professional ambition and cultural survival; whatever Trudeau was trying to do for the French language in the rest of Canada hardly mattered inside Quebec. Indeed, bilingualism and language rights seemed to bolster English in Quebec more than French elsewhere. What mattered was that the corporations and salespeople in downtown Montreal still spoke English. What mattered was that most immigrants were settling among the prosperous, English-speaking minority at a time when French Canada's birthrate was plunging from record highs to record lows.

"Everywhere outdoor advertising continued to throw down on us the unilingual sneer of a dominant minority," Lévesque recalled later. "Nothing seemed able to stop the assimilation of immigrants. Our economic inferiority continued to be carefully maintained from the highest echelons to the level of simple foreman. We weren't told to 'speak white!' any more, but we were still obliged to do so in many cases, right here in our own home."

In 1974 the Liberals had tried to make the issue their own. They had declared French the official language of Quebec, employed carrots and sticks to advance the use of French in business and on the streets, and forced the children of immigrants who could not speak English to go to French schools. Frank Scott had condemned the legislation as a betrayal of the historic right of English Quebeckers – "genocide by erosion" – as had Claude Tétrault during a meeting with Bourassa on behalf of the Montreal Board of Trade, but not even Pierre Trudeau had had the political power to prevent it. Then, just before the election, there had been a nasty controversy over whether it was safe for Quebec's air-traffic controllers to speak French on the job. The issue had become the latest symbol of colonialism's relentless grip and played into the hands of the Parti Québécois.

In 1979, my cousin Guy went to work with Claude Tétrault as a lawyer for Alcan, first at the head office in Montreal and then at Jonquière in the Saguenay region. Eight years in the Saguenay changed his entire perspective. Isolated and almost entirely French-speaking, the people of the Saguenay tended to see Quebec independence as a worthy and even obvious idea, based on their deep-rooted sense of belonging. "They are full of resentment and aggression against *les maudits Anglais*," Guy said. "It wasn't so long ago that you had to speak English to be a foreman or better, and all the management jobs were in the hands of the English. People remember that, and if the situation has improved to an extent, it's because they fought for the French language. Once, I remember, when I was at head office, I circulated a memo in English – 80 per cent of the company's head-office work was done in English, even most of its correspondence with France – and my memo came back from the Saguenay marked, 'Write it in French.' When I got there myself, I understood. English may be the international language everywhere nowadays, but Quebec had the right to try to be a French-speaking place. It did not have to separate, I thought, but it would if Canada didn't recognize Quebec's need to preserve its language."

"Oh?" his father would goad him. "Have we lost our language?"

"No, but thank God we're fighting for it," Guy replied. "The pressure of English is still on us."

"That's because we're in North America, not Timbuktu," Maurice countered.

"Everyone has to accept that when they live in Quebec, they have to know French," his son argued back. "I don't want to take away individual rights, but I want to make sure that my children will speak French. That's all. If the English and the immigrants won't accept that, then we should make them accept it."

"Great," Maurice responded sarcastically, "and they'll all leave."

Theirs was the kind of tense argument that divided every family during the months leading up to the referendum the Parti Québécois had promised to hold before it moved toward independence. (A florist in Montreal noticed a dramatic decrease in sales during this period, because the quarrels had discouraged relatives from sending as many flowers to each other for birthdays, anniversaries, weddings, and even funerals.) The vote was held on May 20, 1980. Like most people in the Saguenay, Guy Prud'homme marked "Yes" to give the Quebec government permission to negotiate a vague new deal based on political sovereignty and economic association; but more than 60 per cent of Quebeckers said "No."

"I wasn't convinced by my separatist friends," Guy explained a decade later. "I just wanted to show English Canada that we were serious, in order to make some progress. I might have voted 'No' if I hadn't been sure that the referendum was going to be defeated, but I wanted to arouse the English, especially the English in Quebec, and the comfortable French Canadians like my parents. They're afraid of losing their standard of living if anything changes, and they're so pro-English they're almost anti-French. But I'm not afraid. Some things may be more difficult, but life will go on. Canada is like a family: we have trouble living under the same roof, but we're stuck like glue."

Shock Treatment, 1977

D on't be afraid," a man had shouted in my ear, in English, while I stood high in the rafters of the Paul Sauvé Arena in east-end Montreal the night René Lévesque and the Parti Québécois won the 1976 election. Tens of thousands of people whooped, embraced, sang, and waved the Quebec flag as though they had been liberated from an oppressor. "We won't hurt you," he said.

Though I had met some cold shoulders and dirty looks in Quebec, the only real confrontation had been in a bar on Rue Saint-Denis when I accidentally took someone's chair. "Calisse de crisse de tabarnak!" he shouted. "Bloody English, the moment you turn your back, they steal something from you! Just like Wolfe on the Plains of Abraham!" And everyone had laughed, including me. This general civility might have been politeness or it might have been fear; it might have been the Catholic tradition of suffering in silence or a Norman respect for the almighty dollar; but I thought it the mark of a tolerant, good-hearted people. Once, when asking a Bell operator for a number in the village of Sacré-Coeur-de-Marie (yes, there is a village called Sacred Heart of Mary), I mispronounced *coeur* as *cour*. "Coeur, coeur," the operator said in the voice of a French Canadian mother. "You have to learn that, because when you want to say, 'I love you with all my heart,' it will be better if you say it in French, 'de tout mon coeur.'"

And yet, in the abstract or among themselves, French Quebeckers can be full of prejudice and suspicion toward *les autres*, the strangers in their midst. "I was taught by the nuns to fear the English and the

Protestants," a friend once told me, "and eventually I had to get out of Quebec City because I couldn't stand the narrow-minded racism of the place."

The psychological roots of this xenophobia go back to the Old Regime of New France, of course, where anyone not French and Catholic was either a rarity or a threat. Huguenots were apostates; Englishmen were enemies; Indians were savages; and blacks were slaves. Esther Brandeau, alias Jacques La Fargue, the only Jew known to have turned up in Canada before the Conquest, was shipped back to France as soon as the best efforts of the cleverest Jesuits proved unable to convert her "flighty" mind; Joseph Hains and Elizabeth Lamax were allowed to stay on condition they assimilate as quickly as possible; and Rose Latulippe was warned not to dance with the Devil. After the Conquest, cut off from the main source of French-speaking immigrants and surrounded on all sides by the English language, French Canada's patriots and priests urged their people to keep a physical and social distance from the corrupting ways of the eternally damned for the sake of their individual and collective souls. Even French-speaking Protestants, Jews, and Muslims were directed toward the English-speaking school system lest their heresies subvert the faith of the French Canadian race.

"We wish to purify this race of foreign growths in order to develop in it intensively the original culture," wrote Lionel Groulx, the influential ideologue whose nationalism had been inspired by the racial theories of Gobineau and Maurras in France and the totalitarian movements of Mussolini and Salazar in Europe. In 1922 he summed up his views in a didactic novel, *Call of the Race*, in which a French Canadian husband realizes that he has betrayed his culture and his blood by marrying an English Canadian woman. Individuals cannot transcend their race, the hero decides, and inevitably the couple must separate. René Lévesque himself cited the book as a childhood favorite.

"Hating the English has been, since 1840, the motor of French

Canadian nationalism, of Quebec nationalism," William Johnson wrote in his survey of "anglophobia" in Quebec literature and politics. "Actually, the English are begrudged because they threaten the realization of the myth that has underlain the intellectual and literary tradition of Quebec from the start: the original earthly paradise, followed by the paradise lost, and, pointing toward the future, the natural aim of history: the paradise regained or the promised land." Time and again, the English have been cast in the role of the snake.

Convenient as a political theory, interesting as an artistic metaphor, as an intellectual precept it was clearly bunk. What of Hugh Munro, who forsook his father and his faith for the love of Angélique Larocque? What of René Moncel, who gave up his language and his heritage for the sake of Edith Brady? What of Emile Nelligan, born in 1879 of an Irish father and a French Canadian mother, who became one of Quebec's greatest poets? What of Mary Travers, born at the end of the nineteenth century to an English-speaking laborer and his French-speaking wife, who became "La Bolduc," one of French Canada's most popular folk singers and song writers? Indeed, what of Daniel Johnson, the nationalist premier of Quebec whom everyone called "Danny Boy" because of his Irish roots, and what of the ultranationalists in Lévesque's own Cabinet named Robert Burns and Louis O'Neill?

If the "French race" was not quite as pure as Groulx wished, the "English race" was even less so. It included the British conquerors, of course, but it soon included American Loyalists, Irish Catholics, and the first Jews. Then, in the twentieth century, the term absorbed every nationality whose immigrants joined the English-speaking community: Russians, Germans, Italians, Greeks, blacks, Chinese – they all became "English" within a generation or two because they did not speak French. By 1981 only 60 per cent of Quebec's anglophones were of British origin, but the nationalists did not look upon the other 40 per cent with greater favor just because they did not live in Westmount or were not related to General Wolfe's occupying army.

From time to time, in fact, French Canadian nationalists have singled out one particular subspecies of *maudits Anglais* for special opprobrium: the Jews. They had killed Christ, after all, which Catholic historians such as Lionel Groulx and fascist politicians such as Adrian Arcand thought even worse than having killed the Marquis de Montcalm. Anti-Semitism in Quebec peaked during the Depression, when nationalist rhetoric strove to blame *les autres* for the economic hardships. The most obvious others were the Jews. Numbering more than sixty thousand by 1931, they were the largest group of neither French nor British origin in Quebec; they lived cheek by jowl with the French Canadian working classes in the buffer zone along St Lawrence Boulevard that divided Montreal into an English-speaking west and French-speaking east; they competed as cheap labor and shopkeepers; and they had started to do well as merchants, garment manufacturers, and landlords. Even Hector Prud'homme and Albert Tétrault, despite their general liberalism, never cared much for the Jews, according to some of their children.

Such prejudice was rarely translated into open persecution – except in English Montreal, where Jews suffered from quotas at McGill University, encountered restrictions in most professions and private clubs, and entered less easily than Roman Catholics into the finer homes of Westmount. The first of Montreal's many large synagogues was established in 1777. The French Canadian voters of Trois-Rivières elected a Jew as their representative in the assembly in 1807. Jewish schools, hospitals, and social agencies flourished, often with government support, and Montreal became the headquarters of the Canadian Jewish Congress. Indeed, Montreal's Jewish community became one of the most successful Jewish communities in the world, whether in politics or business or the arts. But it did so almost completely in English.

English was the language of commerce and the American Dream, after all, when the waves of Jewish refugees poured into Montreal, and the priests in charge of the French school system had no desire to see Jewish children in their classrooms. Even when significant numbers of French-speaking Sephardim began to arrive from North Africa in the 1950s, they were pushed toward the established, English-speaking Ashkenazim, with whom they had little in common.

French Canadians and Jews inhabited the same city like two proud families. Occasionally they intermarried. Occasionally they formed strong friendships, based in no small measure on a mutual dislike of the anglos. In nationalist circles, however, indifference was rekindled into suspicion during the 1960s. The Jews were again made aliens, not because they were Jews but because they were anglophones, and prominent Jewish names began to show up on the FLQ's hit lists. However benign and tolerant most Quebec nationalists liked to think themselves, the Jews saw the emergence of an ethnic nationalism of the sort that too many of them had seen in Russia, Eastern Europe, and Germany. Montreal had an especially high proportion of Holocaust survivors and their descendants, in fact, and their collective memory had shaped the entire community.

"The Parti Québécois," Charles Bronfman, the liquor billionaire not known for undue hysteria, told a synagogue audience on the eve of the 1976 election, are "a bunch of bastards who are trying to kill us!" I myself had not shared his fear (though I did know some Westmount families who spent the night at the Airport Hilton in case they had to flee), but perhaps I should have been more afraid. Though the Parti Québécois was essentially a moderate and democratic movement under Lévesque, it was equally a nationalist one, dedicated above all to advancing the welfare of purebred, French-speaking Quebeckers above the welfare of Quebec's other citizens – of which I happened to be one.

———————

Back in 1961, a Montreal psychiatrist named Camille Laurin had analyzed French Canadians as an immature people full of delusions and bent on revenge against the parent who denied them full power: the English. Now, in 1976, Dr Laurin found himself the new minister in charge of the language laws. With the self-confident zeal of his profession, he set about using these laws to help get French-speaking Quebeckers off the couch and into the world, mature and potent at last. The collective neurosis that contributed to "the weakness, the disorganization, and the vulnerability of the French Canadian man" required, as he once put it, a "collective psychotherapy." The therapy he prescribed was shock treatment. It was called Bill 101.

Passed as one of the first acts of the Parti Québécois government, Bill 101 was designed to make French dominant in every aspect of government and commerce in the province. If English could not be eradicated altogether, it was to be contained by edict and patrolled by the "language police." Only children with at least one parent who had gone to an English school in Quebec would be allowed to go to public school in English – a rude surprise to immigrants from England and the United States, not to mention the rest of Canada. Individual *privileges*, such as freedom of expression, had to defer to the collective *rights* of the Quebec majority. René Lévesque himself had been appalled when he first saw the proposal, but Laurin had persuaded him that it was necessary in order to cure the fundamental neurosis of French Canadians.

Others saw Bill 101 as a symptom of the same immaturity, delusion, and revenge the good doctor had diagnosed fifteen years earlier. Certainly its intention was as much to eliminate English as to elevate French. "The Quebec we wish to build will be essentially French," said a government document that preceded the legislation. "There will no longer be any question of a bilingual Quebec." English signs had to vanish from sight; English schools had to wither away; and according to Dr Laurin, "English-speaking Quebeckers had best learn to see themselves as a minority and not as the Quebec wing of the English Canadian majority."

Often, however, the English-speaking community was erased

altogether. In a first draft of Bill 101, for example, the government affirmed "that the French language has always been the language of the Quebec people" – a remarkable blindness toward those families who had been speaking English in Montreal, the Eastern Townships, the Gaspé, and the Ottawa Valley for at least a century and a half – and in common usage, *Québécois* suggested an exclusivity beyond its simple meaning of Quebecker.

From the early days of New France until well into the nineteenth century, the French-speaking inhabitants of North America had been known as *les Canadiens*. When the English-speaking immigrants to Upper and Lower Canada began to refer to themselves as Canadians, an obvious confusion arose; so, following the Act of Union of 1840, the Canadiens became universally *les Canadiens français*. In nationalist circles during the 1960s, however, French Canadian became the equivalent of Negro, an offensive term that reeked of colonialism and Uncle Tomism. It was rapidly replaced by Québécois, even though – or perhaps because – the new self-definition excluded those French Canadians (like Ottawa politicians) outside Quebec and those English Canadians (like me) inside.

Since then, French-speaking Quebeckers who traced their families back to New France were les Québécois. When a distinction had to be made, their superiority was connoted in the expressions *Québécois de vieille souche* (of original stock) or *Québécois pure laine* (pure wool). English-speaking Quebeckers of whatever ethnic origin were usually *les anglophones, les anglos, les Anglais*, or, more rarely, *les Anglo-Québécois*. Immigrants whose mother tongue was neither French nor English had a special label – *les allophones* or *les allos*, derived from the Greek word for other – though sometimes they were given the dignity of *néo-Québécois*. As if that were not sufficiently caste-like, pure-wool Québécois such as Pierre Trudeau were occasionally stripped of their status for "betraying" the nationalists' ideal, while successful Acadians such as the novelist Antonine Maillet and Franco-Manitobans such as the novelist Gabrielle Roy were often elevated into Québécois for the glory of the Quebec nation.

In the early 1970s, the first sign of a good Quebecker had still been the willingness to function in French. But as more anglophones became bilingual and more allophones were absorbed into the French-speaking community, the standard shifted subtly from language to culture. Haitian blacks, Vietnamese Buddhists, Lebanese Christians, and Moroccan Jews were still *les autres*, even if few of them had any ties to *les anglos* and all of them had French as their mother tongue. They were not likely to carry in their genes the glory of New France, the humiliation of the Conquest, the pride of the Quiet Revolution, or the dream of independence.

"If you speak French but don't have the right name, you still have a problem," a Jewish professor who had emigrated from France more than twenty years earlier once told me. "I'm not considered a true Québécois, I'm a néo-Québécois, and I would be only a little bit worse if I only spoke English."

———————

On a visit to Westmount in 1981 I found a fellow named Heinrich Ribicki weeping in his butcher shop. Ribicki and his wife had come to Canada in 1957 with the dream of owning a family business, and in 1971 they bought Haines Fine Food Market from old Mr Haines himself. Heinrich Ribicki was a good butcher, apparently, and his little business grew with his reputation. Then, in 1979, he started receiving visits from the language inspectors.

"They were bugging me so much, too often," he said in a soft, thickly accented voice, his face reddening. First they had a problem with the "Serve Yourself" notice on the fridge. Then they objected to an expensive hand-painted sign in the window. Then they wanted him to remove the outdoor sign that read "Our Specialty: European Foods." Finally they insisted that the Sunkist orange display had to be in French only. "I was boiling. My wife was born in Czechoslovakia of German descent. She went through this type of persecution when the Communists took away her father's farm and threw her out of the country. She said, 'This is the beginning.'" Rather than change another sign, Heinrich Ribicki sold his store to a young Korean couple.

Nick's restaurant turned into Chez Nick overnight; Tweedy Clothes pulled "Clothes" off its storefront in what looked like a fit of pique. In his century-old shoe shop, a Victorian-looking merchant named George Smithers scratched his head about what to do with all the boxes marked Buster Brown. "They tell me to take down a sign, I take it down," he sighed, sitting at his heavy rolltop desk, surrounded by wood-pegged benches, handmade wooden ladders, and an ancient cash register. With a weary gesture that included his shop, Westmount, and himself, he added, "We're all antiques around here."

Nor were the effects of the language laws merely cosmetic. Because the laws discouraged English-speaking immigrants and opened new doors for French-speaking Quebeckers, French increasingly took over in the boardrooms and on the streets. My father's brokerage firm gave up its Dickensian name of Oswald, Drinkwater & Graham when it merged with Lévesque Beaubien. Dale & Company, the insurance business started by Marian Scott's father, was bought by the father of the PQ's minister of finance, Jacques Parizeau. The Ritz got its first French Canadian general manager.

Between 1976 and 1981 more than one hundred thousand English-speaking Quebeckers left the province, including a quarter of Montreal's Jewish community. Some fled from fear of oppression. Some were unable or unwilling to speak French. Some were simply tired of turmoil. Some were drawn to the oil boom in western Canada or the financial incentives in the United States. Many were young professionals, who left behind an older, weaker, and more despondent remnant that saw nothing but decline for its population and institutions in the future. One of my sisters left Quebec when her husband was offered a better job in the pulp and paper industry in Australia;

my other sister left when she found work in interior design in Toronto. Two of my three brothers ended up in Toronto, too, because it presented more opportunities in corporate finance and urban planning; and my own career as a journalist carried me out of Quebec, first to Ottawa and then to Toronto, though I never gave up my cabin in the Eastern Townships nor my fundamental identity as a Quebecker. (Like a New Yorker in Los Angeles, I defined myself by where I had come from, for Ontario seemed a kind of betrayal and its self-promotion as an "industrial heartland" seemed an oxymoron.) Even my parents moved to Toronto to be near their children. We all started a new life with new friends and new street corners; and if we ever looked back to our old life, we missed our youth rather than Montreal, for Montreal, despite its charms, was no longer the city we had known.

In truth, I had no nostalgia for the British Raj. In practice I had no problem reading French signs and no need to worry about French schooling. But intellectually and emotionally I felt a profound sense of betrayal. The language laws betrayed every English Quebecker – and English Canadian – who had learned French, embraced French Canadian culture, and defended Quebec nationalism as neither extreme nor intolerant. Bill 101 demonstrated an authoritarian, even totalitarian disregard for individual freedoms and minority rights that confirmed Frank Scott's darkest suspicions and proved Pierre Trudeau's argument that ethnocentric nationalism will always lead to reactionary measures.

In the 1960s I had been stirred by the French Canadian plea for justice because it had been argued from two noble precepts: minorities should not be oppressed by majorities, and people should have the right to their language wherever their numbers make it possible. By the late 1970s, however, I was hearing moderate French Quebeckers use exactly the same rhetoric I had grown to abhor in English Canadians: we are the majority here, so everyone should speak our language and assimilate into our culture. Worse, I heard that human rights were now mere privileges, to be given or taken at the whim of a fickle majority to suit the mood of the day.

Had French Canada made no gains since 1960, Quebec's draconian measures might have seemed more understandable. But Pierre Trudeau had brought his own Quiet Revolution to Ottawa, raising French Canadians to unimagined power over the whole country. "French power" became a cliché of the 1970s because of the hold of the French Canadian ministers and bureaucrats over Ottawa. Never again could anyone conceive of a prime minister who did not speak French. Canada had come to define itself, however reluctantly in places, as a bilingual and multicultural nation, with French services available from coast to coast and French-immersion schools in vogue in Vancouver and Toronto. The federal government had become as ardent a defender of the French language in North America as Quebec City had once been (even more ardent, perhaps, because it worked to protect the million or so French-speaking Canadians outside Quebec). In business, the arts, and international affairs French Canadians flourished. Indeed, the government of Quebec itself had never been stronger or wealthier, and the system had proved flexible enough to accommodate even a separatist party and its language policies. Trudeau had made his point: even without special status or independence, French Canadians had been able to overcome the full force of history and numbers simply by showing the will to do so.

Most Quebeckers took the point. They had been used to sending contradictory political signals to Ottawa and Quebec City – voting for Trudeau and Bourassa, or Trudeau and Lévesque, at the same time – for what could have been more advantageous than to have two rival sons in two powerful centers trying to outdo each other for the good (and the support) of the family? But on the only occasion when the choice between federalism and the softest form of independence was put to them directly, in the provincial referendum of 1980, most of them voted for Canada. Four years after the PQ's extraordinary victory, René Lévesque and five thousand of his followers were back in the Paul Sauvé Arena, this time in tears. At one o'clock in the morning I watched them carrying their grief and frustration through the streets of downtown Montreal, waving their flags and yelling, "Next time! Next time!"

"To my fellow Quebeckers who have been wounded by defeat," Pierre Trudeau said on television after the particularly bitter and divisive campaign, "I wish to say simply that we have all lost a little in this referendum. If you take account of the broken friendships, the strained family relationships, the hurt pride, there is no one among us who has not suffered some wound which we must try to heal in the days and weeks to come."

With Lévesque stalemated and Bourassa in a kind of political exile in Europe since his defeat in 1976, Trudeau had finally taken his place at the head of the table. Or so it seemed.

The Dutiful Daughter, 1980

THE DEFEAT of the 1980 referendum marked the low point of my cousin Danielle Daigneault's political involvement. The next day she was too exhausted and depressed to go to work. Exhausted not just from the weeks of campaigning from door to door, daybreak to midnight, on behalf of the "Yes" side, but from fifteen years of argument and activity on behalf of Quebec independence. Depressed not just from the loss of a vote, but from the crushing of a dream.

"It was an enormous disappointment, really tough," she recalled, puffing on one cigarette after another, though radiant with health, confidence, style, and youthfulness. A grandmother at forty-six, she seemed as perky and pretty as Ali McGraw or Geneviève Bujold, and her eyes were as bright as they were blue. "My husband and I watched the results at home on TV, with seven or eight friends, and we were all heartbroken. Quebec had torn itself apart and missed an opportunity that may never come again. There was an energy then, and a caliber of people in the Parti Québécois and the government of Quebec, never again equaled."

Danielle, born in Montreal in 1945 to Arthur Tétrault and his third wife Janine, was living at the time in Sainte-Luce, just outside of Rimouski on the south shore of the lower St Lawrence, with her husband Robert and their three daughters. She had been a separatist since her days as an architecture and history student at the Université de Montréal in the 1960s; and she had become a supporter of René Lévesque the moment he left the Liberal Party in 1968. From then until she joined the provincial civil service she had been a member of the PQ and one of its more enthusiastic volunteers at election time.

There was nothing particularly parochial about her nationalism. She had grown up in Westmount, after all; she had gone to school with English-speaking girls at the Convent of the Sacred Heart and studied abroad in Lausanne and Paris; she had traveled extensively and learned a perfect English. But she had been influenced by the political atmosphere of Montreal in the wake of the Quiet Revolution and by the progressive views of her father, to whom she was especially close after the death of her mother in 1959.

"Papouche," as she called him, "didn't believe in separation in those days. He supported Lesage and Trudeau, like every good Liberal, and I used to tease him for being more Westmount than French Canadian in his subdued way of showing enthusiasm; but he always taught me to insist on being served in French in stores and restaurants. You should be capable of speaking English, he used to say, but you should insist on speaking French. Language was the daily stimulus to Quebec nationalism in the 1960s. We were so frustrated at not being able to express ourselves in our own language in our own place."

Behind language, of course, there was history and economics. "By every statistical measure which we used," the Royal Commission on Bilingualism and Biculturalism reported in 1969, "Canadians of French origin are considerably lower on the socio-economic scale. They are not as well represented by the decision-making positions and in the ownership of industrial enterprises, and they do not have the same access to the fruits of modern technology. The positions they occupy are less prestigious and do not command as high incomes; across Canada, their average annual earnings are $980 less than those of the British. Furthermore, they have two years' less formal education. Quebec manufacturing firms owned by franco-phones produce only 15 per cent of the provincial output."

Though these findings were based on 1961 figures, which did not reflect the profound changes initiated by the federal and provincial Liberals, success was still clearly equated with the English language. When Robert Daigneault, Danielle's childhood sweetheart, whom she married in 1966, wanted to study medicine in French at the Université de Montréal, for example, his father was furious at him for not choosing McGill.

"We were cut off from Robert's family for several years," Danielle said. "His father was a professional whose engineering company was bought eventually by a big Toronto firm, and his brother had an MBA from the University of Western Ontario, so they didn't share our nationalist ideas. Even in my own family, the Trudeaus had been friends of my mother's mother – she had been a Fauteux, a cousin somehow to my father's Grandmother Moncel – and when Pierre Trudeau went to Ottawa, he became like a god to her. I thought him a horror, naturally, but I couldn't say a word against him in her presence. Same with my brother Marc. He was such a Liberal that we didn't speak for ten years."

Nor had Danielle fitted in comfortably on the street in lower Westmount where she and Robert lived for a while. "We were the only French-speaking family around, and our next-door neighbor was a very anglo relative of the Eaton department-store dynasty. She used to say things like, 'Eaton's is an English store, so we shouldn't give any service in French,' and she used to be insulted if someone addressed her in French in what she saw as the *family* store! We had some amazing arguments."

Beyond the humiliation of not seeing a word of French in the local Steinberg's supermarket and not hearing a word of French from the old anglo elite, there had been the demographic threat. While French Canada's birthrate plunged in response to the collapse of Church authority and the advent of the pill, Canada flung open its doors to immigrants in the 1960s, and 90 per cent of the immigrant children in Quebec were going to school in English. "If immigrants continue to opt predominantly for the English language," said one well-publicized report in 1969, "the French-speaking community is bound to see its majority seriously reduced, particularly in Montreal. This would mean losing its only real power: that of making laws and electing governments."

To Jean Dorion, the president of the Saint-Jean-Baptiste Society of Montreal and a contemporary of Danielle's, that future threat to the survival of French Canadians had been more significant than either the colonial subjugation of the past or the economic inferiority of the present. "The working-class district of Montreal where I grew up was full of Italians in the 1950s," Dorion once told me. "Their kids all went to the English schools, and whenever my friends and I ran into them in a restaurant or on the street, they showed nothing but contempt and superiority toward us. They were arrogant and they never spoke French. That became the source, I guess, of my obsession to integrate the immigrants into the culture of the Quebec majority. At first, the French-only law was a message to the anglos: you're no longer the boss here, and the proof is that we won't allow you to have even bilingual signs. That message got through, I think, but then the law became a message to the immigrants: Quebec is not a bilingual place where you can choose which language you want to use."

When I suggested that he was creating the same kind of injustice toward a linguistic minority as Lord Durham and the Eaton's department store had represented, Dorion took offense. "But English isn't on the verge of disappearing in North America, as French is," he argued. "Even in Quebec, English will maintain itself, though some of the English-speaking institutions may weaken. Most anglos keep on functioning in English during the day. Many immigrants keep on adopting English as the language of commerce. Their kids keep on resisting French, because of American television or because their parents use English in their stores and businesses. If we permit both languages to coexist, English will dominate. So we have to reaffirm French, not to bash the English or the immigrants but to defend the interests of the majority."

The issue had become somewhat more abstract for Danielle herself in 1973, when she moved from lower Westmount to Rimouski. Robert had taken a job at the hospital there, in a region that was 90 per cent French-speaking and far removed from regular contact with Eaton relatives, Italian kids, or English-language television. She even began to worry for the quality of her English and whether her children were getting enough exposure to the broader world. Not quite content to settle down as the local doctor's wife, she finished her university degree, raised sheep and marketed the wool products, ran a campground and fish shop for four summers – and voted for the Parti Québécois in 1976.

"I'll remember the night of that victory all my life," she said with magic in her eyes. "I had worked at the polls in Westmount during the previous election, so you can imagine that my expectations weren't very high. I thought the PQ would do better, maybe even well, but I never thought it would take power. We hadn't planned anything special, just us and another couple at home watching TV, but we were so surprised and excited, we stayed up the whole night!"

To make the victory even sweeter, Rimouski had voted PQ for the first time – and so had Danielle's father, Arthur Tétrault.

René Lévesque had come to office promising good, progressive government, and Danielle had become a small part of it, first with the office of consumer protection, then with the department of communications. Beyond the language legislation and behind the regular business of governing, however, there had lurked the intention to hold a referendum on independence, which remained the first principle of the Parti Québécois. Knowing that it had not been elected for independence, suspecting that it could not win a vote for independence, the PQ had concocted an idea called sovereignty-association, which apparently meant political independence accompanied by an economic link to the rest of Canada. Even then, the referendum had not been for sovereignty-association in itself, but for permission to negotiate an agreement enabling "Quebec to acquire the exclusive power to make its laws, administer its taxes, and establish relations abroad – in other words, sovereignty – and at the same time to maintain with Canada an economic association including a common currency." The question had been a ruse, because it presumed that Canada would accept such an arrangement simply because the people of Quebec wanted it.

The people of Quebec did not want it, as it turned out. Federalist Quebeckers had seen through the dishonesty of the question, opted for social stability and economic sense, and affirmed their attachment to Canada. Other Quebeckers, Danielle believed, had been duped by the false promises of Pierre Trudeau for a renewed federation, bought by the millions spent by Ottawa's propaganda machine, and sucked into the scare tactics concerning their welfare checks and jobs. "Lies, money, and fear," was how my cousin summed it up.

After 1980, the Lévesque government never recovered its original dynamism, though it won another election as a reward for its basic competence. The economy turned sour. The unions, the artists, and many of the PQ's other partisans turned away, out of anger or fatigue. A gloom and purposelessness engulfed the leadership and ranks of the party. Its energy seemed transferred into the private sector and individual ambition. Like the rest of North America, Quebec became caught up in the materialism and narcissism of the 1980s. Corporate takeovers and personal comfort pushed aside public debates and collective solidarity. Even the more nationalistic singers and filmmakers in Montreal began to talk about making it in New York and Los Angeles.

Danielle remained in Rimouski, but much of her political interest was redirected into her ever-increasing responsibilities in the department of communications and her obligations at home. Her father, now in his eighties and no longer rich, became more and more senile, and in time she brought him to Rimouski, at first to her home and later to a nursing home. "It was hard for him to have lost everything, including many of his friends," she said, "and I think he deliberately forgot the things that made him unhappy." She hid from him, therefore, the final tragedy of his life: the death of his only son, Marc – "Napoléon II," Danielle called him, because he had inherited his Grandfather Tétrault's exuberance and grandeur, then lost his fortune through wild spending and bad management. Marc had been found shot to death in a car outside a bar in the Laurentians, apparently because of a minor money dispute with the Mafia.

Absorbed in her professional and domestic dramas, laboring to help support her elderly father and give her three daughters a good education and trips abroad, Danielle barely paid attention to the political front. The defeat of the 1980 referendum had given Pierre Trudeau a fresh resolve to achieve the constitutional reforms he had been attempting since 1968. Above all, he wanted to enshrine a bill of rights, particularly language rights, that would guarantee his vision of individual freedoms, official bilingualism, and the multicultural character of Canada. To get it, however, he faced a barrier that had confronted Canadian prime ministers for more than fifty years: there existed no agreement between Ottawa and the provinces about how to change the British North America Act of 1867.

Though Canada had broken its dependency on British foreign policy and British justice decades earlier, any amendment that it wanted to make to the BNA Act still had to be passed by the British Parliament, not because London wanted the anachronistic nuisance, but because Canadians had not been able to produce an amending formula if control of the act were placed in their hands. Should Ottawa be able to amend it alone? Should Ottawa need the consent of all ten provinces to amend it, or most of the provinces, or some of the provinces representing most of the population? Should major provinces such as Quebec and Ontario, or each of the five major regions of Canada, have a veto over any amendment?

Twice, in 1964 and 1971, all eleven governments had neared a compromise solution, but on both occasions Quebec had pulled away at the last minute. "In both cases," Trudeau once remarked, "the reason for backing off was the same: Quebec would 'permit' Canada to Canadianize the colonial document that served as our constitution, only if the rest of Canada granted Quebec a certain 'special status.'" It was not long before most of the other provinces realized what a useful lever their own agreement could be for prying more powers out of Ottawa, and they soon enrolled, as Trudeau put it, "in the school of blackmail of which Quebec was the founder and top-ranking graduate." The victory of the Parti Québécois in 1976 had made a deal even more unlikely: how could a government committed to independence ever assent to a reformed federalism?

But during the 1980 referendum Trudeau had vowed to reform the federation, meaning in his own mind to bring authority over the BNA Act to Canada and append a bill of rights, and he set out to fulfill his vow with an unprecedented determination. He met stiff resistance from René Lévesque and seven of the other premiers, who understood that success would put an end to their power-mongering, but Trudeau was able to prevail by threatening to take his case directly to the people in an election or a national referendum. Since the Charter of Rights and Freedoms was popular in every part of the country, all but one of the premiers decided to strike a compromise with Trudeau to get something for themselves before he sought a mandate from the people to act as he wished. The holdout, of course, was René Lévesque. Since waiting for Lévesque's agreement would have meant waiting forever for a bill of rights, Trudeau pondered a more radical course – to defy all the premiers, the Supreme Court, and the British government by acting unilaterally and then calling an election to get approval for his action – but he did not find much encouragement for such audacity from his provincial allies or many of his own key ministers. He saw no choice but to ignore Lévesque's protest and move ahead with the package of rights and powers accepted by the other premiers.

"Mr Lévesque," Trudeau said later, "knowing that a constitutional deal would interfere with the progress of separatism, played for broke, refused to negotiate, and turned again to the Supreme Court to block the process of constitutional evolution. He lost his gamble." Canada's highest court ruled that Quebec had no veto over the deal and was subject to it even without the provincial government's approval. "A gamble lost; a gamble won – big deal!" Trudeau added. "Quebec public opinion, with its usual maturity, applauded the players and then, yawning, turned to other matters."

So it seemed. When Queen Elizabeth II arrived in Ottawa in April 1982 to bless the revised constitution officially, there were some black armbands in Quebec, a mass demonstration in Montreal, some flags at half-mast, and an all-party resolution of condemnation in the Quebec legislature, but no widespread indignation. René Lévesque was on his way to retirement; the Parti Québécois was on its way to defeat. Most Quebeckers were reluctant to reopen the constitutional battles that had torn apart their families so recently. Even Danielle Daigneault seemed resigned to the reforms. "They were just more of the same thing," she recalled, "but because of the moroseness of the nationalists, they were no big scandal. They became more scandalous later, after the fact."

In 1984 Pierre Trudeau retired after more than fifteen years in power. Independence and special status had been checked, largely because of his efforts, and his vision of making French Canadians full and equal participants in the life of the country, in their own language, had been entrenched in the basic law of the land. It was bound to last, therefore, far beyond his own lifetime – or so he assumed.

"Alas," he said just a few years later, "only one eventuality had not been foreseen: that one day the government of Canada might fall into the hands of a wimp."

A Place in History, 1987

THE WIMP in question was Brian Mulroney, a successful Montreal lawyer who had never concealed his fantasy of becoming prime minister of Canada. Almost everyone agreed that he had some qualifications for the job. Born an electrician's son in 1939 in the papermill town of Baie Comeau on the remote north shore of the St. Lawrence River, he was clever, perfectly bilingual, as charming as an Irish publican. He had used his street smarts and ambition to build a reputation as a labor negotiator, and then to land himself in a stone mansion near the top of Westmount as president of the American-owned Iron Ore Company of Canada, all the while serving his political addiction by acting as an indefatigable backroom organizer and strategist for the Progressive Conservative Party. Though he never fought for a seat in the House of Commons until 1983, his name was often bandied about in the party's many leadership intrigues.

Mulroney's qualifications were marred by some weaknesses. His hard work often reeked of crude careerism; his fashionable appearance hinted at superficiality; his Irish warmth masked a vengeful nature; and his most sincere voice oozed insincerity. When he first tried to take over the Tories, in 1976, he lost to a young, uninspiring, and ungainly member of Parliament from Alberta, Joe Clark. Full of Catholic piety and gentlemanly platitudes in public, Mulroney was an unpleasant drinker before he gave up alcohol in 1979 and a bitter loser before he began to win.

The biggest strike against him, however, had nothing to do with his personality. He was a Conservative in the Liberal stronghold of Quebec. Rarely in recent times had the Tories been able to win more than one or two of Quebec's seventy-five ridings. Those long odds explain why Brian Mulroney had not dared to run for election in his home province.

In 1983 he had a second and rather unexpected chance to beat Joe Clark for the Conservative leadership. For the most part Clark did himself in, by incompetence and personal unpopularity, but Mulroney was shrewd enough to turn his Quebec liability into his main asset. "French Canadians are *your* salvation," he used to tell English-speaking party members, who were beginning to accept the distasteful idea that they needed more Quebec seats if the Liberals were not to remain in power forever. "All they want is a bicultural, bilingual leader who can reach out and say, 'Vous avez un foyer chez nous,' you have a home with us!" The only candidate who fit that description, of course, was Mulroney himself.

This was Trudeauism painted Tory blue, and Mulroney's Quebec policies seemed as Liberal as his stylish suits and Gucci shoes. As a private citizen he had campaigned hard to help defeat the 1980 referendum. In 1982 he had not disguised his enthusiasm for Trudeau's constitutional reforms – "not because he had thought about it for five minutes," one of his closest friends told me, "but because he was so thrilled by the sheer bravado of it all." At law school in Quebec City in the early 1960s Mulroney had known many of the people who became major figures in the Parti Québécois, and he neither trusted their politics nor expected them to be satisfied with anything less than Quebec independence. "Before I give away a plugged nickel," he shouted again and again, "I want to know what Lévesque is going to do for Canada!"

I heard him shout that once myself while interviewing him during his 1983 leadership campaign at his Westmount home, just around the corner from where I grew up. At noon he was still in his silk dressing gown, recovering from another tough week of speeches and flesh-pressing and a long morning of urgent phone calls. His deep baritone was hoarse with fatigue and du Maurier cigarettes, though it boomed with indignation or self-confidence whenever he attacked his opponents. I had seen him around town over the years, at social events and football games and the bar in the Ritz, and I had friends who liked his fun and admired his talents, but I was perhaps too Irish myself to be impressed by his conceits, his rants, or his renditions of "Danny Boy." More to the point, I did not believe that he sought power for any principle higher than his own vanity. Now, however, hearing the vehemence with which he attacked the Parti Québécois, I thought I had discovered one policy Brian Mulroney would not sacrifice for the sake of his own skin.

"Brian's supporters in Quebec, by and large, are spoils politicians," Joe Clark explained to me soon afterward. "They have probably never voted Parti Québécois and they identify with the traditional, often anglo elite. My people are more nationalist and more rural. They're part of another elite, which is French-speaking and associated with the PQ but not necessarily separatist."

Instead of trying to attract Liberal voters by lambasting René Lévesque and the Parti Québécois, Clark had hoped to build a new coalition: one-time devotees of Maurice Duplessis, disgruntled farmers and businessmen, nationalists who could not abide the federalist vision of Pierre Trudeau, old *bleus*, and Catholic traditionalists. "In the past there was no substantive reason to be a Conservative in Quebec, except anger at the Liberals and the prospect of reward," he argued. "We were on the sidelines because Quebec is an idea-oriented province and we weren't involved in policy." So Clark had begun to develop policies and a rhetoric that moved toward decentralized power, the special interests of Quebec, and an accommodation with the moderate wing of the Parti Québécois.

No sooner had Brian Mulroney won the leadership from Clark than he began to change his tune. Heading into the 1984 election, Mulroney faced the old question of where to find Tory candidates, organizers, and voters in Quebec. The answer was in the nationalist alliance that Clark had begun to assemble. So Mulroney began to vacillate between his own Trudeauism and Clark's decentralist vision of "a community of communities." Instead of praising the constitutional reforms of 1982, he now condemned Trudeau for ostracizing Quebec. Instead of being suspicious of the separatists, he now welcomed them into the Tory fold and offered to deal with the Parti Québécois if he became prime minister. His ploy succeeded in attracting support from many Quebec Liberals and the PQ government. Helped by Canadians' ennui with almost twenty years of Liberal government and their lack of enthusiasm for Trudeau's bumbling successor, John Turner, the Conservatives won an overwhelming victory in the 1984 federal election – including three-quarters of the ridings in Quebec. Rimouski voted Tory, for example, electing a woman who had campaigned for the "Yes" side in the Quebec referendum.

"Ya dance with the guy what brung ya," goes one of Mulroney's pet adages, and in Quebec he was brung by the nationalists. Most of his Quebec members of Parliament were frankly shocked to find themselves in Ottawa. Many were recent converts to the Conservative Party; some had been active partisans for the Parti Québécois; indeed a few of the most powerful remained ambivalent about the Canadian federation. To keep them quiet and to keep the province Tory, Mulroney made real and symbolic concessions to the Parti Québécois government and Quebec nationalists. He allowed the Quebec premier to take a seat at the 1986 conference of French-speaking nations in Paris, for example, and he appointed as Canada's ambassador to France a former PQ supporter named Lucien Bouchard, a lawyer from the nationalist Saguenay region, who had already been instrumental in softening Mulroney's attitude to Quebec nationalism. Later, when Mulroney's "spoils politicians" rocked his government with repeated scandals, he summoned Bouchard to become a major Cabinet minister and key Quebec adviser in Ottawa. One can perhaps deduce the tenor of Bouchard's advice from the fact that when his wife went into labor, he rushed her to a hospital across the Ottawa River so that their child would be born in Quebec, not Ontario.

By the end of 1985 Quebec nationalism was still in the doldrums – not because of Mulroney's soft stance, as he liked to brag, but because the separatists had been trounced by Trudeau's hard line in 1980 and 1982 and were still mired in their own dejection. The PQ had muted its cry for independence to an ambiguous mumble before the 1985 provincial election, yet lost anyway, even in Rimouski. Its defeat seemed the last nail in the coffin of the independence movement.

Who could have guessed that it would be resurrected within a couple of years, more potent than ever? Who could have known that its resurgence would be triggered by Brian Mulroney, the Quebec nationalists around him, and the old ambitions of Robert Bourassa?

———

Like Richard Nixon or a bad penny, Robert Bourassa kept turning up no matter how often he was tossed out. After his whipping at the hands of René Lévesque in 1976, he had fled to Europe, teaching in Paris and studying the European Common Market in Brussels. But he did not let go of the seemingly preposterous idea of one day returning to Quebec in triumph. That day came in 1983, when, older and shrewder, after years of patient and discreet groundwork, he regained control of the provincial Liberal Party. He succeeded not only because there was no better candidate at the time; both he and the province had developed along the same lines. His economic priorities, technocratic methods, and pragmatic approach to federalism suited the new mood of Quebeckers, who were more interested in entrepreneurial success than constitutional wars, as long as their pride and their profits were respected.

Bourassa felt pressure from the nationalists to do something about Quebec's never having formally agreed to the 1982 constitutional changes, however, and he decided to press the issue with his old friend Brian Mulroney. Mulroney, for his part, had come to power with the ambition "to be remembered in history," according to his friendly biographer. What better way than to do what Trudeau had failed to do and sign an agreement "to give Quebec back its rightful place in Confederation," as Mulroney said in a speech written by Lucien Bouchard. When his Irish luck removed the most obvious obstacle – the Parti Québécois – and replaced it with a tacit supporter to whom the Tories owed a debt, Ottawa and Quebec began to talk seriously about bringing Quebec back into "the constitutional family."

"While I couldn't ask for everything in every sphere," Bourassa later said, "I summed up everything that I regarded as essential." That included provincial control over immigration to Quebec, limits on Ottawa's ability to spend money in areas of Quebec jurisdiction, a veto on future constitutional changes to Canada's national institutions, participation in the appointment of Supreme Court judges, and – most important of all – the recognition in the constitution of Quebec as a "distinct society." The expression was never defined precisely; Bourassa said only that "'special status,' 'associated states,' and 'distinct society' are concepts that work together in a certain way."

On April 30, 1987, Brian Mulroney set out to sell Robert Bourassa's five demands to the other nine premiers by gathering everyone together at a secluded retreat on Meech Lake, north of Ottawa. The negotiation was no easy task, but it was made easier by the prime minister's experience as a labor arbitrator and his willingness to surrender anything to anyone to get Quebec's signature on a deal and secure his own place in history. His main challenge was to overcome the hostility among the English-speaking provinces to any recognition of special status or special powers for Quebec. Whatever Quebec got, they wanted too.

Mulroney settled the first four points, therefore, by offering every premier what Bourassa had demanded – and he threw in a fifth concession, provincial participation in the appointment of federal senators, for good measure. But Quebec alone was to be considered "a distinct society," and its government alone was to be commissioned by the constitution "to preserve and promote the distinct identity of Quebec." Mulroney downplayed this as merely a matter of political and sociological fact, with no additional powers or privileges attached, and all the premiers decided to believe him – all except Bourassa, that is, who went home crowing that it meant "new ground" for language, culture, and Quebec's political and economic institutions.

"We are getting a major gain that is not limited to the purely symbolic," he claimed, "for the country's entire constitution must henceforth be interpreted to conform with this recognition." In other words, Quebec could argue for any power or push aside any right on the grounds that it had to "preserve and promote" its distinct identity, whatever that meant. "It must be underlined that the entire constitution, including the Charter of Rights, will be interpreted and applied in the light of the article on the distinct society. This directly involves the exercise of legislative powers, and will allow us to consolidate our gains and make even greater advances."

To his apparent surprise, he had been handed the special status he had long sought. The clause was an open-ended and deliberately ambiguous change in process by which Quebec could procure more substantial powers through the Supreme Court – whose membership it now influenced. In fact, Bourassa had accepted so few changes precisely because they were procedural changes; their very ambiguity would keep the power-mongering in play while increasing the likelihood for success. The Meech Lake Accord was the triumph, then, of the old nationalist strategy of *étapisme*, the step-by-step accumulation of powers, each step seeming a reasonable and necessary price for peace, each step leading inevitably toward autonomy.

Indeed, Mulroney sold the Meech Lake Accord itself as a reasonable and necessary step for peace. "We must never forget that, in 1982, Quebec was left alone, isolated, and humiliated," the prime minister now argued. "How could we, for a single moment, accept Quebec's being excluded from national life? It was the worst injustice ever inflicted on Quebeckers." Unless the new deal was passed by every provincial legislature within the three-year limit, Bourassa chimed in, Canada would be "a country with an unfulfilled destiny, with a major partner not a part of the constitution."

Quebec was very much part of the constitution, in fact, and had never been excluded from national life. Bourassa himself acknowledged as much by using one of Trudeau's constitutional amendments to prop up Quebec's language law after the Supreme Court decided that Bill 101's prohibition of English-language signs was a violation of freedom of expression. In December 1988 he applied a technical rule to override the Charter of Rights in order to reinforce the ban on outdoor signs in any language but French. ("Never mind the English," he was told by his advisers. "All that counts is social peace.") He sent a chill into Quebec's English-speaking community by saying that the "distinct society" clause would take precedence over freedom of expression in the future. Nothing dampened the ardor of English Canada for the deal more effectively than this highhanded display of what the Quebec government might do with it.

As for "humiliation" and "injustice," they came as news to most Quebeckers, who evidently had missed the insult and injury at the time. Trudeau and most of his caucus had been Quebeckers, after all. But suddenly both their prime minister and their own premier were telling them in unison that Quebec had been isolated and abused by the national government and the premiers of English Canada. Then their media began to exaggerate a rare instance of the Quebec flag's being stomped upon by anti-French demonstrators in Ontario, suggesting this was the mood of English Canadians everywhere. No wonder Quebeckers began to get enraged.

"Do you think the queen would have come over here and there would have been a big party in front of Parliament Hill with everybody in striped pants celebrating a constitution without the industrial heartland of Ontario?" Mulroney sputtered, with his typical Irish exaggeration. Ignoring the reality of a Parti Québécois government that had been determined to sign nothing in 1982 – and his own approval of Trudeau's actions – Mulroney argued that the interests and feelings of the people of Quebec had been trampled in a way that would not have happened to anyone else in Canada. The accord, exactly as framed, became the very least that Quebeckers needed to make up for the grave "injustice" they had suffered. Saying no to even one jot or tittle would be another slap in the face of Quebeckers. It would be a rejection of the ordinary people of Quebec by English Canadians.

As one, Ottawa and Quebec City worked the province into a lather about the accord, which became more a symbol of dignity than a constitutional arrangement. Throughout Quebec, everyone – journalists, academics, businessmen, union chiefs – felt the pressure, by tempting offer or direct threat, to defend the accord, since opposition implied the continued humiliation of the Quebec people. And when this take-it-or-leave-it blackmail prompted a backlash among English Canadians, who objected to parts of the accord or the way it was being rammed down their throats, Mulroney and Bourassa were quick to accuse them of an arrogance toward Quebec that would have dreadful consequences. Everyone had to put water in his wine, they maintained, except Quebec, which had been grievously wronged. It was Meech or separation.

It became a self-fulfilling prophecy, of course. Months before the final deadline at the end of June 1990, polls showed that a majority of Quebeckers – driven by the rhetoric of humiliation and the myth of personal rejection – favored independence. Even then Mulroney did not try to calm the waters or prepare for a failure of the accord. He could not, because of the pressure from the Quebec nationalists in his caucus. Some, including Lucien Bouchard himself, had quit in May at the very hint of appeasement, and they formed a new party, the Bloc Québécois, to work for the independence of Quebec in the House of Commons. Other Tories were expected to follow if Meech did not pass. As the fatal hour approached, therefore, Mulroney chose to "roll all the dice" and bring the premiers together again for a make-or-break conference that lasted most of a hot week in early June. A country's unity was on the table.

Three provinces had yet to approve the accord (elections having thrown out the premiers who had endorsed it in 1987): Manitoba, New Brunswick, and Newfoundland. Mulroney's tactic was to lock everyone in a room from morning to midnight, like hostages in a ter-rorist hijacking, for as long as it took to reach unanimity once more. By day four the premiers were swearing at each other, storming out, being dragged back in, and terrifying the dissidents with apocalyptic scenarios. The strongest of the three holdouts, Clyde Wells, the premier of Newfoundland, was reduced to tears by sleep deprivation and the relentless brainwashing. "If you don't give in, you are going to destroy Canada," he was told again and again. "No matter what you think intellectually, you have to do it to save Canada."

By week's end, when the three recalcitrant premiers finally suc-cumbed and went home to pass the accord in their legislatures, it looked as if Mulroney's gamble had worked beautifully. He even boasted to the press about how clever he had been. Within days, however, his boast proved premature. New Brunswick passed the accord at once, but Manitoba's attempt to ram it through the system ran into technical delays because of the opposition of the only aboriginal member of the provincial legislature, Elijah Harper, who refused to give unanimous consent because Meech had done nothing for his people. That insurmountable obstacle gave Clyde Wells, who had regained his composure and his principles, the excuse not to hold a vote in the Newfoundland legislature. At midnight, Saturday, June 23, the deadline came and went. The Meech Lake Accord was pronounced dead and buried.

The sudden collapse resounded across Quebec like a bugle call. Thirty years after the Quiet Revolution, twenty years after the FLQ crisis, ten years after the referendum, Quebec was in turmoil again. The Meech Lake Accord had not been a separatist cause. Most separatists had opposed it, in fact, as conferring only an unsatisfactory "special status" within Canada. That did not prevent them from twisting its failure to their own ends. Since English Canadians had "rejected" Quebec – despite the fact that almost all the provinces had passed the accord, and despite the fact that the federal Liberal Party had just elected yet another French Canadian, Jean Chrétien, as its leader – Quebeckers were urged to find succor and safety among themselves. They were summoned as they had been summoned whenever under threat from the English in the past: to defend themselves by acting with a single mind and uniting into a single body. Exactly three hundred years after Frontenac's heroic response to the English siege of Quebec, French Canadians again rallied to the cry, "We will answer from the mouths of our cannons!"

The Mohawks Return, 1990

THE MILITARY siege of Quebec in 1690 had coincided with the Iroquois terror following the massacre at Lachine. The psychological siege of 1990 coincided with a new armed conflict between Mohawks and French Canadians at Oka. Nothing much had changed in three centuries: the inhabitants of the St Lawrence Valley were trapped again between the English and the Indians.

The Oka conflict was based on a centuries-old quarrel over the ownership of a pine forest twenty miles west of Montreal. The Pines had been part of an ancient Iroquois settlement known as Kanehsatake; it had also been part of a huge tract of land granted by Louis xv to the Sulpician priests in 1717. In the nineteenth century the priests began to sell off the grant to farmers and timber merchants – over the objections of the Mohawk chiefs, who claimed the land as "ours by right of possession, ours as a heritage" – and in 1945 the remaining fraction was sold to the federal government for an Indian reserve. Even that protected morsel was encroached upon when the municipality of Oka leveled a section of the Pines in 1959 to build a nine-hole golf course. Thirty years later the municipality proposed to level another section, bordering the Mohawks' burial ground, to add another nine holes.

In early 1990 the thousand natives of Kanehsatake organized a protest with sit-ins and roadblocks. Responding to reports of an imminent raid by the Quebec provincial police, they armed themselves with hunting rifles and reinforced their ranks with members of the Warrior Society, a militant and paramilitary association that had arisen with the revival of Mohawk pride and the defense of Mohawk rights in the 1970s. Its Warriors were a powerful, controversial force on all the reserves in Quebec, Ontario, and New York State, where they controlled bingo halls and gambling casinos, brought cheap American cigarettes for sale in Canada, and vowed to defend the Mohawk Nation with AK-47 weapons and their own blood. Now, their faces hidden behind kerchiefs and masks, their identities hidden behind nicknames such as Lasagna and Mad Jap, they came to the defense of the Pines at Kanehsatake. There, less than three weeks after an Ojibwa-Cree member of the Manitoba legislature had triggered the collapse of the Meech Lake Accord, the Mohawks repelled an attack by a hundred provincial policemen, who tried to smash the roadblocks in a pandemonium of tear gas and smoke bombs. Gunfire was exchanged; when it stopped, a corporal lay dead.

Mohawks at Kahnawake, across the St Lawrence from Montreal, established a blockade of the Mercier Bridge as an act of solidarity, thereby involving hundreds of thousands of south-shore commuters as well as the residents of Oka in the dispute. After three weeks of unproductive negotiations between the representatives from Ottawa and Quebec and the leaders at Kanehsatake and Kahnawake, ten thousand angry commuters began their own series of demonstrations and blockades, insulting the natives, threatening violence, and calling for the army. Following a request from Premier Bourassa to Prime Minister Mulroney, more than twenty-five hundred soldiers moved into the Montreal region, with jeeps, tanks, helicopters, howitzers, jet fighters, and a navy boat. A few days later the troops replaced the Quebec provincial police, who were exhausted and dispirited after almost six weeks of round-the-clock duty against both the Indians and the commuters. The army, now numbering over four thousand, was ordered to advance for a final assault against the barricades and the few hundred Mohawks waiting with submachine guns, shotguns, and dynamite. Thousands of residents, white and native, fled the front lines in anticipation of a bloodbath. When the Mohawks at Kahnawake tried to evacuate their children and elders to safety, commuters terrorized the sixty-car convoy with rocks and fists.

Ultimately, the crisis dissolved. First, the Mercier Bridge was reopened to traffic. Then the last two dozen Warriors walked out of the alcohol-treatment center that had been their bastion, and surrendered – narrowly escaping the fate of their eighteen ancestors who had been slain nearby in 1689 in revenge for the attack on Lachine. Their struggle had cost one life, eleven weeks of tension, the mobilization of the armed forces, and more than $100 million in expenses, but the Mohawks kept the Pines.

"The state is once again criminalizing a valid social protest," said Pierre Vallières, the former FLQ ideologue who, a month later, would lead two hundred and fifty demonstrators to a rally outside Pierre Trudeau's Montreal home to commemorate the twentieth anniversary of the War Measures Act. "It is trying to dismiss social demands, demands for sovereignty, as criminal activities."

This time, however, many Quebec nationalists did not nod with sympathetic understanding as they had when the FLQ resorted to kidnapings in 1970. For one thing, these Mohawks all spoke English – and hadn't some of their ancestors come with the British conquerors in 1760 and the British Loyalists in 1783? For another, Indian sovereignty over bingo halls and golf courses seemed to challenge Quebec's own hallowed sovereignty. Most wounding of all, the natives had made Quebeckers – the Quebeckers who had launched the police raid, the Quebeckers who had called in the army, the Quebeckers who had thrown the rocks, the Quebeckers who had coveted the Pines – look as arrogant and racist as the *maudits Anglais!*

In the wake of the Meech Lake fiasco, Quebeckers were supposed to be the aggrieved and jilted minority. Suddenly they were being perceived as the hardhearted and oppressive majority, compared to southern rednecks and reactionary Afrikaners, subjected to the ethical preachings of Bishop Tutu and Jesse Jackson, visited by representatives of the International Federation for Human Rights, and held to a draw (if not actually defeated) on the moral plane by Spud-wrench, Blackjack, and the other gunslinging cigarette smugglers in Halloween masks and war feathers.

Oka was, according to one Quebec nationalist, "the last alibi of English Canada," a convenient excuse to characterize Quebec as a fascistic and bumbling place, and the Warriors had been the unwitting pawns in this sinister design. "I think," said a senior official of the Parti Québécois, with a bit more moderation, "this crisis has been exploited by some people to consolidate their anti-francophone positions and perceptions."

———————

Oka was but one front during "the Summer of the Indians." The other involved, on one side, about ten thousand Crees and five thousand Inuit, and, on the other, Hydro-Québec, the government of Quebec, the business leaders of Quebec, the unions of Quebec, and – if this side was to be believed – the future prosperity of seven million Quebeckers.

At stake were not a few dozen acres of pine forests but thousands of square miles of territory around the Great Whale River in the James Bay region of northern Quebec. The territory was slated to be developed into an enormous hydropower project that would divert at least four rivers, flood an area the size of Lake Champlain, and cost more than $12 billion. It was the latest in a series of megaprojects undertaken by the province, beginning in 1971 with the construction of fifteen colossal dams on the La Grande River. Several more were already being planned for other significant rivers in the decade ahead.

These megaprojects were Robert Bourassa's particular obsession, a passion for a man of so little passion, for they blended prudent economic planning with the verve of nationalist glory. "Quebec is a vast hydroelectric plant in the bud," he once proclaimed, "and every day millions of potential kilowatt-hours flow downhill and out to sea. What a waste!" Harnessing that "waste" became his chosen way of creating tens of thousands of jobs, injecting billions of tax dollars into Quebec companies and the Quebec economy, attracting industries with cheap electricity, and netting billions of American dollars with sales to the northeastern states. "Bourassa is probably in favor of the death penalty," I was told, "if electric chairs mean more business for Hydro-Québec."

There were two immediate snags, however. The dams, the roads, and the construction camps would damage an especially sensitive environment, one of the largest and most fragile wildernesses left on the planet, and – more bothersome, since moose and tundra cannot address the United Nations – they would disturb the lives of the native peoples who still fish those rivers, hunt those woods, and honor that land. The La Grande projects had been completed thanks to an agreement, reached in 1975, with the Crees and Inuit, who chose to "cede, release, surrender, and convey all their native claims, rights, titles, and interests" over most of the territory in exchange for hundreds of millions of dollars in cash, land guarantees, and compensatory promises. The aftermath proved no happy precedent for the Great Whale project. Money, airports, workers, and development had brought more miseries than benefits, including consumerism, venereal disease, alcoholism, television, fast foods, and the devastation of Eenou Astchee, "the people's land," otherwise known as New Quebec.

"We have already lost most of our traditions," said the Inuit mayor of Kuujjuarapik, whose four hundred inhabitants faced being overwhelmed by more than four thousand construction workers in the area in the next five years. "Our traditional way of life is gradually being abandoned by our young people, and recently our school has started to teach our youngsters the history of our land as seen from the south. I suppose that's called progress."

The Cree leadership resolved to stop the Great Whale development and every other megaproject. Shortly before the failure of the Meech Lake Accord and the standoff at Oka, some Crees paddled a canoe from their home on James Bay to the financial towers of Manhattan, where they got the mayor of New York and scores of reporters to hear their message that New Yorkers should neither buy Quebec power nor lend Hydro-Québec money until the environmental and native issues were settled. Comparing Quebec's hinterlands to the rainforests of Brazil and their own plight to genocide, they enlisted the support of international ecological activists such as Greenpeace, the Sierra Club, and at least one Kennedy; David Byrne and Jackson Browne performed in a Ban the Dam Jam; legislative lobbies in New York, Maine, Vermont, New Hampshire, and Massachusetts worked on their behalf. In July 1991 even Ottawa risked the fury of the Bourassa government by opening a public examination of Great Whale's environmental impact.

"There are seven million Quebeckers who need this project," Bourassa said angrily, citing the sixty-three thousand jobs it was expected to create and the billion-dollar contracts already signed with the American states. "The natives blocked the ratification of the Meech Lake Accord. Now should they block the Great Whale?"

Hydro-Québec began fighting back too, with the help of an international public-relations firm and a chunk of its annual $14-million communications budget. It needed both. In January 1992 the *New York Times* published a cover story in its Sunday magazine subtitled "Flooding Quebec To Light New York." "Do the land and its natural inhabitants have certain rights that outweigh the demands of urban, industrial society?" it asked. Two months later the New York State assembly voted 122 to 17 to set up its own inquiry into the effects of the Great Whale dams; two weeks after that the governor of New York canceled a long-term, $17-billion contract with Hydro-Québec. There wasn't the need any more, he said, and the price had become too high. Quebec's energy minister, however, fingered the natives' campaign.

"I blame them for discrediting Quebec all over the world," said

Lise Bacon, declaring that work on the Great Whale would proceed in any case, though in three stages and at a slower pace. "This land still belongs to Quebeckers, and Quebeckers are the ones who will develop it. Natives are not going to stop us from doing that." And then, perhaps sensing the semantic quicksand at her feet, she asked, "Are they Quebeckers or not?"

———————————

Nothing makes Quebec nationalists more frustrated and enraged than charges of racism, anti-Semitism, or even ethnocentrism. They quickly point to their Vietnamese restaurants and Jewish schools, or the statistics favorably comparing the percentage of Quebec's native population living in poverty or prison to that of Manitoba's. They draw attention to their business trips to Latin America and the exotic wives of some prominent *indépendantistes*: the leader of the Parti Québécois had married a Pole, the president of the Saint-Jean-Baptiste Society a Japanese, this union leader a Haitian and that a Lebanese, the head of the Bloc Québécois an American, and the bard of Quebec nationalism an *anglo* no less! Finally, when all else fails to convince – when Quebeckers throw rocks at Indian children or deny the Hassidim a new synagogue for fear that "soon Outremont won't belong to us any more," when Quebeckers kill a twenty-four-year-old black in a police chase without asking any questions or suggest that the novelist Mordecai Richler should have died in the Holocaust for writing about them without flattery – the nationalists dodge the issue by dismissing it: sure, they say, but Quebec is no worse than Ontario or Nebraska.

Perhaps not, but neither Ontario nor Nebraska is striving to attain political sovereignty for the fundamental purpose of promoting one language group and one distinct culture. Multilingualism and multiculturalism are still seen as alien threats to the survival of French Quebec. Though the demographic projections are not nearly as ominous as they seemed in the 1960s, allophones are expected to make up 10 per cent of the population in fifteen years and 20 per cent fifty years later. That increase among those least likely to vote for independence is one reason separatists have been pressing so hard for an immediate referendum.

Even cosmopolitan Québécois sense a growing problem, especially in Montreal, the magnet for immigrants. Accustomed to seeing themselves as a homogeneous people, French Canadians have had to adjust to the astonishing number of black cab drivers and Asian shopkeepers in their midst. Where once the English, the Jews, the Greeks, and the Italians kept to their own streets and districts, now – thanks to Quebec's own language laws and integration policies – the more visible minorities are filling the buses and wooing the girls. About a quarter of Montreal Catholic schools currently have an allophone majority, and in several years more than half the children in the Catholic system are expected to have neither English nor French as their mother tongue. It is common for them to speak their native tongues at home, French where they have to, and English everywhere else (or, as one Italian put it, French for love, English for business, and Italian for quarreling).

"Young Québécois *de souche* don't feel comfortable being made a minority," wrote a group of teachers from one school containing eighty-seven ethnic groups, forty-five languages, and nine religions. "Either they behave like everyone else and speak English, or they become hostile and feel even more like foreigners themselves." In 1990 the Montreal Catholic School Commission even thought of banning the use of English in its buildings and playgrounds. "It is totally unacceptable for two Vietnamese to speak to each other in English," said one official. "It's a menace that weighs heavily on the French character of our schools."

In 1991 Quebec's immigration minister sponsored a National Intercultural Week, replete with folk dances and exotic foods "to celebrate the benefits that the cultural communities bring to the

French-speaking collectivity." *La Presse* duly reported that Huu Trung Nguyen had not been prevented from becoming a vice-president of banking services, that Felipe Batista from Portugal felt "perfectly Québécois," and that Olga Saraguro from Ecuador was "happy to integrate into French Quebec" because of the "exceptionally generous heart" of the Québécois. Before long, however, the immigration minister had to admit, as delicately as possible, that "the social consensus in favor of a substantial increase in immigration was not sufficiently broad for the government to raise the levels at a much faster rate."

"Allez-vous-en, maudits nègres!" a working-class crowd shouted less delicately the next day, as a group of Jamaican and Ethiopian blacks were led away under police protection after several nights of racial brawls near Olympic Stadium in east-end Montreal. "Go back to Haiti!"

The new fear of disappearing into a sea of immigrants has become as great as the old fear of disappearing into a sea of English. "We keep hearing about multiculturalism," Roger Prud'homme said when I visited him in his Outremont apartment, where he has lived by himself since his divorce in 1977 and the departure of his four adult sons. Like his father, my great-uncle Hector, he has a loud voice, a nervous energy, a bald head, a debonair style, and some unabashed opinions about foreigners. "Multiculturalism is a nice idea, but it can be difficult to live with."

As vivacious and hospitable as his older brother Maurice, Roger hopped back and forth between French and English, which he too spoke with a heavy accent. "I speak it maybe once or twice a year, now that I'm retired," he said, "but even in the hardware store, almost all our customers were French." After graduating from the Ecole des Hautes Etudes Commerciales, for years French Quebec's only business school, he had remained in the family firm for most of his working life, then run his own picture-framing shop for a decade, more for fun than profit. "I'm a federalist," he said, "even though I think Ottawa has too much power. I used to be in the same class as Jacques Parizeau, you know. Funny, he used to be as thin as a finger. Now he's so full of shit! But I can understand where separatism comes from. In the past, a lot of people up in Westmount – I'm sorry, your family comes from Westmount, doesn't it? – used to know French Canadians only by their maids. They thought of us as servants, or so we were taught, and I believed that to an extent. I think it's important that we speak French properly and maintain the French language. The problem now is we have too many allophones. How can you make a Chinese into a French Canadian? Even the French-speaking ones, from Haiti or Morocco, they may get along a little better with French Canadians, but if they're another color or religion, there's a problem. You can't turn a Haitian into a pure-wool Québécois in one or two generations. Look at the problems the United States is having with its Hispanics. I'm not a racist, but if we want to maintain a certain kind of country, maybe we should ask for European immigrants who aren't too exotic."

Quebec nationalists still find it harmless sport to bully the English minority who arrived a mere two hundred years ago with their mink coats and cocktail shakers. They still find it sensible to herd the grateful immigrants into the one true language and culture. They seem bamboozled, however, over how to handle the natives. Accustomed to portraying Quebeckers as a disadvantaged and colonialized people who need power to resist assimilation by the dominant society, the nationalists have come face to face with a more disadvantaged and more colonialized people who want power for the same reason – except that the dominant society is now Quebec's.

"To be unable to live as ourselves," René Lévesque said in 1968, "in our own language and according to our own ways, would be like living without an arm or a leg – or perhaps a heart." His sentiment was echoed almost twenty-five years later when Ovide Mercredi, the national chief of the Assembly of First Nations, said, "What we would like is to be able to preserve a way of life, to be able to use our own institutions of self-government, to deal with the social and economic needs of our people, to heal our communities, to make some progress."

In fact, Mercredi told the Quebec national assembly, "It is not clear to whom the term Québécois refers. Does it imply that people of all racial, national, and ethnic origins living in Quebec are a single people? Are the French, English, Italians, Greeks, Haitians, Irish, Germans, Jews, Arabs, and other ethnic groups living in the province all one people with one right to self-determination? Are French Quebeckers and First Nations within Quebec part of a single people? If this is your view, then it is contrary to our right to self-determination and self-identification."

Mercredi had struck at the Achilles' heel of Quebec nationalism. If French Canadians are defined as a people or a nation in the way that the Jews and the Crees are a people or a nation, then Quebec cannot speak for those who live beyond its borders. However, if Quebec is defined as the homeland of French Canadians, as Israel is for the Jews and Eenou Astchee for the Crees, then what are the rights of those who are not French Canadians within its borders? Do they too have the right to the survival of their traditions or the right of self-determination? To answer no would make a mockery of two hundred years of high-sounding principles about collective rights, minority rights, national liberation, social justice, and the tyranny of the majority. To answer yes, however, would invite a degree of pluralism beyond the tolerance of most Quebec nationalists.

Thus, when Quebeckers protest that they have been generous to the aboriginals, they sound – even to their own ears – like the anglos who remind them of British generosity in 1791 and 1867. When Quebeckers offer concessions toward aboriginal autonomy as long as the "democratic majority" and "territorial integrity" of Quebec are maintained, they sound – especially to native ears – like Ottawa politicians inventing new forms of federalism to keep Quebec from real sovereignty. When Quebeckers talk about being a distinct society, with one distinct language and one distinct culture, they sound – to democrats and progressives around the world – like the merchants and governors who dreamed of one race, one tongue, and one Church in the dark ages of a conquered Canada.

The problem has less to do with insincerity than with the fatal flaw of ethnic nationalism itself. "To insist that a particular nationality must have complete sovereign power is to pursue a self-destructive end," Pierre Trudeau wrote, when still unelected, in 1962. "Because every national minority will find, at the very moment of liberation, a new minority within its bosom which in turn must be allowed the right to demand its freedom." Thirty years later that was obvious, not only in the civil wars amid the ruins of Yugoslavia and the Soviet Union, but in Quebec. "If Canada is divisible," said a Cree leader in early 1992, "then so is Quebec."

Most of the scenarios for the violent partition of an independent Quebec have been fantasies in which the anglos of west-end Montreal and the Eastern Townships remain Canadians within a corridor between Ontario and the Maritimes. There is a more realistic possibility: that the Crees and Inuit of northern Quebec would choose to stay with Canada. Their eternal pacts are with the British monarch, after all, and though Quebec was given authority over their land by Ottawa in the first quarter of the twentieth century, Ottawa is still responsible for their rights and well-being.

"Should Quebec unilaterally declare sovereignty," Ted Moses, a Cree chief, told a United Nations group in 1991, "it is not likely that indigenous peoples will passively surrender their rights and lands to the new state. A conflict will occur that, like it or not, will involve the most fundamental issues of international law."

If the natives called for help with shouts of genocide and oppression, would Canada and the world community remain unmoved?

"We are not opposed to the constitutional claims and aspirations of Quebec; we are not opposed to the independence of Quebec," said Matthew Coon-Come, the grand chief of the northern Crees. "However, none of these political changes can or will be made in disregard of our legitimate rights, interests, and aspirations."

My cousin Danielle Daigneault thought that the natives were exploiting the situation "for their own profit and on the backs of Quebeckers." Jacques Parizeau pledged that sixty thousand Amerindians, representing less than 1 per cent of Quebec's population, would never impede the wishes of the Quebec people.

So it has been since that day in 1657 when a young pioneer named Jean Saint-Père was captured during an Iroquois raid on Ville-Marie, slain, and beheaded. Miraculously, his severed head uttered a final prophecy, in perfect Iroquoian, to his captors: "You murder us, you commit a thousand cruelties against us, you want to destroy the French, but you will not succeed. The day will come when they will be your masters, and you will obey them. It is vain for you to struggle."

The Relief Guard, 1991

QUEBEC is basically business-oriented now," said my cousin André Tétrault, one of Albert's four anglicized sons, a broker at Midland Walwyn, where he specializes in American stocks. He is a tall, good-looking man with a patrician confidence and a passion for tennis. "A lot of English Canadians still think of French Canadians as priest-ridden, rural folk who don't know what's going on in the world. That's long gone! Quebeckers are 'with it,' and now they're asking if Canada is 'with it' too. I find their business guys intelligent, interesting, energetic, and open. I think my father made the right decision about his sons' education, given the circumstances, but maybe we have come to regret it more than he ever did."

These business guys – collectively known as *la garde montante* (the relief guard) or "Quebec Inc." – are the product of Quebec's educational reforms, language laws, and economic transformation since the Quiet Revolution. Some were bright young bureaucrats in the 1960s who moved over to the top floors and higher salaries of the private sector in the 1970s. Some were the lucky beneficiaries of Ottawa's development programs and Hydro-Québec's gargantuan projects. But many came as if from nowhere in the 1980s, with Harvard MBAS or regional factories or a smart idea. With names such as Nadeau, Dutil, Chagnon, Sirois, and Gaucher, they became as well known and venerated as the hockey stars of the Canadiens thirty years earlier.

More than a mere manifestation of the 1980s, when the entire Western world seemed possessed by a mania to take over companies and buy BMWs on credit, Quebec Inc. was a reflection of Quebec's modernization. It represented – and inspired – the growth of a new Québécois middle class, able to fill the jobs of the departing anglos and eager to move into the vacant houses in Westmount. In 1990, as opposed to the balance in 1960, francophones were earning the same as anglophones on average, controlling most of Quebec's companies, and working for the most part exclusively in French. Quebec was producing more MBAS than any other province; it had a higher percentage of stockholders than any other province, thanks largely to the tax incentives of the Stock Savings Plan initiated by the Parti Québécois in 1979; and, until the latest recession hit, it had the highest economic growth of any province. The life of the founder of the Desjardins credit unions, with over four million members and $44 billion in assets, became a comic strip in *La Presse*. The life of the inventor of the snowmobile became a miniseries on television. The proud name of Louis-Joseph Papineau, the nineteenth-century nationalist hero, was carried by a real-estate promoter selling condos on Nun's Island.

Quebec Inc. was more than a business elite. Like the French language, it had replaced the Roman Catholic Church as a symbol of pride and identity. Where once the nationalists had aroused the masses by appealing to the Holy Trinity, now they appealed to the Mouvement Desjardins, Hydro-Québec, and the Caisse de Dépôt et Placement.

The Caisse had been created in 1965 to manage the money of the province's pension and insurance plans. It was the brainchild of Jacques Parizeau, now the leader of the Parti Québécois but at the time an economic adviser to the Liberal premier, Jean Lesage. While its first purpose was to make profits, its very existence reduced the ability of the anglo bond traders to bully the Quebec government, and its sheer size eventually had an impact throughout the Quebec economy. By 1991 the Caisse had become one of the five largest pools of capital in North America and the largest stock-market player in Canada, with over $35 billion in assets and more than $12 billion in corporate investments.

Federalists in Quebec and Ottawa had always assumed that the creation of a prosperous, French-speaking business class would rebut the arguments for independence. Just as Pierre Trudeau had demonstrated that French Canadians could take power at the central level – by political will more than constitutional change – so tycoons such as Paul Desmarais and Jean de Grandpré had been expected to show how French Canadians could take hold of the economic levers. "I don't agree that French Canadians should live in a sort of ghetto," Desmarais once said. "We have much better opportunities within a great country where we can develop our businesses and our ideas. We have always done well politically and culturally, but we have never really participated in the economic life of Canada. We weren't players. Fellows like René Lévesque said, 'We can never be players, so let's stay home and have our own game.' I was against that, of course, and I think in my own way I've proven we can be players. We're not being locked out. All we have to do is get out there and do it."

Just as Trudeau's "French power" had required the introduction of official bilingualism in Ottawa, so the *émergence* of a French-speaking business class required institutional and administrative reforms at the federal level, from regional-development subsidies to shaming the anglo corporations into finding French Canadian directors. After that, the federalists supposed, market forces and self-interest would encourage francophone businessmen to pick up the struggle for a progressive, bilingual, and individualistic Quebec within Canada.

"I still think Trudeau was right," Claude Tétrault told me. "Sure, French Canadians experienced discrimination in the past, but so did Jews in Montreal – and look what happened to them. The Jews went into open areas like retail and real estate, and they pulled themselves up by their own bootstraps. Once the French Canadians got rid of the Church influence and Church schools, they did the same. Those who didn't spend their time blaming someone else for their situation just went out and changed it."

That certainly seemed the case up to the referendum in 1980. The independence movement had been confined mostly to the intellectuals, the unions, the *chansonniers*, and the students; the Parti Québécois had been seen as anti-business. Even those nationalists who fretted about the survival of French Canada's culture had been concerned about the economic effect of separation on their jobs and pensions. Even those businessmen who benefited from the language laws had been worried about the flight of anglo capital and the closing of Canadian markets.

When Parizeau became minister of finance after the election of the Parti Québécois in 1976, therefore, he had set out to develop a business sector that would be sympathetic to nationalism. Among other moves, he deliberately increased the Caisse de Dépôt's nationalist and interventionist role, primarily through the appointment of Jean Campeau, a like-minded bureaucrat, as chairman. Soon the Caisse was taking a more active stance on company boards and in financial circles to promote and protect the economic development of French Quebec. It used its clout to ensure that the ownership of Quebec's major supermarket chains remained with Quebeckers, for example, and it grabbed a controlling interest of the forestry giant Domtar in what some analysts called "nationalization by other means."

"A lot of the talk about Quebec Inc. smacks of outsiders saying, 'These crazy guys couldn't have done it by themselves, so there must have been a vast conspiracy,'" said Michel Bélanger, an influential Quebec bureaucrat at the time of the creation of Hydro-Québec and the Caisse, now an important business leader. "In fact, some businessmen emerged, they weren't stupid, and they used the Caisse wisely. And if the Caisse had to lend money, why not lend it locally? Most of its portfolio is not Quebec-centered and is run reasonably well. And if there's the appearance of all these people being in cahoots together, that's not Quebec Inc., that's Quebec. They're all part of the same family, in which everyone has a brother-in-law who is married to the sister-in-law of someone else."

Instruments such as the Caisse and the Stock Savings Plan weakened the entrepreneurs' dependency on anglo capital and federal patronage while tightening their links to Québécois institutions and provincial power. Those links formed a French-speaking equivalent of the interlocking directorships and private-club deals of the Canadian establishment. They connected the francophone banks to the francophone credit unions to the francophone insurance companies to the francophone brokers to the francophone manufacturers, retailers, managers, and professionals, and then – usually through the Caisse or Hydro-Québec – they connected Quebec Inc. to the Quebec government.

Unlike the Canadian establishment, Quebec Inc. had come of age in a period of enthusiasm for laissez-faire economics and globalization. The practical need to look beyond Quebec's limited population for export markets met the psychological hunger of Quebec's businessmen to play in the world at large. Having been confined for so long in the parochial mentality of Old Quebec, they seemed giddy with the new possibilities. They dashed off to do deals in French in Europe and Africa, Asia and the United States. Often, in their quest for greater horizons, many of them flew right over English Canada. Sometimes Canada seemed too small for their ambitions. Sometimes there was not enough decision-making power left in the branch-plants of Ontario and Alberta to bother with a stop en route to New York or Houston. Sometimes Quebec companies got better deals from foreigners, who were less likely to believe that independence would happen and less likely to care if it did. Many times, however, there was just too much history for comfort.

"If we're dealing with Americans," Bélanger explained, "they assume they're dealing with a different place. Toronto often expects Quebec to be the same place and adjust to its ways. And why pay someone in Toronto to deal with the Americans? Why not cut out the middleman?"

The arrogance of Toronto apart, a remarkable number of French Canadians have preferred to test themselves at the Harvard Business School or on Wall Street, where intelligence or money softens their accent and renders meaningless their roots. That kind of test lay behind Robert Campeau's spectacular – and ultimately disastrous – foray into the American retailing industry. When the anglo elite of Montreal repelled his attempt to take over Royal Trust in 1980, not least because it saw him as a French-speaking property developer from Ontario, he turned south and was able to borrow billions of dollars to buy Allied and Federated Stores, including Bloomingdale's, Brooks Brothers, and Bonwit Teller. Nobody cared where he came from.

The Harvard kids and Robert Campeau may have been ardent federalists, but their glorification of free enterprise and free trade played into the strategy of the Quebec nationalists. The election of Brian Mulroney's Conservatives in 1984 had led to significant dereg-ulation and decentralization – both of which were encouraged by the Quebec nationalists in the Tory caucus – and their fight against high deficits had handicapped Ottawa's traditional means of buying support for Canadian unity with tax dollars. Then, in 1988, the Con-servatives had won a second term in office on the issue of the Canada–United States free-trade treaty, which in effect loosened the political bonds between east and west for the sake of the economic currents between north and south. Mulroney won the election because he won Quebec, and he won Quebec because its govern-ment, its opposition, its business leaders, and even its unions were in favor of free trade with the Americans. Among its other benefits, free trade reduced Quebec's reliance on English Canada, and that in turn reduced the economic threat of independence. Indeed, when Quebec's business leaders were pressed into service by Mulroney and Bourassa to support the Meech Lake Accord, many of them did so by declaring that the alternative – independence – was more possible than in 1980 because it was now economically viable. Some even said it was desirable.

"The impact here was extraordinary," Jacques Parizeau said. "Remember, the main objection to sovereignty has always been eco-nomic, and that argument was all the more impressive for people who didn't know anything about business. But when they heard business people saying, 'You know, it might work,' the impact was very strong."

This rush of self-confidence produced a rather cocky attitude that nothing was impossible. In some executive suites, including those of the powerful Mouvement Desjardins, Quebec's place in Canada was no longer deemed to be an asset. Federal debt, federal monetary policy, federal restrictions, federal duplication, federal priorities, federal politics – all now seemed to be hindering Quebec's develop-ment. Federalism did not look as profitable as it once had. Indepen-dence did not look as costly.

"Constant language and cultural conflicts are now magnified by a financial and economic crisis without precedent in the history of Canadian federalism," declared a report of the Quebec Liberal Party in 1991. "Structural problems sap the economy and go unresolved for lack of consensus among the country's provinces and regions. It is becoming increasingly obvious that the Canadian federal state is based on centralizing practices dictated by an inflexible will to standardize public services to the utmost and the pursuit of grand so-called 'national' policies. But these federal concerns are poorly suited to the real needs of the provinces, business, and people. In addition, the federal state no longer has the financial means to carry out its policies."

And that was the opinion of Quebec's *federalist* party.

Most nationalists admit Quebec's own role in creating this situation. From its founding in 1867, Canada has been denied the efficiency and flexibility of a centralized, unitary government primarily to accommodate the interests of Quebec. Since 1960, it has become the most decentralized federation in the world largely because of the pressures of Quebec nationalism. "I think we had to go through the exercise, during the sixties, of divesting Canada of a great deal of its fiscal and budgetary muscle. And we did one hell of a job," Jacques Parizeau once confessed. "We were all federalists. But for any one of us who had any knowledge at all about economic and budgetary policy, we knew very well we were bringing the country into a state where, it was well known, it would be very difficult to govern."

If few important businessmen were prepared to apply Parizeau's solution – independence – to the problem, few argued that Ottawa should be reinvested with the powers and resources necessary to deal with Canada's economic problems. Many argued, instead, for a special status and a massive transfer of authority so that Quebec could become "master of its own development."

"The people I meet," André Tétrault said, "they never talk of separation. They want a framework that will let them get down to business, some sort of special status that doesn't go overboard. And why the hell shouldn't they have it? It's not going to hurt anyone else."

Behind this decentralism was the old corporatist vision of Quebec: a small, homogeneous, and harmonious society in which all the sectors volunteer to work together, taking on the world for the benefit of the collectivity. The vision stretches back to the mercantile regime of New France, where government directed and funded the fur trade, the iron forges, and the shipyards according to a master plan in the head of the king or his chief minister. As one historian wrote about an intendant in the early part of the eighteenth century, "Hocquart soon threw himself into the task of developing a Quebec-based entrepreneurial group that he hoped would be the salvation of the Canadian economy. The pursuit of this policy was inseparable from a politics of patronage, the doling out of monopolies, subsidies, contracts, and jobs."

In 1991 Hocquart was resurrected as Gérald Tremblay, Quebec's minister of industry, commerce, and technology, who was also on the boards of Hydro-Québec and the Caisse de Dépôt. Educated as a lawyer and a Harvard MBA, experienced as a businessman and a civil servant (in charge of loaning money to Quebec businesses), he unveiled an elaborate industrial strategy designed to mobilize entrepreneurs and workers into thirteen key "clusters" that government money and policies would help to make productive and competitive. "It's the government that must show the way and define a global strategy for the economic, social, and cultural development of Quebec," he said in a major speech in September 1991. "In sum, a defensive strategy based on individualism and the status quo, in the context of the globalization of markets, will lead straight to collective hell. But an offensive strategy calling for the mobilization of all the players, founded on value linked to work well done, can again realize our greatest hopes."

Quebec Inc. was not Reaganomics or Thatcherism. If English Canadians tend to see politicians as the agents of businessmen,

French Canadians tend to see businessmen as the agents of politicians. "Individualism must make room for the common interest," Tremblay declared, establishing a series of industrial task forces made up of businessmen, union leaders, and government officials. They were to do for economics what the nationalists wanted to do for politics: assume there is a single will of the Quebec people, determine what it is, and make it effective.

Nothing better illustrated that spirit than the huge banquet, held a couple of weeks after Tremblay's speech, at which more than two thousand politicians, chief executive officers, and union representatives honored Louis Laberge on the occasion of his retirement as president of the Quebec Federation of Labour. A fiery separatist and socialist who had been jailed by the Bourassa government for his strike activities in 1972, Laberge was being fêted not only because he remained a powerful influence with labor. He was a useful business partner too, for he had just taken over the union's Fonds de Solidarité des Travailleurs du Québec, which had almost $500 million to invest in Quebec companies.

———————

"For the majority of businessmen in Quebec," declared Jean Campeau, who had left the Caisse de Dépôt to become chairman of Domtar, "the question is no longer if sovereignty will happen, but when it will happen."

If that had ever been true, it was no longer so certain by the fall of 1991. The majority of Quebec's business leaders had supported the Meech Lake Accord by beating the drum of special status and raising the specter of separation, but now they were feeling the same heavy pressure from Bourassa and Mulroney to speak up for a renewed federalism. Even if some of them were, as Jean Campeau argued, "federalists 'by convenience,' because it is more profitable in the short term," they were still federalists and Canada was still profitable. The biggest names with the biggest companies and the biggest clout at home and abroad – Paul Desmarais of Power Corporation, Raymond Cyr of Bell Canada, Guy Saint-Pierre of SNC Group, Laurent Beaudoin of Bombardier – organized themselves into the Regroupement Economie et Constitution to fight against independence.

"This commitment to search for new solutions of a federal nature is shared by the majority of the French-speaking leaders of the largest Quebec corporations," Laurent Beaudoin claimed, "despite the widespread opinion, particularly in English Canada, that the Quebec business elite is now *souverainiste*."

Beaudoin's claim seemed proved a year later when Jean Campeau organized his own feeble business group to support independence. He boasted a hundred members (compared to the Regroupement's twelve hundred), but their names were kept secret so as not to jeopardize their federal and provincial contracts or subsidies, and there were no important business leaders among his fourteen directors, except perhaps for Campeau himself. Besides political pressure and peer pressure, Quebec Inc. was feeling economic pressure. Quebec had been hit by the effects of free trade, the deindustrialization of the American northeast, high interest rates, a high Canadian dollar, Ottawa's new sales tax, the downturn in its Ontario and American markets, the virtual collapse of the Stock Savings Plan following the market crash in 1987, and a particularly deep and stubborn recession. Unemployment in the province jumped above 12 per cent. Layoffs and bankruptcies became daily headlines, particularly when they concerned the heroes of Quebec Inc.

One by one, many of its brightest lights lost their golden glow – including Jean Campeau at Domtar, which reported losses of almost $350 million in 1990–91. Marcel Dutil dumped his half of Quebec's largest gas utility on the Caisse and another government agency in order to save his steel-products firm. Raymond Malenfant lost control of his hotels and office buildings in part to cover his debts to the Mouvement Desjardins. Most spectacularly of all, Lavalin Inc.

was forced to merge with its archrival, SNC Group. Like Hydro-Québec itself, Lavalin – a colossal engineering firm with thousands of employees, dozens of affiliates, and contracts around the world – had become a metaphor for Québécois know-how and gutsiness. Its boss, Bernard Lamarre, had become as mythic as Napoleon, charming, cunning, dictatorial, with a fabled art collection in his office and a politician from every party in his pocket. Like Napoleon – or Napoléon Tétrault – his overreaching ambition and overconfident autocracy finally brought him down, and his fall shook the province.

"Unfortunately, some of these guys didn't have any long-standing experience," my cousin André Tétrault said. "They got into things they knew nothing about, they got too big for their boots. Worse, they didn't have anyone to put the brakes on them."

The more prudent were still doing well, of course, but the comeuppance of the high fliers and high rollers cast a shadow over the entire business class. Was Quebec Inc. as viable as it claimed, or simply the privileged recipient of taxpayers' money? Had the boom been merely a lucky phase of the North American economy? Certainly the cockiness had been kicked out of Quebec's entrepreneurial spirit. The Coopérants Mutual Life Insurance Society, founded more than one hundred years before in the Catholic parishes of Quebec, collapsed after a disastrous acquisition spree. Shares in the National Bank, the only major bank controlled by French Quebeckers, plunged after a series of bad loans. Michel Gaucher, the shipping magnate who had been supported by the Caisse in his bid to buy the Steinberg's supermarket empire and keep it Québécois, sold it at a discount after two years of losses. Analysts even began to take a closer look at Hydro-Québec because of its enormous debt load and the uncertainties about its American contracts.

The impact was greatest in Montreal, of course. Manufacturing was down. Taxes were up. Construction was down. Office vacancies were up. Tourism was down. Bankruptcies were up. Rows of stores were boarded up. Countless houses were for sale. In some poorer districts, unemployment exceeded 20 per cent and the kids were turning to drugs or crime. "Montreal has the highest level of unemployment of any city in North America," said Marcel Côté, a noted consultant to both Mulroney and Bourassa. "It's normal to lose old industries. It's less normal not to replace them."

In a report to the Quebec government, Côté committed a kind of heresy by apportioning some blame to the language laws. The laws had driven out English-speaking businessmen just when Montreal needed to modernize its economy, he argued, and they discouraged talent, investors, and head offices from coming in. Since there was nowhere else for labor and management to go if they wanted to work in French, Montreal was "the end of the line" and, as such, was stuck with a certain level of chronic unemployment. Furthermore, Côté claimed, French Canadians had been able to take over the economy of Montreal in the 1960s only because Montreal had already started its decline from national powerhouse to regional metropolis, due to such factors as the opening of the St Lawrence Seaway, the loss of head offices, and the investments of the American auto industry in southern Ontario.

The Quiet Revolution might not have been quite so quiet if many anglos had not been ready (perhaps even delighted) to pack up their sagging businesses or sell off their outmoded factories. For almost two decades the rot in Quebec had been camouflaged by the political and "catch-up" spending of the federal, provincial, and municipal governments – highways, schools, hospitals, airports, subways, Expo 67, hydro dams, the 1976 Olympics, grants and loans and write-offs and bail-outs – but by 1990 the public debt had forced every agency at every level to cut back. That, and the wane of protectionism, exposed the underlying weakness of the Quebec economy. Typically, the Quebec government responded at the end of 1991 with yet another agency (Innovatech Grand Montréal), yet another five-year plan, and yet another infusion of hundreds of millions of dollars, to which the Ottawa government added hundreds of millions more in the form of military contracts, development programs, and a plethora of new museums dedicated to art, history, and even humor.

———————

Revolutions usually grow out of bad times, but Quebec separatism has generally been a fair-weather phenomenon. Economic hardships turn the debate from language and pride to dollars and cents. Québécois who think that independence might be nice begin to ask at what cost. All through 1991 and into 1992, therefore, nationalists and federalists engaged in "la chicane de chiffres," the war of numbers, with the nationalists accusing the federalists of practicing "economic terrorism" and the federalists accusing the nationalists of hiding the net benefits of Canada from the people. Almost everyone agreed that Quebec had the means and resources to be a functional country, on the scale of Austria or Denmark. They disagreed on whether it would be as prosperous as it has been within Canada.

First, a separate Quebec would have to assume its quarter-share of Canada's $400-billion debt, which would push Quebec's annual deficit from around $2 billion to more than $10 billion. Even with additional revenues and increased efficiencies, Quebec would probably have to raise taxes from a base that is already overburdened, and pay a premium to capital markets that are already demanding a price for uncertainty. Uncertainty would also inhibit investment, not because Quebec is in danger of becoming another Cuba but because its trade with English Canada and the United States cannot be guaranteed if it separates. The free-trade deal was signed between Canada and the United States, after all. It seems unlikely that an independent Quebec could operate inside its rules without some tough negotiations, which might begin with Washington's querying the cosy arrangements of the Caisse, Hydro-Québec, the government of Quebec, and Quebec Inc.

As for English Canada, reason and self-interest suggest that Ontario and the other provinces might wish to assure their own lucrative markets in Quebec. But anger and revenge are as likely to prevail. As in 1980, an economic association cannot be guaranteed in advance. Even the most amicable divorce seldom remains civil when the time comes to divide the furniture and the bank accounts.

Oddly, however much the separatists rage against the pernicious effects of federalism, few advocate a unilateral declaration of independence. They understand the advantages of a common market with Canada, in its own right and in the eyes of foreign investors who hold tens of billions of dollars of Quebec's debt. Odder still, however much they roar about the devastating consequences of Ottawa's monetary policies, many propose to keep the Canadian dollar for its practical benefits. Jacques Parizeau has even talked of keeping the Canadian passport. Even if Canada went along with such deals for its own purposes, however, how would two majorities work together in the central institutions without perpetual conflict or paralysis? Ironically, the republic of Quebec might well have to give up more control over its affairs than the province of Quebec.

Economic issues could make or break the cause of independence, as they did in 1980, but they are not the force behind it. It is not driven by the misery of the working class, and, unlike the Quiet Revolution of the 1960s, it has not been instigated by the frustration of a French-speaking middle class. For all the efforts of the separatists to make Canada the cause of poverty and unemployment, they face a major contradiction every time they crow about the success of Quebec Inc., argue for an economic association with Canada, or recognize Quebec's high standard of living. What is so bad, then?

"Separation is an emotional thing for most people," Jacques Tétrault said when I visited him one Saturday afternoon in his elegant cottage in North Hatley, next door to where I had argued with Frank Scott during the FLQ crisis twenty years earlier. "'If

English Canada doesn't want us,' people are saying, 'we'll go on our own.' They feel hurt and they need to be loved."

A Knife to the Throat, 1992

HOW TO HEAL the hurt, how to show love – that became English Canada's challenge after the death of the Meech Lake Accord in 1990. In the aftermath, polls showed support for sovereignty-association at an unprecedented 66 per cent; straight-out independence garnered 58 per cent. The Bloc Québécois, the pro-separatist faction in the House of Commons, led by the Tory renegade Lucien Bouchard, was the most popular party at the federal level among Quebeckers, and it proved its popularity when its candidate won a by-election in downtown Montreal. The Parti Québécois was the most popular party at the provincial level, and it scored a significant victory by capturing a Liberal stronghold near Quebec City in a provincial by-election. All through the fall of 1990 and into the spring of 1991, French and English Quebeckers were engaged in furious arguments about the pros and cons of independence. For better or worse, most thought it inevitable.

"Oh, isn't it terrible?" said Jeanne Vanier, the sister of Albert and Arthur Tétrault, when I visited her. "Why can't Canada just be Canada? Why don't we just stick together? All my life I've had English friends and French friends, there was never any problem. It's the same where I'm living now. There are English people and French people, and we all get along. We play bridge together, we play bingo together, we go on trips in the minibus together. I don't see the problem."

"I can't understand it myself, but it might well happen," said her daughter Nicole, who clearly did not share the views of our cousin Danielle in Rimouski. Recently retired as head of social-services research at the Université de Montréal, Nicole reminded me of Simone Signoret, not least because of the pleasure with which she dragged on one Matinée after another. Unlike the French actress, she had no trace of a French accent in her English. As a child she had spoken English to her father and French to her mother; over time she had alternated between English and French schools, English and French universities, and English and French jobs. "Certainly there's a feeling around town of 'This time, we're going to get it.' Outside of work, most of my friends aren't separatists. It's natural in Montreal for people of the same affinity to stay together. But, at work, I'd guess that all but a few of the couple of hundred people are separatists. It's a semi-public, semi-academic milieu, of course, so it may not be representative, but I'm always surprised by how many of my graduate students can't even read English. Some of them take pride in not knowing a word of English, as if that's proof that they don't need it. There's enormous peer pressure not to defend Canada. Everybody assumes that I'm a federalist because they know that my Uncle Georges was the governor general, but I usually don't bother to argue about it. It's pointless. If you're not with it, you're out of it – and generally I prefer to be out of it."

According to Lysiane Gagnon, Quebec's most astute journalist (and no doubt another "cousin" of mine through the Gagnons of Ile d'Orléans), "Fifteen years ago the typical *indépendantiste* was a rebel or a free-spirited individual. Today the average sovereigntist is a conformist who likes to go with the crowd. In most circles it is seen as 'normal' to be a sovereigntist; an unabashed federalist is a curiosity." Indeed, went the joke, you could always guess the federalists at a party: they were the ones who never said anything. One Outremont couple I know were afraid to put a pro-Canada sticker on their car, so they resorted to a decal with the first four musical notes of "O

Canada" – safer, no doubt, but hardly effective propaganda.

"I come from a strong federalist family, but even my sister has become a separatist," a French Canadian woman told me during the winter of 1990. "Her husband's a doctor, and I asked her what would happen if he couldn't earn his present salary in an independent Quebec. 'We'd just move out,' she said. Does that make any sense? But that's the kind of thinking I hear these days."

———

When Meech failed, Robert Bourassa vowed not to return to the bargaining table with the other premiers. He did not want to submit to the humiliation of another failure, and he saw no point in endlessly repeating the five basic demands – recognition of Quebec as a distinct society; control over immigration; guaranteed representation on the Supreme Court; limits on federal spending; and a Quebec veto power over changes to federal institutions – that the accord had promised him in exchange for his signature on Trudeau's 1982 constitutional reforms. Now, Bourassa argued, it was time for English Canada to decide what it wanted and produce a binding offer for Quebec's consideration. It had to be at least Meech, and, as a kind of penalty, it should be more.

Considerably more, said his party when the Quebec Liberals gathered for a policy convention in early 1991. They endorsed almost all the proposals of a committee that Bourassa had set up in 1990 to prepare for "a second round of negotiations in the event of the ratification of the Meech Lake Accord, as well as alternative scenarios in the event of the accord's failure." (There, in black and white, was more clear evidence that the accord was to have been the means to further power-mongering by the Quebec government, not the end to its demands.) The committee's report – known as the Allaire Report, after its chairman – presented a devastating portrait of Canadian federalism and a bleak outlook for its future.

"Under the existing federal structure," it said, "the Quebec government lacks the essential powers it needs to enable Quebec to develop fully as a distinct society, as well as the tools to allow it to secure the future of the French fact in North America. The current structure fails to reflect the realities of Quebec and Canada, and gives rise to incoherence, abuse, and duplication of government efforts. It frequently encourages inaction, exacerbates the crisis in public finances, and perpetuates budgetary imbalances."

The solution, according to the report and the party convention, was an entirely new constitution, with a complete overhaul of the central institutions and a massive transfer of powers from Ottawa to Quebec City. The central government would be left with exclusive authority in only four areas: defense, customs and tariffs, currency and common debt, and subsidies to the poorer regions. Quebec would have exclusive or shared authority over everything else, from the post office to foreign policy, and a veto over anything Ottawa did regarding the shared responsibilities. Canada had to dismantle itself, in other words. If it did not, the Quebec Liberal Party would support a referendum to give Quebec "the status of a sovereign state."

On paper, at least, there were now two separatist parties in Quebec, for the Liberal resolution went far beyond anything Canada was likely to offer. Meech had been possible only because the prime minister and premiers paid no attention to the majority of English Canadians. This undoing of Canada was clearly impossible. Just as many Quebec separatists blithely assumed that Canada would agree to economic association, these fair-weather federalists blithely assumed that Canada would agree to political suicide. In fact, though English Canadians love to bitch about the federal government, few want to see it disappear. They may want it to listen, they may want it to work, but they want it. Even the angriest westerner, who often sounds like a Quebec nationalist when on a rant about the sins and stupidities of Ottawa, usually wants more power over it rather than less power for it. According to one poll, 62 per cent of Canadians preferred outright separation of Quebec to any more concessions that would cripple the effectiveness of the central government.

Robert Bourassa, now as in the past, did not want outright independence. Ever the pragmatic economist, he feared the consequences of uncertainty and upheaval. Apparently he had lost control over the report during his extended convalescence from a cancer operation. He certainly tried to soothe the wounded feelings of his federalist supporters by closing the Liberal convention with a tribute to the history, values, and job benefits of the Canadian union. The party resolution was not binding on his government, after all, and its wild demands were no doubt negotiable. But the pressure from the nationalists in the province, and in his own ranks, was useful in his own quest for special status, more autonomy, and whatever profit could be milked from the federation. So he decided to play an audacious and rather dangerous game. While trying to check the momentum of the separatist option by delaying any referendum until the fall of 1992, he did not try to crush it.

A short while later he passed a law committing his government to hold a referendum before October 26, 1992, on full sovereignty for Quebec. It was his response to another report, that of the Commission on the Political and Constitutional Future of Quebec. The commission had been conceived at the hour of the death of the Meech Lake Accord when Jacques Parizeau extended his hand toward Bourassa and pleaded for Quebeckers to "get together and discuss among ourselves – not with all sorts of other people, *entre nous* – our future and what must happen to us." As such, the commission, drawn mainly from the elites of politics and the public service, of business and labor, of education and the arts, had evoked the memory of French Canadians rallying as they had done during the Iroquois attacks and English invasions to defend, with one proud heart and one collective will, the survival of the race.

Alas, even by ignoring the Maurice Prud'hommes, Claude Tétraults, and Jeanne Vaniers who thought that the status quo had served them well, even by dismissing the André Moncels, André Tétraults, and Nicole Vaniers who were fed up with the entire wrangle, even by neglecting the aboriginal peoples and the non-white immigrants, even by manipulating which briefs could be presented at the televised hearings and which economists or demographers would be invited to provide research, still the commission had trouble finding the one great will of Quebec. Indeed, there were two chairmen – Michel Bélanger and Jean Campeau, one a federalist and the other a separatist – because Bourassa and Parizeau had been unable to agree on one. The commission shared the Allaire Report's assessment that "Quebec's relationship with the rest of Canada, within the political system and the constitutional order which govern them, has reached a stalemate," but it could not come up with a solution. So it came up with two.

"We all started from the premise that Canada couldn't go on as it had," Bélanger told me, "but we divided over whether to go out or stay in. Going out is feasible, but is there a better way to get the same objectives at less cost? Staying in may be less costly, but what basic powers does Quebec need to maintain its identity, protect its policies from every goddamn federal program that comes along, and not be a pain in the neck for all the others all the time? So we said, if we're staying in, what are Canadians willing to do for us? If it's only the status quo, well, forget it, maybe we'll all suffer, but we're getting out. And if we're getting out, let's figure out the details beforehand and go."

Unlike the Allaire Report, the Bélanger-Campeau Commission did not itemize the conditions for Quebec's remaining in Canada. Canada was to come up with an offer Quebec could not refuse. A good offer would affect the question or even annul the referendum, presumably, since it would give Bourassa the excuse to change the legislation. An inadequate offer would see Bourassa himself leading the way to independence. It might have been an enormous bluff, but Canada had been given eighteen months to save itself.

––––––––––––––––

In the words of one strategist, Quebec had put "a knife to the throat of English Canadians." Almost at once, however, the knife began to quiver. In poll after poll, support for sovereignty slipped. By the spring of 1991 it was less than 50 per cent. Without constant provocation, most Quebeckers had been unable to sustain the pitch of indignation and humiliation; and given the diversity and conflicts of Quebec society, it had not taken long for the myth of a single national will to reveal itself as a flimsy illusion. Even the most optimistic separatists recognized that their recent numbers had been artificial – which was why one prominent nationalist called Bourassa a "traitor" for evading the opportunity to hold a quick and successful referendum. The Société Saint-Jean-Baptiste de Montréal itself was having trouble finding the money and enthusiasm for another big parade in June. Whether because of the downturn in the economy or the surlier mood in English Canada, more and more Quebeckers were taking a harder look at independence.

Still, the odds on Canada were no better than fifty-fifty. A strong defense of federalism remained something of a social gaffe, for anything less than "a clear message" weakened Quebec's negotiating position. With the collapse of the Roman Catholic Church, it seemed, federalists confessed their shameful sin only to the anonymous ear of the pollster. Nor did the swing away from independence translate into a swing toward the status quo. Give us liberty or give us a distinct society, went the cry of a majority of Quebeckers, and at the same time polls reported that most Quebeckers no longer feared any adverse effect of independence on their jobs, their taxes, their retirement benefits, their health care, or their personal financial situation.

"The challenge," said Joe Clark, who was named minister for

constitutional affairs in April 1991, "is to try to define changes that can be acceptable across the range of different perspectives in the country."

His challenge was made tougher, not easier, by the one obvious change that would have met with almost universal acclaim: the immediate resignation of Prime Minister Mulroney. "There is fury in the land against the prime minister," the federal government's own commissioner on Canada's future reported, and polls showed that more people believed Elvis Presley was alive than believed Brian Mulroney was doing a good job. Many Canadians still held Mulroney personally responsible for creating the constitutional crisis in the first place. Many more doubted whether he could clean up his own mess.

Though he had begun at last to attack the fallacies and economics of separatism, Mulroney's power base still depended upon the Quebec nationalists in his Cabinet, his caucus, and his constituencies; and though he had been forced to open the agenda to the hopes and desires of English Canada, both his future in politics and his place in history still depended upon appeasing Robert Bourassa. "The people who haven't got the message – and don't want to hear it – are the politicians, particularly our prime minister," one witness told the government's commissioner. "He will do his desperate best to go the decentralized route even if it means the dismemberment of the country."

It seemed so that September, when Ottawa unveiled twenty-eight proposals for general discussion. There was something for everybody: aboriginal rights for the native peoples; property rights for businessmen; an elected Senate with better representation for western Canada; a surrender of Ottawa's authority over job training and its shared responsibilities in six other areas; more influence over immigration and culture for all the provinces; and a "distinct society" clause that would allow Quebec to protect its French-speaking majority, "unique culture," and civil-law tradition from the impact of the Charter of Rights. One new proposal, however, was something the federal government wanted for itself: the power to "exclusively make laws in relation to any matter that it declares to be for the efficient functioning of the economic union."

The intention had been to harmonize economic goals and strengthen the Canadian common market, which was beset by all sorts of provincial barriers designed to impede the free flow of beer, bricks, and architects. To Joe Clark, the new proposal seemed to suit the kind of economic association advocated by the Allaire Report, the Bélanger-Campeau Commission, and the Parti Québécois. Within hours of its suggestion, however, it met a volley of fire from Quebec's politicians, businessmen, union leaders, and editorialists – and not just the nationalists – who feared it would threaten everything from the Caisse de Dépôt to the myriad of incentives and taxes designed to promote development and jobs in Quebec. "If this is accepted," Jacques Parizeau intoned, "it will be the end of what we call Quebec Inc."

"Isn't it ironic," Lysiane Gagnon commented, "to see Quebec, so wild for free trade with the United States just three years ago, rise up today as one against a proposal for free trade inside Canada? The fearless go-getters of three years ago, who used to talk only of risk-taking, competitiveness, excellence, and entrepreneurship on a continental level, now huddle close to themselves, in panic at the idea of leaving their hothouse, speaking only of protectionism, guarantees, and acquired rights."

That aside, the proposals were generally seen as "less than Meech." Where was Quebec's veto, for example, and what powers had been lost by the more precise definition and more limited application of the distinct-society clause? Bourassa knew that he could not reject the package completely without tilting Quebec toward independence, but he also knew he could not accept what he described as "authoritarian federalism." "What was offered Quebec made it possible to maintain a dialogue," he explained, "but only just."

Ottawa went back to work to improve the offer. It sent an all-party parliamentary committee across the country to seek advice from experts and plain folks. It assembled still more experts and plain folk to discuss the key issues at a series of weekend conferences in early 1992. The federal government planned to gather together all this advice, add its own thoughts, and come up with better, firmer proposals in April, just months before Quebec's deadline.

After seventy-eight meetings, seven hundred witnesses, three thousand submissions, and a final week of political arm-twisting, the parliamentary committee produced one hundred and thirty pages of platitudes and contradictions – the obvious results of the pressure to find a Canadian consensus, pleasing to every region and interest group. The qualified distinct-society clause was back, for example, but it had to be compatible with the "vitality and development" of Quebec's English-speaking minority. The federal politicians had stretched themselves to the limits of politics and logic to accommodate Quebec. Now everyone awaited Bourassa's response.

Again, he did not reject the proposals. Again, he did not accept them. Though the economic-union idea had been stripped of real power, Bourassa was still bothered by Ottawa's "reflex to dominate," as he put it, "a domineering federalism where it must be present in every sector and in the end have the final word." Clearly, he did not feel he had enough to take to the people in lieu of independence. He needed more powers, exclusive powers, distinct powers.

What did he have in mind? Perhaps, Bourassa once hinted, instead of holding a referendum on full independence, he would pose a different question: "Do you want to replace the present constitutional system with two sovereign states associated in an economic union and responsible to an elected parliament?"

Canada, in other words, would become a union in the way that the European Economic Community is a union. Two independent countries would submit to a common legislature, presumably as equal partners in some kind of dyarchy. As Bourassa never tired of reiterating to the separatists, from René Lévesque to Jacques Parizeau, "You can't have a monetary union without an economic union, and you can't have an economic union without a political union." Since some sharing of sovereignty is inevitable, he reasoned, "why should we take back powers that will then be redelegated, with all the transition costs involved for Quebeckers and for Canadians?" Why not instead work for sovereignty through federalism, by building binational institutions at the center?

Here, then, was the long-term, step-by-step purpose of special status and distinct society. In time Quebec would be so strong and so different that it could demand representation by "nation" rather than representation by population in Ottawa. Bourassa had taken a step closer to that goal by withdrawing from the constitutional negotiations and compelling English Canada to deal with Quebec one on one. That was the design behind his deliberate ambiguity regarding the meaning of distinct society in the Meech Lake Accord and his growing irritation with the narrowing of its definition and application: it had to mean new powers, or it was useless. And if it was useless, he wanted new powers now.

When Bourassa's version of *souveraineté* was put to the people by the pollsters, it did not fare better – or worse – than Parizeau's. More powers sounded like a nice thing to get, but there had been no groundswell of public opinion demanding them and no widespread faith that the Quebec government was necessarily a better government. "In the abstract," wrote Stéphane Dion, a young political scientist at the Université de Montréal, "Quebeckers tend to cast a favorable eye on the transfer of powers to their provincial government. But in practice, sector by sector, they are hard-pressed to identify the areas where the removal of the federal government would serve their interests."

Even some leading members of Quebec's arts and film communities, traditionally the standard-bearers of Quebec nationalism, had doubts about becoming poorly paid instruments of the provincial ministry of culture. "If we have in Quebec a literature, a dramaturgy, a song industry that testify to our existence," wrote the novelist Jacques Godbout, "we owe them to the indefatigable and enlightened support, over the past fifty years, of a few federal institutions. These institutions have access to significant funds, and their staffs have not been subjected to the dictates of prelates and politicians."

Such voices were lost, however, in the loud clamor of Quebec's political and business elite for a distinct society and increased power. A noteworthy number of English Canadian politicians, academics, and journalists were even prepared to strip the disguise off distinct society and concede special status and special responsibilities to Quebec. Quebec *is* the only province with a French-speaking majority and *has* "a unique culture," they argued, noting that French Quebeckers have their own version of "Happy Birthday" and smoke more cigarettes than English Canadians, so what was the point of decentralizing the entire federation just to keep Quebec from being recognized as different in the constitution?

I had asked the same question in the 1960s. Twenty-five years of constitutional conferences had provided the answer. The demands for more power would never be satisfied. Granting a general license to pursue special powers would only encourage their pursuit. Inevitably, Quebeckers would lose their enormous influence in Ottawa, as other Canadians began to wonder why Cabinet ministers and members of Parliament from Quebec should have authority over matters from which Quebec would be increasingly exempt. Inevitably, the identification of Quebec as the national state of the Québécois people would only be strengthened. Inevitably, Canada would return to the deadlock of the double-majority regime of the 1850s or pull itself apart once and for all.

There was something sad, even pathetic, about the spectacle of hundreds of earnest people spending thousands of hours and millions of tax dollars, scrambling against the ticking clock to feed the insatiable appetite of a relatively few power-mongers. At best their efforts proved to ordinary Quebeckers the sincerity and affection of ordinary Canadians. At worst their efforts threatened to emasculate the country for another short-term peace. Either way, they seemed to assume that a positive result would appease the sovereigntists and convince the separatists. It was, as Samuel Johnson said of the man who remarried immediately after the death of an impossible wife, yet another example of "the triumph of hope over experience."

———————

In March 1992 Canada's two northern territories and four native organizations joined the federal and provincial governments at the next round of negotiation. Quebec remained apart. "If it was difficult to reach an agreement with eleven," Robert Bourassa observed from the distance, "it is obvious that it will not be easy with seventeen."

The others ploughed ahead without him, as much to secure the best deal for themselves as to deliver an acceptable offer to him. They set the end of May as the new deadline for their work, not enough time to bind all their legislatures to a final offer but time enough for Bourassa to consider whether the offer was sufficiently binding and alluring to affect his October referendum.

It soon became apparent at the negotiating table that everyone had some reservations about the parliamentary committee's recommendations. The concessions to Quebec were not the most serious. More intractable were native self-government and Senate reform. The native leaders threatened to block any deal unless they got the autonomy and rights they wanted; several provinces held out for a federal Senate that was elected, effective, and equal in terms of provincial representation – more like the American Senate, in other words, than the British House of Lords. Lurking over everyone's shoulders was the ghostly presence of the Quebec government, which was known to be wary of a "third order of government" for natives that would intrude upon Quebec's own power and of

provincial equality in the Senate that would give seven million Quebeckers the same weight as the one hundred thousand citizens of
Prince Edward Island.

Bourassa gained at least one advantage by his absence from the
table: no one could accuse Quebec of being the spoiler at these talks.
The risk he took, however, was that the talks would succeed without
his input, isolating Quebec of its own volition. But success did not
come by the end of May. The deadline passed. Weeks passed. Then, at
the end of June, two years after the fatal efforts to save the Meech
Lake Accord, Prime Minister Mulroney once again summoned the
players to Ottawa for a final attempt to break the impasse.

"If Mr Bourassa is offering Quebeckers the choice between
renewed federalism and separation," he said, "it is essential that he
have a tool which is called the federal offer. In the absence of an
agreement between the premiers, we are going to formulate our own
offer."

Certainly no one expected an agreement. Mulroney even flew off
to an economic summit in Germany, leaving Joe Clark to deal with
the nine premiers. By getting nothing for Ottawa, by surrendering
anything for peace, Clark achieved unanimous support on July 7 for
a "premiers' package." Out went Ottawa's hope for more authority to
strengthen the Canadian economic union; in came an equal, elected,
and effective Senate. Out went Ottawa's jurisdiction in several areas;
in came new provincial powers and native self-government. Quebec
was still to be recognized as a distinct society as that pertained to the
Charter of Rights, but there were new qualifications to protect
Quebec's anglophone and aboriginal minorities, and efforts to
prevent the phrase from becoming a means of grabbing further
powers through the courts. "What does Canada want?" Robert
Bourassa had asked after the collapse of the Meech Lake Accord. Now
he knew what the premiers of English Canada, at least, wanted: they
wanted Quebec to be a province like the others.

Brian Mulroney, as amazed and dismayed as every other thinking

Canadian by what Clark had wrought, did not rush to embrace the agreement or brag about how he had again achieved consensus where no consensus seemed possible. One premier had been absent from the table, after all, and there was remarkably little in the premiers' package for Robert Bourassa to take to Quebeckers as an alternative to independence. Not only had Quebec's special status and special powers been reduced to almost nothing; Quebec's proportion of seats in the Senate had been reduced to less than 10 per cent.

"I cannot say today: no deal," Bourassa responded at first, for no deal would have forced him to hold the referendum on independence. He still did not want immediate independence, nor did he believe that most Quebeckers wanted it. Most were worried about the economy and sick of almost five solid years of constitutional brinkmanship. With an eye on the polls, Bourassa had already hinted that the referendum would not be about independence, for he was reluctant to hold a vote he was unsure of winning; otherwise, as had happened in 1980, Quebec's best weapon for blackmailing Ottawa would lose its potency. Instead, Bourassa wanted more negotiations. He wanted more time, more adjustments. For starters, just to get him back to the table, he wanted a broader and stronger distinct-society clause, almost exactly the one that had been in the Meech Lake Accord. It would apply to the interpretation of the entire constitution, not just the Charter of Rights, and it would override the rights of Quebec's minorities. If he could not get special powers now, in other words, he wanted to resume his step-by-step quest for them later.

Incredibly, Ottawa promised him that, and the process began again. Canada was back to where it had been two years earlier, still hunting for a deal to satisfy Quebec, still being bamboozled into granting special status by the threat of independence, even though the threat had proved somewhat empty. While most Quebeckers felt more Québécois than Canadian in their daily lives, and a third of them would probably never give up the dream of independence, the overwhelming majority still described Canada as an important part of their personal identity. A third of all separatists were even prepared to make a significant sacrifice for Canada, according to one poll, and a third of the population still believed that if Quebec became a sovereign state, it would be a part of Canada! Despite a decade of separatist propaganda and nationalist posturing, independence was no more popular than it had been in 1980.

Political and economic pressure had brought Robert Bourassa back to the bargaining table, in fact, though he had not received all five minimal conditions of the Meech Lake Accord, not to mention the preposterous demands of the Allaire Report. The same pressure pushed him to reach a compromise settlement on August 22, after five intensive days of negotiation, with Prime Minister Mulroney, the other nine premiers, the two territorial leaders, and the four aboriginal representatives. In exchange for conceding an equal (though less effective) Senate, Quebec was guaranteed at least a quarter of the seats in the House of Commons whatever its share of the population. In addition to getting the set of new powers that were offered to all the provinces, as well as the possibility of negotiating bilateral arrangements for even more from Ottawa, Quebec was to be recognized for the purposes of judicial interpretation as "a distinct society which includes a French-speaking majority, a unique culture, and a civil-law tradition."

"Quebec will finally enter the Canadian constitutional family with its head held high, with dignity and with more powers than it has ever had to protect and develop its distinct society within Canada," Mulroney immediately crowed.

Like the Meech Lake Accord, the tentative deal was presented as all or nothing, this Canada or no Canada. On that basis Bourassa decided to direct the October 26 referendum from sovereignty to the federal offer, and Mulroney and the other premiers decided to hold a national referendum on the same question on the same day. Though the deal fell short of the expectations Bourassa had raised, he was gambling that he could put the tiger of nationalism back in its cage without being eaten.

If so, and if the new accord passed elsewhere in Canada, the Quebec political class – federalist and separatist alike – would have a host of new devices by which to continue its march toward a double-majority union of two equal nations. If not, it would again pursue its goal of political sovereignty and economic association more directly. Either way, the elites' old game of maximizing the economic benefits from the federation while minimizing the political connections to the center would not stop unless the people of Quebec – or the people of Canada – make clear that they have had enough of the game itself.

Scattered Seed, 1992

"THE Moncel name has gone to hell," Maurice Prud'homme once joked.

Worse, in fact. It had gone to Toronto.

Never a common name, even in France, it was near extinction in Quebec. I found a couple of very distantly related Moncels in the Montreal telephone directory; and there was André Moncel, who had lent me the family genealogy, in the Town of Mount Royal. Beyond Quebec there was only my Uncle Robert in Nova Scotia and André's son and young grandson in Toronto. The son was named Charles, after my grandfather's brother, but I did not miss the coincidence that the first Moncel to Canada, almost two hundred and fifty years ago, had also been Charles. This latest Charles, born in 1954, and his son Leo, born in 1985, may well be the last bearers of the French soldier's nom de guerre in Canada.

Unlike my Uncle Robert, who inherited the military vocation of so many of our ancestors, the current Charles Moncel is no soldier. He is an automated-funds transfer agent with the Canadian subsidiary of American Express. He has a shy and thoughtful manner, a kind round face beneath dark curly hair, and remarkably clear eyes. I was surprised when I first met him – he lived within a long walk of my house in central Toronto – that he had no accent in English.

"It's because I grew up on a solid dose of American television," he said, "three or four hours a day, Captain Kangaroo and all that. I still pronounce words like 'been' and 'again' in the standard American, rather than Canadian way. At first I had a French accent. I spoke French at home and at school, though most of my friends on the street in the Town of Mount Royal were English-speaking. But when I was about seven, I was sent to a day camp where some kids teased me for my accent. I said 't'ree' instead of 'three,' things like that. It was the first and only time when people made an issue of my being French. I worked hard to speak English perfectly afterwards."

Television had not been his only American influence. There were the weekend excursions to New York State, where his parents kept a boat on Lake Champlain. There were the summer weeks at a New Hampshire camp run by Franco-American priests, where Charles picked up the strange blend of Yankee habits and Catholic values that characterize the French Canadian community of New England. There were the motor vacations across Canada and the United States. From an early age he had developed a taste for travel and a sense of life beyond 1950s Quebec. (He may also have received his professional destiny, for American Express traveler's checks, American Express cards, and American Express brochures lay deep within his childhood memory.)

"I was always aware of two worlds, one that spoke French and one that spoke English," he said. "They didn't clash. I had good feelings about both. I loved when the nuns made us pray for snow in December and told us Bible stories. That felt positive, not restricted. Gradually, however, the English world attracted me more than the French.

There was so much *more* of it. Later I understood the beauty of the French language and attitude, but I had picked up American values as well as American English from TV. Some of the nationalistic teachers at the Collège Notre-Dame in the 1960s didn't like me speaking so much English, but I wasn't attracted to what they were offering."

Even then, while still a high-school student in the midst of the Quiet Revolution and the FLQ bombs, Charles preferred to look outward. During one Christmas holiday he went to Haiti with a teacher and was led on an "eye-opening" excursion into the realities of the Third World by some French Canadian missionaries there. After graduation he went to Japan with an exchange group and spent two months living with Japanese families and frequenting Buddhist temples. Fascinated by Asian life and Asian philosophy, he interrupted his studies again to spend a year with Canada World Youth, mostly with families and students in Java. He hitchhiked around Europe; he studied Chinese and Japanese at McGill; he led tourists from France to every corner of Canada.

Predictably, like his father and mother, he was a federalist. "I felt that whatever Trudeau did was a good thing. In hindsight, perhaps he should have sealed his constitutional reforms by getting Quebec's agreement, but he was clearly the best possible man for the times. The election of the Parti Québécois in 1976 did not worry me especially. Nothing was going to change overnight, though the English saw the writing on the wall and the ones who stayed understood the risks. There will always be a place for the anglos in Quebec. But being a Québécois is something else. I myself didn't feel entirely at home in Montreal, which was one reason I moved to Toronto."

Love and money were other reasons. A Winnipeg woman of Polish and American roots, whom Charles had met in Asia, was intending to move there, and the tour company for which he was working offered him a job in its Toronto office. He went, he married and bought a house, he had a girl and a boy, he found a more secure position, and he lived happily ever after.

An ordinary story, but when multiplied by hundreds of thousands or even millions over time, one of tremendous consequence. "My parents left me lots of choices, too many choices, perhaps because they had had so few choices themselves," Charles said. "That's the real story of Quebec today. The declining birthrate, the French Canadian women marrying Italian men, the French Canadian men marrying Oriental women. The social network of family has fallen apart."

———————

Wherever I went in my extended family, I encountered the same story. The seed of Guillaume and Alphonsine Moncel had scattered to the United States, the Netherlands, the Dominican Republic, Greece, and South Africa. There were young Prud'hommes and Tétraults in Ottawa, Toronto, Calgary, and Vancouver. Sometimes whole families had gone; sometimes only the old, the impractical, the nostalgic, and the mentally deranged had stayed. And of the remaining, a remarkable number are ready to leave on a moment's notice.

All of them, anglophones and francophones, weighed a score of political, financial, irrational, and personal factors and made an individual decision to go or not. In this they were no different from Zacherie Cloutier, who had decided one day in 1634 to quit Mortagne with his wife and children, traverse a dangerous ocean, and spend the rest of his days in New France. Nor were they different from the explorers, Indian interpreters, coureurs de bois, guerrilla warriors, loggers, prairie pioneers, northern engineers, Franco-Americans, and federal bureaucrats who had left their parents and farms in the St Lawrence Valley to seek food, fortune, or simple liberty. They were no different, either, from the current emigration of Québécois professionals and Québécois pensioners to the Sun Belt of the United States.

According to one estimate, the seventy-five thousand Canadiens at the time of the British Conquest produced more than twelve million North Americans. Only half of them still speak French or live in Quebec. I have met others living as artists in New York (where a Franco-American named Jean-Louis Lebris de Kérouac became better known as the Beat novelist Jack Kerouac), businessmen in Los Angeles (where a French Canadian expatriate became mayor in the 1870s), doctors in West Africa, miners in Australia, and Hindu ascetics in the Himalayas. At some point they or their ancestors had perceived what the French philosopher Ernest Renan once articulated: "Man is bound neither to his language nor to his race; he is bound only to himself because he is a free agent, or in other words a moral being."

So, too, many French Canadians kept their maternal language and remained in Quebec as acts of individual choice, as expressions of their personal freedom, not because they felt bound by blood. They were the heirs of the individualistic and irreverent habitants whose lack of obedience and respect had been denounced over the centuries by priests, administrators, and British governors. Among their ranks were many of the politicians, missionaries, entrepreneurs, and artists who had looked beyond French Canada, espoused unorthodox ideas, understood the realities of the English language, and confronted the challenges of the modern world without fear.

There were risks, of course, especially the risk of overambition, which had stretched the resources of the fragile colony on the St Lawrence across an unmapped and hostile continent, and the risk of assimilation, which had befallen the families of Alain de Lotbinière, Albert Tétrault, the Franco-Americans, and René Moncel. But there were also rewards: the historical success of Champlain and Frontenac, the political success of La Fontaine and Laurier, the commercial success of Joseph Masson and Paul Desmarais. To them, there could have been no rewards without the risks, and without the rewards there could have been nothing but individual and collective atrophy.

They were just one side of the French Canadian family, which was divided as profoundly as the human family between the nomadic and the sedentary. Against the continent was the valley. Against the fur traders were the farmers. Against the merchants were the priests. Against the federalists were the nationalists. Against the voyageurs were the other habitants who had always warned their children about the dangers beyond the boundaries of the parish. Those who left for the west or New England or Ottawa, for adventure or opportunity or freedom, jeopardized the security of those who remained behind for safety. They became traitors, *vendus*.

"In every generation," Hugh MacLennan observed in *Two Solitudes*, "there arose French Canadians who tried to change the eternal pattern of Quebec by political action, and nearly all of them had been broken, one by one." They were broken by the strength of the collectivity, the power of every family. "If they went far enough, they were bound to find themselves siding with the English against their own people, and if nothing else broke them, that inevitably did."

Though they represented an old and legitimate line of Canadiens, they were often broken because the other side had monopolized the traditional, psychological, even moral ground. Family duty, religious faith, personal sacrifice, national destiny, and filial obedience were the instruments of control. The tiny settlement was under siege; the true faith was under siege; the mother tongue was under siege – only a selfish and treacherous sinner would desert his kin in such circumstances. This was the message from the pulpit and in the press, from teachers and novelists and local heroes. This was the dark side of Quebec nationalism, in which dissent amounted to betrayal.

Anglos, aboriginals, and immigrants are often portrayed as dissidents because they are not part of the one body, one mind of the Québécois people. In 1990, for example, the novelist Yves Beauchemin spoke of a revelation that had struck him in a doughnut shop when he overheard people speaking Greek and English. "All of a sudden, despite the warm and familiar atmosphere of the place, I had the impression of sitting on top of a bomb. The whole of Quebec was there. Two cultures occupying the same territory. A majority, French-speaking and good-natured, with weakening demographic projections; and the immigrants who do not seem to be living in Quebec, but in America, that's to say in a massively English-speaking continent. The two groups seemed, in a dangerous way, like strangers." Why dangerous? "Simply because two cultures can't expand in the same linguistic space. Quebec, after all, is not elastic! If English takes more room, French will take less. If French takes more room, English will have to take less."

But the nationalists' ire has not been confined to strangers. It has been directed at anyone who transgressed the boundaries of the parish. In 1977 the nationalists went after Robert Scully, then a precocious editor with *Le Devoir,* for describing Quebeckers as "spiritual cripples" to an American audience. "French Quebec is such a small, forgotten, culturally deprived, hyperactive, and insecure community," Scully wrote in the *Washington Post,* "no one would want to live there who doesn't have to, i.e., who isn't born into it. Lots of people are happy there, but always in spite of it, never because of it." Scully was swamped with hate mail, repudiated by his own newspaper, and after passing through "the worst days" of his life, pressured into recanting. Like some Chinese writer during the Cultural Revolution, he declared himself "terribly repentant" and exiled himself to Maine.

More recently, the pressure has been felt by any French Quebecker who opposed the Meech Lake Accord, other than for nationalist reasons. Bourassa himself seemed bullied into the proposed referendum, just as he had been bullied into the language laws, and most federalists have been shouted into silence by the charge that they are not "good" Québécois. Few shouted back, as the father shouted to his separatist son in a play by Gratien Gélinas, "that 'valiant defenders of our threatened country' can be found outside the fort as well as inside."

The silence often gives the impression that there is one answer to the old question, "What does Quebec want?" In fact Quebec has been split into at least two camps since the days of Champlain's colony. French Canada has never been the absolutist heaven imagined by many nationalist historians or the totalitarian hell portrayed by many liberal commentators. It has always been torn between traders and settlers, coureurs de bois and habitants, *rouges* and *bleus*, federalists and nationalists.

Currently, according to most studies of the Quebec mind, a third of the population weigh toward federalism, a third toward independence, and a third remain confused. When the confused are probed for their tendencies, they divide equally. Hence the polls that place support for federalism and sovereignty at 50 per cent each. Quebec is literally of two minds. This dualism exists in many individuals too. Just as many pioneers were seasonal fur traders as well as farmers, just as many patriotes were political democrats as well as social conservatives, so a large percentage of Québécois are federalists and nationalists at the same time. The contradiction is a part of their patrimony.

"Between the world of furs and the world of the River's Lowlands, there were always tensions," the historian Fernand Ouellet wrote of New France. "Agriculture, the seigneuries, the parish, and the family (this last dominated by the wife) required stability, commitment to traditional values, withdrawal into oneself, isolation from the outside world, and austerity. The fur trade, in contrast, led to adventure, military exploits, escape from rigid surroundings, luxurious tastes, and a certain looseness of living. The Canadian habitant was not a product of only one of these worlds: he belonged to both at once."

Agriculture prevailed in the early nineteenth century, and with it nationalism. Industrialization prevailed in the early twentieth century, and with it federalism. But the psychological dichotomy remained in the family's memory, perhaps even in its genes. It has made Quebec quite an enigma over the decades. Quebeckers voted for Trudeau and Lévesque at the same time. They have supported fiscal conservatism and social democracy at the same time. They have opted for free trade with the United States and trade barriers within Canada at the same time. They have been warriors and pacifists at the same time. They have been pious Catholics and notorious libertines at the same time. They have banned English signs outside and permitted them inside. They have worshiped their land tearfully and desecrated it shamelessly. They have puffed with pride and cowered with inferiority. They have been generous of spirit and petty of mind. They have fought for the survival of their language and culture and abandoned both for a condo in Florida. They have wanted to remain in Canada and be an independent nation at the same time.

"Montreal is a weird place," Charles Moncel remarked. "It's so controlled in some ways and so lawless in other ways. It has a west end, which isn't that different from the American style of Toronto, but then it has an east end, which is allied to the Quebec countryside and still authentically different from the rest of North America. That difference is behind Quebec nationalism. It is a kind of ignorance, which is both a strength and a weakness. The strength allows this pure French Canadian spirit to grow. The weakness perpetuates an ingrained hatred of having to speak English to get ahead – not because of the anglos, but because of the world."

That underlying ignorance, both as strength and weakness, explains why the nationalists have failed in their attempts to cast themselves as the coureurs de bois of the twentieth century: the heroic ones exploring new territory, the fearless ones leaving the old family farm, the freedom-loving ones seeking broader horizons. In this reversal the federalists are the old and timid peasants clinging to past traditions and personal security in the form of a Canadian flag and a federal welfare check. True, neither Jacques Parizeau nor Danielle Daigneault is unsophisticated in experience or cautious in temperament. But despite all the rhetoric of nationalist businessmen taking on global markets and nationalistic politicians thinking in global terms, the goal is still to pull back from the continent to the valley, close the posts in the west, give up the east coast, and retreat behind the barricades to defend New France from the onslaught of Englishmen, Indians, and foreigners. It was not a coincidence that in 1990 more than half the population of Quebec tuned in weekly to a soap opera about habitant life at the end of the nineteenth century.

Once the intendants tried to regulate the colony (and protect their own interests) by preventing individual traders from voyaging among the Indians and the English. Once the bishops tried to secure the faith (and protect their own interests) by dissuading rural Quebeckers from emigrating to the cities and the United States. Now the nationalists are trying to create a nation (and protect their own interests) by guarding ordinary Quebeckers from the advantages of Canada and the English language. The language laws did more than ban English signs and compel immigrants to go to French schools: they deliberately curbed the trend among young Québécois toward American culture and English education. While making sure that their own children had access to the private schools that would open the doors to Harvard and international commerce, the nationalist elites removed the choice from most people. They understood all too well the temptations and benefits of the broader world.

Just as the traders had gone beyond the law, just as the migrants had gone beyond the border, countless French Quebeckers have gone – and will continue to go – beyond their language and culture for the sake of prosperity and liberty. "The Canadien is lively, proud, haughty, strong, hardy and industrious, capable of enduring extreme hardships," a French priest commented in 1709. "He likes to travel and roam through the woods, has much trouble remaining in one place, and takes after the uncivilized in loving independence."

My grandfather was that way, and so is my cousin Charles Moncel. "I don't speak French to my children," he said, "because I assume that if they want to speak it, they can learn it later. And they will want to speak it if the need is there. That is the big question: will the need be there? At the moment, it doesn't appear that it will."

Ultimately, the need can only be born of individual choice, not government coercion. People have to be drawn to the French language by the excellence of Quebec's education system, by the dynamism of its economy, by the richness of its culture, or else they will be condemned to exile or to life imprisonment in a folkloric theme park. Canadian bilingualism, which imposes the learning of both languages on relatively few federal public servants so that all citizens can have more individual choice about the language they speak, recognizes that reality.

"I would like to see Canada return to Trudeau's vision," Charles Moncel said, "but the circumstances and players have taken an unfortunate direction. Are the forces great enough to save the country? If 40 per cent of Quebeckers want independence, is 60 per cent enough to stop them, particularly if half are only lukewarm federalists? I don't know. Things change from day to day. Right now Quebec has everything it needs but the final declaration that would allow Bourassa to go around calling himself the president of the republic. The wrangling will continue for a long, long time. I can't see going back to Quebec myself. I visit two or three times a year, but I already feel like a refugee. My wife and I are thinking of moving to Vancouver some day. Even my parents are thinking of it. The only question is whether or not I'll be buried in Montreal in the Moncel plot."

The Blessing, 1992

IN 1977, between the election of the first Parti Québécois government and the enactment of its language law, I was offered a job with the Canadian Broadcasting Corporation in Ottawa. I did not want to leave Quebec, even temporarily, but the job was a good one and I had found nothing as interesting in Montreal. Before moving, however, perhaps to distinguish myself from the anglo exodus, perhaps to guarantee my return, perhaps to secure a piece of my childhood wherever I wandered for the rest of my days, I bought ninety acres in the Eastern Townships near the Vermont border, not far from where I had gone to school, summered on Lake Memphremagog, and visited Frank Scott.

Beside a trout stream in a pastoral valley, I put up a log cabin and filled it with books and mementos. By the stone fireplace in the living room or from the hammock on the porch I looked on pine trees, rushing water (rushing all the way to the Atlantic, I liked to muse), and the sun dropping behind the western ridge. On the valley's eastern ridge I dammed the springs and created a deep pond, which was soon visited by deer, ducks, moose, and blue herons. Swimming in summer or skating in winter, I contemplated a storybook domain, almost Swiss in its smallness and neatness: a couple of working farms on the far slope, their fields a changing quilt of subtle colors; Holsteins moving to and from the barn with soft bells; smoke rising from the sugaring shack hidden in a grove of maples; days and seasons and years revolving with a smooth predictability.

It was a cliché, this cabin in the woods, which bore little relation to most of modern Quebec, but it had the power to become a true refuge none the less. Whenever I can, I hasten back to it. Whenever I leave, I long to return. The sight of its landscape in a movie is enough to bring tears to my eyes, and I found neither the plains of Tanzania nor the ranges of Nepal more beautiful than its gentle hills.

In addition to its own charms, it is set amid one of the happiest – and oddest – societies in North America, a droll realm where conversations hop from English to French, where anglicisms are a basic part of the French vocabulary and gallicisms common to the English, where people have the pleasure of speaking their mother tongue while understanding – and being understood by – everyone else. In this realm there are families in which small children grow up believing that all men speak English and all women French, or vice versa. There are Ryans who do not know a word of English and Tremblays who wear Scottish kilts, and they live in places called Sainte-Marguerite-de-Lingwick and Saint-Isidore-d'Auckland. Side by side are farms that have been owned by families that moved north from the United States early in the nineteenth century and farms that are occupied by families that have never needed to speak English. Amid them, within a mile of my cabin, are a trilingual couple from Lithuania, a trilingual couple from South Africa, several Jews from Eastern Europe, a retired couple from England, a few American draft dodgers tending organic gardens, and a Japanese sculptor whose wife and artistic partner is a French Canadian woman from Montreal. ("At least your mother is *normal*," their three handsome sons have been told at the local school.)

Despite the pull of my work and travels, I have spent many seasons and whole years here, and for the past three summers I have decamped from Toronto with my wife and children to share the peace of the place with them. At picnic lunches beside the pond I fed my newborn daughter her bottle, watched my two-year-old son chase our duck across the sand with his toy shovel, waved back to my young stepson during his ride on Monsieur Lefebvre's tractor, and discussed the prospects for the Atlantic provinces if Quebec seceded. At late-night dinners on the porch I savored the scent of mown fields and pine forests, admired the tanned faces of my friends in the flame of the kerosene lantern, felt my heart lift at the sight of my bright and lovely wife across the table, and argued fiercely about the true meaning of distinct society.

Private happiness, public strife: that was the mood of those summers, as the Meech Lake Accord collapsed, the economy weakened, the referendum threat was made law, the Mohawks and the Crees protested, and the constitutional negotiations persisted like a chronic illness. In some ways, of course, the private happiness was not reality. A two-month stay in the Eastern Townships did not reflect life in urban, unemployed, or unilingual Quebec. In other ways, however, it was the public strife that seemed unreal. Quebeckers, both French- and English-speaking, show a remarkable ability to have a good time in bad times, and the dour headlines rarely represented the general atmosphere. Like individual license versus collective control, like indoor tolerance versus outdoor repression, like the open arms of the family versus the doors closed to strangers, private happiness and public strife are another expression of Quebec's duality.

Into this relatively harmonious corner of Quebec, as genuine and as exceptional as every other corner of Quebec, there came in the summer of 1991 a nineteen-year-old Montreal student named Philippe Tremblay. He was the president of Action-Québec, a voluntary group dedicated to enforcing the language laws and partly financed by the Parti Québécois. "We want to francize Quebec," he said, armed with a camera and notebook, after he pulled into Ayer's Cliff. While most visitors find it an attractive and rather sleepy village of eight hundred, lying in a pastoral valley at the southern end of Lake Massawippi, Tremblay found it full of crime and subversion. There was nothing he could do about its English name – it had been settled by Americans around 1820, after all, and remains two-thirds English-speaking despite the exodus that has laid waste many old Scot and Yankee families to the point of extinction – and the municipality had already followed the orders of the Commission for the Protection of the French Language to whitewash "Stop" from its "Stop/Arrêt" signs and "Street" from its street signs. But there (in broad daylight!) was the word "Garage," and there (just across the road!) was the word "Snack Bar," and there (where even children could see it!) was the word "Milk Shake."

More galling, no doubt, to Philippe Tremblay was the apparent indifference of the locals and cottagers, who were flipping back and forth from French to English as they passed from Houde's supermarket to the Cliff House tavern. Tremblay clearly had a lot of work to do. Such was the insidious grip of British colonialism that many of the illegal signs had been put up by French Quebeckers!

The signs do not have much to do with the Conquest of 1763. They have to do with the convenience of American tourists, who might want to know that *auberge* means inn. They have to do with courtesy to anglophone customers, who might prefer to shop where people respect their very existence. Above all the signs have to do with freedom and community. To most people in Ayer's Cliff the two languages are not political issues or abstract principles. They are part of one's friends, one's relatives, oneself. Where Philippe Tremblay saw arrogance and threat, the locals see neighbors and family.

In truth there is not much arrogance and threat left in the anglos of the Eastern Townships and Quebec. They have never been weaker in proportion or clout; they have never been poorer in opportunity or hope. Many of their farms and businesses are for sale. Many of their schools and community associations are closing down. Many of their children and grandchildren are moving away. Conversely, French is on the rise in Quebec households and at work, and while most French Quebeckers have remained unilingual, most English Quebeckers have learned both languages. "If French is threatened today, it's rather by the lamentable state of the spoken and written word," says Jacques Henripin, a demographer who issued dire projections about the survival of French and subsequently changed his mind. "And on this subject, it's no use burying our head in the sand. This is not the fault of *les Anglais* or of the constitution."

Les Anglais are still the villains to the likes of Philippe Tremblay. In the spring of 1990, Montreal saw a new opera about the life of Emile Nelligan, the romantic poet who had written all his masterpieces before he was twenty, after which he was committed to a lunatic asylum for the remaining forty-two years of his life. In the libretto by the renowned playwright Michel Tremblay, Nelligan's schizophrenia and institutionalization are clearly the fault of his English-speaking father, who is portrayed, despite all the documented evidence, as anti-French and anti-art.

"What is wrong with our family?" he screams at his tragic wife.

"An English father. A French mother," she answers sweetly, *très doucement*. "Children forced to choose between their father and their mother. A family divided in two from the start, doomed to failure."

In this mentality, there can be no easing of the ban on English signs, no concessions to allow English-speaking immigrants to go to English schools, no recognition of those anglos who – for selfish or for altruistic reasons – persevered through the political turmoil of the 1970s, adapted to the language laws at work, sent their children to French schools, and waved goodbye to two hundred thousand departing friends and relations. Reluctantly or enthusiastically, these English Canadians transformed themselves from Colonel Blimps to bicultural middlemen somewhere between Quebec City and Toronto, with their own distinct opinions and their own distinct language. ("I'll pick up a Cuvée des Patriotes at the *dépanneur* near the *métro* on my way home from the *exposition*," an English Montrealer might say, meaning he'll get some wine at the corner store near the subway after seeing an art exhibition.) In return for their efforts, their own traditional party overruled the Charter of Rights and delegitimized the public existence of their language. It was like being kicked in the groin when already down.

"Being an English Quebecker is like living in a hotel," a friend once said. "It's comfortable for the moment, but you always know that someday you will have to leave." Almost 30 per cent of English Quebeckers now expect to leave the province within five years. Another 14 per cent say they will go if Quebec separates. Meanwhile, they have become feistier. Bourassa lost three important anglos from his Cabinet in protest against the sign law; the Liberals lost four

English-speaking ridings in the 1989 provincial election to the Equality Party, an English-rights movement with heavy support in Montreal's Jewish community. In June 1991 the tenth annual meeting of Alliance Quebec, an organization claiming to speak on behalf of forty thousand English Quebeckers, resolved to set aside its defensive and conciliatory approach and fight for the growth, not just the preservation, of their language and community.

Much of the fight had been inspired by Reed Scowen, a bilingual native of the Eastern Townships and former Liberal member of the Quebec assembly, who published a provocative manifesto called *A Different Vision* in 1991. The time has come, he argued, to put behind apologies for the injustices of the past and guilt about speaking English in Quebec. The English-speaking community can no longer be characterized as privileged or even of British origin. The anglos have slipped from 24 per cent of the province's population at the time of Confederation to barely 10 per cent now. Their average income is no greater than that of French Quebeckers; their political strength is practically nil. So why must their rights be curtailed and their numbers decimated? For the sins of their English Quebec forefathers, it seemed, and for the power of the English language around the world. "The government," Scowen claimed, "and those who influence it, can admit no limit to the expansion of French in Quebec."

"The actual banning of other languages is a measure of hysteria, frankly," remarked Charles Taylor, the eminent McGill philosopher, himself half French Canadian and wholly sympathetic to the survival of French Quebec. "It's a product of mass neurosis." To which Lysiane Gagnon of *La Presse* added, "Who wants to integrate into a people so paranoid that it can't stand the sight of another language? Who wants to join a culture so fragile that it is threatened by a sign and so unattractive that it can only survive thanks to a battery of laws?"

Gagnon's questions were significant because she gave voice to the majority of French Quebeckers, including those in Ayer's Cliff. That majority rarely speaks up or marches in the street, but it did express itself in early 1992. Under the language law, the town of Rosemère lost its bilingual status, which would have allowed it to provide certain signs and services in English, once its population passed from mostly anglophone to mostly francophone. The mayor of this suburban community north of Montreal decided to hold a plebiscite to see whether its twelve thousand residents, more than two-thirds French-speaking, wanted to stay bilingual out of respect for its past and consideration for its anglos. Amazingly, 77 per cent voted for bilingualism, though they had little to gain by doing so.

Even Jean Dorion of the Saint-Jean-Baptiste Society admitted that most Québécois oppose the French-only sign law most of the time. "When things are quiet," he explained, "people can't understand why we have to ban other languages. They see it as vengeance. But when things are hot, when the English start putting up English-only signs at the least hint of flexibility, when the immigrants start speaking English in the stores and schools, we get a chance to justify the ban and our support increases."

It is to the advantage of the nationalists to keep things hot, of course, if only to prevent the Liberals from making any concessions to their English-speaking supporters. Thus, Philippe Tremblay was paid to go into communities such as Ayer's Cliff and provoke linguistic tensions. While he and his sort succeeded in spooking Robert Bourassa, who spooks at the very notion of a nationalist protest, elsewhere they sometimes succeeded only in solidifying the opposition to such narrow-minded paranoia. In Ayer's Cliff storekeepers and local officials began campaigning against the language laws and declaring themselves proudly bilingual.

Too often, however, the nationalists have shamed or bullied the other side into complicity. They have propagated the illusion that Quebec is of one mind – *must* be of one mind – and that they alone articulate the will of the people. At the same time they demean the ambitions and interests of federalists. Nationalist ambitions are for the glory of the nation; federalist ambitions are for twenty pieces of silver. Nationalist interests are for the well-being of the French-speaking majority; federalist interests are craven and petty. In the 1980 referendum, the "Yes" supporters described themselves as idealistic, altruistic, and heroic; they dismissed the "No" supporters as bought by Ottawa dollars, preoccupied with security, and weak of purpose.

But that neat fabrication was destroyed, in what may have been the pivotal moment of the referendum campaign, when a Parti Québécois Cabinet minister accused the federalists of wanting to create a Quebec "full of Yvettes," a common name for those French Canadian women whose only role in life is "to give pleasure to others, to serve them, to be gentle and submissive." In response to that insult, fourteen thousand women gathered in the Montreal Forum to wave the Canadian flag and sing "Vive la Canadienne." They wanted to show that the separatists had no monopoly on the courage and dignity of Hélène Desportes and the other heroines of New France.

"Canada is a country that is probably too big for small minds," the novelist Roch Carrier recently remarked. "Canada is a country that is probably too varied for simple minds."

The forces against its survival are certainly great. Quebec by itself seems cosier. French Quebeckers *entre eux* seem safer. The nationalists are a permanent and sizable bloc. They have enough power to intimidate the politicians and manipulate public opinion. They have created the infrastructure of an independent state, with all the necessary political, economic, and even international instruments in place, and they have fostered the prejudice among many young people that independence is both normal and inevitable. Many federalists will continue to leave the province; more immigrants will become sympathetic to Quebec's self-determination. Someday the economy will improve. Someday the Parti Québécois will be elected. Someday fresh leaders will emerge and fresh humiliations will occur.

Above all, the memory of the Conquest and the minority status of French Canadians within Canada will not disappear. The psychological desire to be liberated from the shame of history, to be the majority in a state whose flag flies at the United Nations, cannot be appeased by political compromise or economic progress. It remains the driving force behind Quebec nationalism. Isaiah Berlin, the political philosopher, once explained the power of that force by means of a tale. A sultan sealed his wife and son into a barrel and set them adrift on an ocean. They were safe as long as they did not stand up. In time, however, the son longed to stretch. "Don't, we'll drown!" his mother cried, but the boy could endure his captivity no longer. "So be it," he said, "but I must stretch – just once." He got his moment of freedom, and then they both perished.

All at once, or step by step, a variety of conditions could come together by which Quebec would achieve independence, but besides creating many new problems, that would not resolve many old ones. What about the political and economic association with Canada? What about the fate of the French language in North America? What about the usefulness of the English language around the world? What about the anglos, the immigrants, and the native peoples? What about the French-speaking communities outside Quebec? What about the signs inside Quebec? What about the exodus of French-speaking professionals? Most of all, perhaps, independence would not eradicate the powerful portion of Québécois who do not desire it. It would not erase the tensions within the family, because they are based on conflicts and contradictions that have rested in the soul of French Canada since the seventeenth century.

I encountered them, for example, in the soul of my cousin, André Prud'homme, a gentle and rather childlike man with a thin white beard, a pipe in his mouth, a hole in the elbow of his sweater, sandals on his feet, and a cat sleeping in his lap. Though he had been forced to work for twenty-six years in his father's hardware business, he was in style and vocation an artist with a spiritual longing. He had

306

married Jacqueline Champagne, a psychoanalyst who was the daughter of a famous composer, and they have always lived in the world of culture and ideas. First as a passion, then as a profession, André had sculpted in bronze and stone, painted, and made jewelry, and on a sideboard in his dining room he had created "a little world of little people," small and brightly painted wooden gnomes at a wedding in the forest.

"I was a Liberal in the 1960s," he said. "I liked Trudeau a lot at the beginning, less at the end, and now I don't like him at all. In 1976 I voted for the PQ. In 1980 I voted 'Yes' in the referendum. I was never an angry French Canadian. I felt we needed a chance to experiment with risk and challenge, and I didn't feel I had anything to lose. I have as a Quebecker what I need to live: a language, a certain mental structure tied to language, an education, a faith, and some special values beyond money and materialism. And we have as Quebeckers the talent and creativity to do things, as long as we have the power and money, in our own fashion.

"But things are becoming more complicated. One morning the Mohawks picked up guns in Oka and we faced an entirely new situation which we didn't know how we got into or how we were going to get out of. Up north, the Crees could blow up a few pylons and we would be in the dark, in more ways than one. The uncertainty about an economic entente with Canada could put us in the gutter. Everywhere there is less and less talk of borders and countries. The days of isolation from the outside world are over, and in fifty or a hundred years there could be more immigrants than French Canadians in Quebec – even an independent Quebec. Who knows what is going to happen? I'm waiting. I'm reading. I'm watching the news. I'm not sure what I'm going to think."

Our cousin Danielle Daigneault knew what she was going to think, but she did not know if it mattered. "I intend to support independence," she said, "even if the leaders aren't as good, even if the economic situation isn't as good, even if, even if. Quebec needs independence to put energy back into its people and give the society a dynamic that can change everything. But Quebeckers have become more individualistic, more confused about where they and the world trends are going, and they don't like confrontation by nature. They will usually take the route of least resistance, even if it leads back to Canada. Maybe the next generation will have the courage to do what needs to be done. Maybe not. Independence is not inevitable."

Arrayed against independence is another set of formidable forces. National economies are integrating everywhere, and with integration comes a diminution of national sovereignty. The new countries of Eastern Europe and Central Asia, at first an inspiration to nationalists in Quebec, are suffering malaise and even bloodshed. The vast majority of Quebec's immigrants oppose separation, and most of the business class has realized which side its bread is buttered on. Most Quebeckers feel no keen sense of oppression; the high emotions of humiliation and rejection have subsided; people want to get on with their personal dreams. The doors to the whole world have been thrown open, and more Quebeckers have ventured beyond them. Two of Danielle Daigneault's daughters, though still nationalistic, are heading abroad to study, and one has even married an English Canadian from Toronto!

Many Quebec nationalists have moved beyond the need for a national state, as La Fontaine and Laurier did in the nineteenth century, and many Quebec federalists have moved beyond fear and tradition as primary motives for remaining Canadian. If Canada is to flourish as well as survive, however, more Quebeckers will have to fight for it as a social vision, not just a grim necessity or a useful advantage. They will have to develop a crystal-clear appreciation of its flexibility, its diversity, its humanity, and its example to the world. They will have to accept certain realities: that French Canadians will always be a minority within Canada; that Canada can only function as a contract between individuals rather than between two or three founding peoples; that the Charter of Rights is a better protector of their language and freedom than any special status; that English Canadians are stronger allies in the undertaking to preserve and expand the French language and culture in North America than the Americans or even the French; that the attempt to rally the Québécois into one national mind and one dominant culture is less the path to survival than the road to totalitarianism.

Not the easiest realities to accept, perhaps, but experience has demonstrated that they are compatible with nationalist goals. French Canadians may have been a minority in Ottawa since 1867, but they have been a minority so powerful and effective that they kept the Conservative Party out of office for most of the twentieth century, and they have controlled the office of the prime minister for most of the past fifty years. Quebec may have been treated as a province like the others, but that did not prevent it from fashioning its own society and altering the entire country in thirty years. The Charter of Rights may have struck at the excesses of the language laws, but it guaranteed ways to advance the cause of the French language. English Canada may have harbored its share of imperialists and bigots, but French Canadians have never been pressured into the fate of the Franco-Americans or abandoned as they were by France. Ethnic solidarity may have kept Quebeckers pure in their faith and content on their farms, but individual dissent drove them to gain a continent and discover the world.

The quiet strength of outward-looking Quebeckers can force the political class and its cronies in the media, the universities, and the boardrooms to take the knife from English Canada's throat. If that strength becomes less quiet, ordinary Quebeckers can amend the more repressive aspects of the language laws and halt the more unproductive elements of the constitutional haggles. They have been empowered by history to speak up with the same pride and justification as the nationalist elites, for both are legitimate heirs of New France and guardians of the patrimony.

Quebeckers need not accept the status quo, nor must they cease agitating for what works best. They do not even need to love Canada or lose their primary identification with Quebec, but they have to see through the phony politics of humiliation and the self-serving manipulations of their elites. They have to decide whether they want to live within Canada or strike out on their own. Whatever the decision, they should be prepared to accept what follows as their own responsibility, without requiring special status if they stay or guaranteed association if they go. That, more than any flag or embassy, would mean true freedom from the Conquest.

———————

As for myself, I am beyond the pale. Once a Westmount anglo, now an ex-Quebecker in Toronto, I lost more than the right to vote: I lost, in the eyes of many Québécois, the right to an opinion. My background permits me nothing but remorse and acquiescence; my departure strips me of sincerity and credibility. There is an irony in this. In 1955, when I stood in the window of the Ritz and looked down on the French Canadian crowds at the Saint-Jean-Baptiste parade, a privileged and protected child who knew nothing of their history or their language, no one would have said that I did not belong. In 1990, when I stood on Sherbrooke Street and watched the demonstrators waving flags and chanting slogans in the wake of the Trojan Sheep, decades after I had left the Circle and become infatuated with French Canada, I was judged little better than a regular tourist.

Like all principles and preferences, my federalism stems from my past, but it is not more knee-jerk or self-interested because of that. Listening to some of my cousins, I realized I might now be an *indépendantiste* if my grandfather had not assimilated into English Montreal – what a nice idea to snuggle *entre nous* and build, like André Prud'homme's gnome wedding, "a little world for little people"! – but I hope I would have had the wit and wisdom to see beyond it. I had, after all, left the walled garden on the Circle, as much a paradise in reality as New France was in myth; I had learned another language, delighted in other cultures, known Africa and Asia, and still felt true to the land and people of Quebec.

My federalism, then, is not the prejudice of those who hate the sight of French on cereal boxes or long for the much-delayed assimilation of French Canadians. Nor is it the weakness of those who preach concession after concession in the hope of appeasing the nationalist beast and, when the hope proves vain, feel betrayed, turn back in on themselves, and suggest Quebec go to hell. I do not want Quebeckers to leave Canada, and I do not think they must. Conversely, I do not believe that Quebec politicians should get everything they ask for simply because they ask for it, and I do not want to see Canada rendered dysfunctional merely to avoid Quebec's independence. Neither advocating nor dreading independence, I pound the picnic table and provoke my nationalist friends as a kind of civic duty, both as a citizen of Canada and as a friend of Quebec.

Now, too, in the course of exploring my French quarter, I have discovered another duty. It commanded me to speak up, and it gave vehemence to what I had to say. I found it by accident one summer morning when, my wife being away from the cabin, I took my two small children into Montreal for the day. We were going to meet Claire Hoult, a niece of my great-grandparents and an invaluable repository of family lore. She was going to show me the home where my grandfather Moncel had lived as a boy. I had known it only as an address on Sherbrooke Street, as a Victorian interior in a photograph of the Moncels at lunch. When we reached it, we saw that it was now the headquarters of the Saint-Jean-Baptiste Society of Montreal!

"Grandpa Moncel must be rolling in his grave," Claire said. In the front hall there was a portrait of René Lévesque. The upstairs bedrooms were the offices of such ultranationalist organizations as Action Nationale and Mouvement Québec Français. The wood-paneled room where Laurier had danced and my great-grandmother had played the piano, now the Salon Lionel Groulx, contained Pap-

311

ineau's flag from the Rebellion of 1837, stained-glass windows with portraits of French Canada's heroes, and Massicotte prints of peasant life in New France.

One of the prints showed the New Year's Day blessing, an old French Canadian custom in which each family's father, as head of the household and representative of God, blessed his wife and children for the coming year. "Your great-grandfather used to do that when I was a girl, and he probably did it in this room before that," Claire said. "He sat in one of the big leather armchairs. All his children and their families lined up in front of him, and each in turn knelt down at his feet and asked for his blessing: 'Voulez-vous me donner votre bénédiction, Papa?'"

I imagined the scene: a fire in the large fireplace, the candlelight on the mahogany mantel, my great-grandfather plump and satisfied with fresh turkey and creamed sweetbreads and the éclairs known as *religieuses*, the silent family members clutching the gold coins they had found in the floral centerpiece by pulling the red ribbons that had bedecked the Limoges plates.

And, given the history on the walls, I imagined, in a long line, the generations of ancestors who had stood for a blessing for almost four hundred years. There was Zacherie Cloutier, ready to kneel before Guillaume Moncel as he had not done before Robert Giffard. There was Hélène Desportes, remembering that this was the time of year when Samuel de Champlain had died. There was Jean Gervaise, eager to abase himself before the current warden of Notre-Dame. There was Louis Boulduc, preparing to curry favor from another wealthy patron. There was François Lorit, hoping that the others would not laugh when he stammered for the blessing. There were Joseph Hains and Elizabeth Lamax, sharing memories of their New England childhoods in a thick *patois*. There was Madeleine Gagnon *née* Deblois, already exhausted from cooking the holiday feasts in Sainte-Famille. There was Charles Leret *dit* Moncel, daydreaming of military glory when his regiment marched with Lévis to overcome the disgrace of

Montcalm's defeat. There were Hugh and Angélique Munro, as madly in love as they had been when Hugh lost his own father's benediction. There was Charlotte Leduc, just back from a Christmas visit to her half-brother François-Antoine Larocque. There was Louis Fauteux, holding a turquoise brooch from Paris as a gift for his daughter Alphonsine. There was my great-grandmother herself, risen from the grave in the "back and beyond" of Notre-Dame-des-Neiges cemetery. There were her seven children: the boy and girl lost in their youth, Ninette Tétrault bearing her troubles without complaint, Willy being badgered by Albertine, Charles ever jovial and full of tales, Cocoune Prud'homme eternally quiet, and my grandfather René in his gray suit and polka-dot tie. There were the fifteen grandchildren who survived childhood, and the four who did not. There were the great-grandchildren, and the great-great-grandchildren, and the great-great-great-grandchildren of Guillaume and Alphonsine Moncel, stretching as far back from them as they had been from Count Frontenac.

But when it came my turn, I held back. I did not really belong. I had left the family, after all, and was ashamed to ask for my great-grandfather's blessing in an English accent. He looked up at me from his armchair with amusement in his eyes and a smile beneath his mustache – and he beckoned me to approach.

"Are you not also mine?" he asked.

And so in the living room of his home, now the Société Saint-Jean-Baptiste de Montréal, beneath Papineau's flag, while Claire prattled on, I bent to tie my son's shoelaces – and, on my knees, *entre nous*, silently beseeched my forefathers to bless me.

They did, but now I owed them *foi et hommage* too. Now I, too, had a family duty.

Way's Mills, Quebec
August 1992

Acknowledgments

Like every Canadian, I owe a tremendous debt of gratitude to the editors and contributors of the *Dictionary of Canadian Biography* (University of Toronto Press). I have relied on its essays for many facts and insights about New France, Quebec, and the historical figures – whether among the family or the famous – mentioned in the text. I have taken some liberties when constructing dialogue or setting scenes, and I have made some arbitrary decisions when faced with conflicts and uncertainties in records. Otherwise, I have tried to make the history as accurate as possible. The DCB has been an invaluable teacher, though any errors of fact or interpretation remain mine.

I am also grateful for the research done by Richard and Elizabeth Hubert of Greenwich, Connecticut, on our Munro ancestors.

I would like to thank the Canada Council for its assistance.

Thanks, too, to John Macfarlane, Jan Walter, and Gary Ross for their kindness, patience, and inestimable help. They have been the best of publishers, editors, and friends. I have also benefited from the labor and talent of Susan Kent Davidson, Gordon Robertson, and Anne Holloway. I owe much to the long hours and infinite considerations of Eileen and Bob Harbinson of Ultra Word Processing.

Above all, thanks to my wife Gillian, whose work, intelligence, support, and love have made every page of this book – and every day of my life – better.

Further Reading in English

Armstrong, Joe. *Champlain*. Toronto: Macmillan, 1987.

Cohen, Andrew. *A Deal Undone: The Making and Breaking of the Meech Lake Accord*. Vancouver and Toronto: Douglas & McIntyre, 1990.

Coleman, E.L. *New England Captives Carried to Canada*. Portland, Maine, 1925.

Douville, Raymond, and Jacques Casanova. *Daily Life in Early Canada*. New York: Macmillan, 1968.

Dufour, Christian. *A Canadian Challenge / Le Défi québécois*. Lantzville, BC: Oolichan Books, 1990.

Eccles, W.J. *France in America*. Toronto: Fitzhenry and Whiteside, 1990.

Fournier, Pierre. *A Meech Lake Post-Mortem*. Montreal and Kingston: McGill-Queen's University Press, 1991.

Fraser, Graham. PQ: *René Lévesque and the Parti Québécois in Power*. Toronto: Macmillan, 1984.

Fraser, Matthew. *Quebec Inc*. Toronto: Key Porter, 1987.

Levine, Marc V. *The Reconquest of Montreal: Language Policy and Social Change in a Bilingual City*. Philadelphia: Temple University Press, 1990.

Linteau, Paul-André, René Durocher, and Jean-Claude Robert. *Quebec: A History 1867–1929*. Toronto: James Lorimer, 1983.

McRoberts, Kenneth. *Quebec: Social Change and Political Crisis.* Toronto: McClelland and Stewart, 1988.

Mathews, Georges. *Quiet Resolution: Quebec's Challenge to Canada.* Toronto: Summerhill Press, 1990.

Miquelon, Dale. *New France 1701–1744.* Toronto: McClelland and Stewart, 1989.

Monière, Denis. *Ideologies in Quebec: The Historical Development.* Toronto: University of Toronto Press, 1981.

Ouellet, Fernand. *Economic and Social History of Quebec 1760–1850.* Ottawa: Carleton Library, 1980.

Reid, Malcolm. *The Shouting Signpainters.* Toronto: McClelland and Stewart, 1972.

Thomson, Dale. *Jean Lesage and the Quiet Revolution.* Toronto: Macmillan, 1984.

Trofimenkoff, Susan Mann. *The Dream of Nation: A Social and Intellectual History of Quebec.* Toronto: Gage Educational Publishing, 1983.

Verney, Jack. *The Good Regiment.* Montreal and Kingston: McGill-Queen's University Press, 1991.

Wade, Mason. *The French Canadians.* Toronto: Macmillan, 1968.

Westley, Margaret. *Remembrance of Grandeur: The Anglo-Protestant Elite of Montreal 1900–1950.* Montreal: Editions Libre Expression, 1990.

Young, Brian, and John A. Dickinson. *A Short History of Quebec: A Socio-Economic Perspective.* Toronto: Copp Clark Pitman, 1988.

Index